Silver Lake BOHEMIA

A HISTORY

MICHAEL LOCKE AND VINCENT BROOK

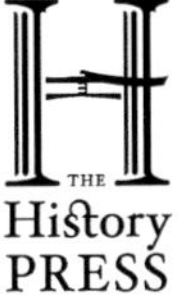

Published by The History Press
Charleston, SC
www.historypress.net

Front cover, top left: Silver Lake Reservoir. *Photo by Michael Locke; top right:* life partners Harry Hay and John Burnside, circa 1960s. *Courtesy of ONE Archives at USC Libraries; center right:* Anaïs Nin portrait by Peter Gowland. *Courtesy of Anaïs Nin Trust; third row, left:* protest at the Black Cat tavern, 1969. *Courtesy of ONE Archives at USC Libraries; third row, middle:* Eugene Kinn Choy residence, Eugene Kinn Choy, 1949. *Photo by Michael Locke; third row, right:* Loren Miller portrait. *Courtesy of Robin Miller Sloan; bottom:* Harry Hay marching with Radical Faeries, Gay Pride Parade. *Courtesy of ONE Archives at USC Libraries.*
Back cover, top row, left: Effa Manley at home in Silver Lake with Cy Young Award winner Don Newcombe, August 7, 1973. *Courtesy of Negro Leagues Baseball Museum; top row, middle:* Mako Iwamatsu portrait. *Author's collection; top row, right:* James Eads How portrait. *Author's collection; bottom row:* Silver Lake Reservoir. *Photo by Michael Locke.*

Unless otherwise indicated, photographs are by Michael Locke or are in his collection.

First published 2016

Manufactured in the United States

ISBN 978.1.46713.532.0

Library of Congress Control Number: 2016943914

Notice: The information in this book is true and complete to the best of our knowledge. It is offered without guarantee on the part of the authors or The History Press. The authors and The History Press disclaim all liability in connection with the use of this book.

CONTENTS

ACKNOWLEDGEMENTS

We couldn't have written this book without the gracious support and invaluable contributions of the following people and institutions: Betty of the Holyland Bible Knowledge Society; Gilbert Brebes and Joy Pae of Rose Scharlin Cooperative Nursey School; Deborah Ching; Barton Choy; Richard Chylinski; Charlie Conrad, Lindsay Kennedy and Dean Malouf of The Black Cat; Raymond Droswell of the Negro Leagues Baseball Museum; Diane Edwardson; Genevieve Fong of the Eames Office; Jocelyn Gibbs of the Art, Design and Architecture Museum at the University of California–Santa Barbara; Baylis Glascock; Thomas S. Hines; Wes Joe; Megan Laddusaw, Rick Delaney and the staff at The History Press; Michael Lehrer; Sarah Lorenzen of the VDL Research House; Bill and Annie Macomber; Marvin Malecha of North Carolina State University College of Design; Michael, Miriam, Andrea, Katya, Tommi and Dorothy Meyer; Barry Milofsky; Dion and Dr. Raymond Neutra; Jim Overmeyer; Jennifer Palmer-Lacey, Michael Masterson and Cheryl Revkin of the Silver Lake History Collective; Patrick and Julie Pascal; Loni A. Shibuyama of ONE National Gay & Lesbian Archives at USC Libraries; Judge Robin Miller Sloan and her husband, Michael Sloan; Alexei Romanoff and his husband, David Fahar; Ruth Ross; Sarah Sherman of the Getty Research Institute; George Smart of North Carolina Modernist Houses; Mark Thompson; Antony Unruh; Phyl and Ronald van Ammers; Mark Vieira; Kent Wong; Eric Lloyd Wright, Mary Wright and Tree Leyburn Wright; Momo Yashima and her husband, Ralph Brannen; Peter "Bart" Yates; posthumously, David Hyun and Julius Shulman; and last but not least, our ever patient, loving and inspiring wives, Karen Brook and Donna Locke.

PREFACE

Our first book on Silver Lake, *Silver Lake Chronicles: Exploring an Urban Oasis in Los Angeles* (2014), covered a broad swath of the area's history from the nineteenth through the mid-twentieth century. Topics included the construction of the reservoir that gave the place its name, the first families to build homes in the area, the moguls who founded the city's earliest movie studios here and the stars they discovered and other local figures who rose to prominence in the fields of medicine, philanthropy and religion.

The second book, *Silver Lake Bohemia: A History*, is more narrowly focused. As the title suggests, it deals with artists, intellectuals and political activists who, in their achievements and lifestyles, established the area's progressive tone and reputation, which persists to the present.[1] Another unique aspect of the sequel is the amazing network of interconnections among the people and places we chose to spotlight. The locally based, modernist designers who put Silver Lake on the international architectural map, most of whom led unconventional lives and leaned to the left, interacted freely with and built innovative homes for local avant-garde writers and politicos who intermingled socially and supported one another's efforts.

Musicologist Peter Yates's Evenings on the Roof concerts exemplify this harmonic convergence. Yates and his wife, Frances Mullen, established groundbreaking salons featuring the latest in classical music written and performed by renowned composers and musicians. These salons were held in a Silver Lake home redesigned by modernist icon Rudolph Schindler and attended by luminaries including writer Anaïs Nin, who lived in a Silver Lake home built by Eric Lloyd Wright, grandson of Frank Lloyd Wright, whose historic Hollyhock House, built for socialist, experimental theater producer Aline Barnsdall, had brought Schindler to the area in the first place.

As longtime residents of the area, versed in its rich history, we were aware of some of the congruencies at the outset. However, we only discovered their remarkable extent and complexity in the process of researching and writing the book. As the individuals and locations we highlight are extraordinary in their own right, this discovery added yet another layer of appreciation and enjoyment to the enterprise—one we hope will enhance the reader's overall experience as well.

1

IT ALL BEGINS WITH BARNSDALL

ALINE BARNSDALL AND THE HOLLYHOCK HOUSE

Aline Barnsdall's historic Hollyhock House, atop Olive Hill in what would become Barnsdall Park, is actually located in East Hollywood, a mile or so from Silver Lake. Frank Lloyd Wright, whom she hired to design the house and a theater and arts complex and who went on to build several other buildings in Los Angeles, designed none in Silver Lake proper. Yet Aline's avant-garde spirit and Wright's modernist masterpiece were seminal ingredients in the mix of art, architecture and activism that turned Silver Lake into the city's bohemian hub.

Though Wright would spend limited time in L.A., other architects lured here by his presence—notably Rudolph Schindler, Richard Neutra, Gregory Ain and John Lautner—would transform Silver Lake into a modern architectural mecca. The built environment, in turn, boosted the area's attraction to artists, intellectuals, politicos and others of independent mind who had begun populating the larger area known as Edendale (encompassing Silver Lake, Echo Park, Elysian Heights, Los Feliz, Franklin Hills and East Hollywood) in the wake of the movie industry's westward migration.

An iconoclast before her arrival in Los Angeles in 1916, Aline brought with her from Chicago, where she had been producing experimental theater since 1914, a strong feminist streak, a passion for the arts and radical politics and, soon, a child out of wedlock, a social taboo at the time.[2] After producing successful plays at the Los Angeles Little Theater downtown in 1916, she embarked on her theater and arts project on the aptly named Olive Hill property—thirty-six acres of olive tree–dotted parkland bordered by

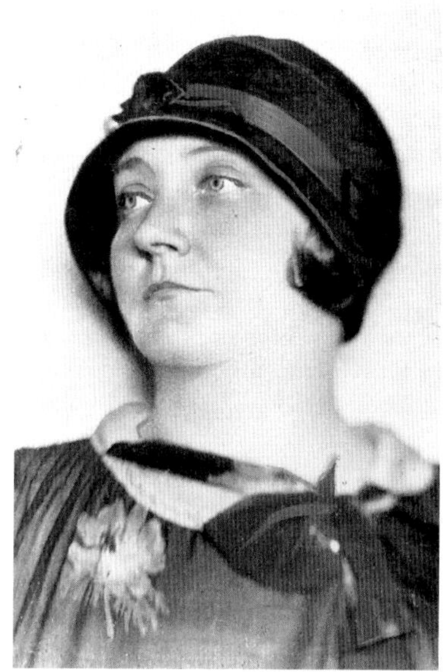

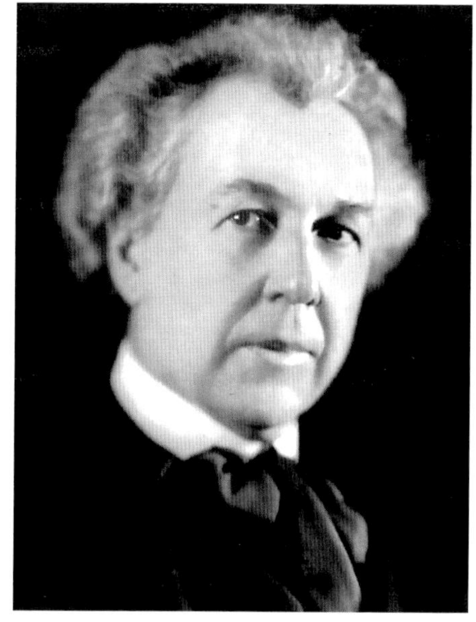

Left: Los Angeles cultural leader and philanthropist Aline Barnsdall, circa 1934.

Right: Portrait of Frank Lloyd Wright.

Vermont Avenue and Edgemont Street to the east and west and Hollywood (then called Prospect) and Sunset Boulevards to the north and south. At the crest of the hill, Wright eventually built Aline's residence, named the Hollyhock House—after her favorite flower and/or because the flowers grew wild there.[3]

Though the choice of the notoriously mercurial Wright proved unfortunate for Aline personally—the arts complex floundered and she found the Hollyhock House unlivable—the house and surrounding greenspace, with panoramic views of (eventually) Griffith Park Observatory and the Hollywood sign, would become one of the city's greatest treasures. The site was nominated in 2014 by Interior Secretary Sally Jewell to join the likes of the Statue of Liberty and the Acropolis on UNESCO's World Heritage List of natural and cultural wonders.[4]

Oilman's Daughter

Louise Aline Barnsdall was born with a silver spoon in Bradford, Pennsylvania, in 1882 and raised in nearby Titusville. Her father, Theodore Newton Barnsdall, had turned his grandfather William's pioneering Barnsdall Oil Company (William had drilled the world's second well in Titusville in 1859) into the country's largest independent oil and gas producer. An unlikely sire for a future socialist, Thede (as her father was called) bequeathed Aline a steely sense of purpose tempered by integrity and compassion. "Both were loyal and generous, supporting those less fortunate," biographers Norman and Dorothy Karasnick aver; "both used innovative means to advance their ideas and ideals."[5] From her mother, Angie, who had dreamed of a life on the stage and who died in 1907 when her daughter was fifteen, Aline acquired her artistic sensibility and love of the theater.[6]

Her first trip to Europe, in 1911, which turned into a year-long study of theater and music, broadened her horizons artistically and politically. "There's a new kind of woman in the world today," she proclaimed, evoking the feminist current of the time.[7] But along with an embrace of the new came a grounding in the tried and true. It was her great fortune (in more ways than one) to study with legendary actors Eleanora Duse and Dame Ellen Terry and Terry's son, esteemed director and set designer Gordon Craig. Besides the expertise she gained from this illustrious trio, Aline acquired the inspiration for her Olive Hill project, which clearly paralleled the Teatro d'Albano theater complex Duse had planned for her lover, Gabriele D'Annunzio, the noted Italian poet, playwright and war hero.[8]

Aline's own love life began to flourish in Europe as well, via an affair, begun in Berlin, with American attorney and theater enthusiast Lawrence Langner, who was eight years younger than the thirty-year-old Aline. "We were the same age in our enthusiasm over the theater and Bernard Shaw," Langner explained away the generation gap, "and she was even younger when it came to discussing politics and Victorian morality, against which she was in even greater revolt than I was."[9] Though the romance fell short of marriage, Langner helped further Aline's theater career by introducing her in 1914 to the Fine Arts Building in Chicago, "the center of [the city's] artistic life." Along with providing the venue for her early stage productions, the building initiated contact with Frank Lloyd Wright, who, for a short time, had a studio on the top floor.[10]

Theater, architecture and politics all came together during Aline's two years in Chicago. The Players Producing Company, which she founded and directed plays for, was a critical and financial success. With Wright, whose career had stalled after his cook burned down Wright's Wisconsin home and murdered his mistress and her children in 1914, Aline began planning her theater project. And with Emma Goldman, the notorious anarchist and free-love advocate, who also had offices in the Fine Arts Building, she struck up a lifelong friendship that "would have a profound impact on Aline's future."[11]

Theater, oil and the movies came together in Aline's move to Los Angeles in 1916. From previous visits to the city, she had already chosen Olive Hill as the perfect place for realizing her dream of bringing "culture to the West."[12] She also was attracted to the young motion picture medium, whose base of operations had only recently migrated to L.A., where her father, in addition to owning a small movie house, had extensive oil interests. With the theater building, her top priority, in the planning stages, Aline wasted no time in resuming her own productions. The Los Angeles Little Theater she started downtown at Ninth Street and Figueroa Boulevard, like her project in Chicago, followed the precepts of the Little Theater movement. Begun in Europe in 1910, the Little Theater approach featured bold new works, provocative treatment and promising young talent.[13]

All three facets were more than satisfied in her first L.A. production, the aptly named new play *Nju*, directed by Richard Ordynski with set designs by Norman Bel Geddes. Ordynski had worked with legendary Austrian impresario Max Reinhardt and was called the Polish Reinhardt; Bel Geddes, on his way to becoming one of the nation's premier industrial designers, was, one year later, designing sets for the Metropolitan Opera. The play was a hit with the public and garnered rave reviews, and its premiere in October 1916 drew the cream of Hollywood, including Charlie Chaplin, Douglas Fairbanks, Gloria Swanson, D.W. Griffith and Cecil B. DeMille.[14]

Though the Little Theater continued to thrive, other developments proved bittersweet. Aline's father died in early 1917, leaving his estate to be divided between her and her half-sister, Frances, who bought out Aline's interest in Barnsdall Oil Company for $3 million (a princely sum at the time). Ordynski, with whom Aline had begun an affair and from whom she became pregnant, left her and her theater company after a bitter falling out. Louise Aline Jr., nicknamed "Sugartop" (later called Betty), was born in Seattle, where Aline went to escape the limelight and literally papered over the "illegitimate" birth by having a friend, Roy George, list himself as father on the birth certificate.[15]

Not that anyone in the know bought the ruse—least of all the FBI (or BOI, Bureau of Investigation, as it was then known), which had placed Aline

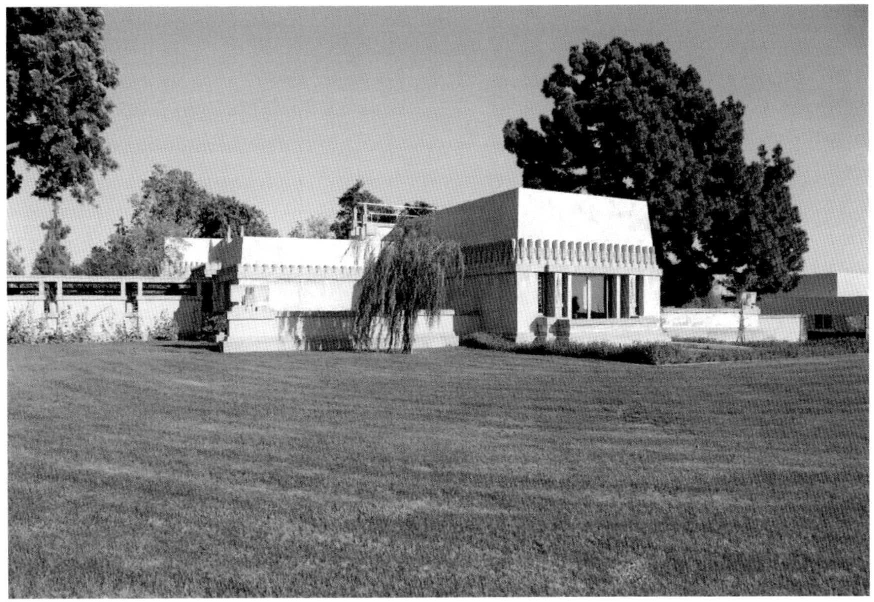

Hollyhock House, Frank Lloyd Wright, 1921.

under surveillance since her renewed contact with Emma Goldman in Los Angeles in 1916. Goldman's anarchist taint was bad enough for the anti-leftist bureau, but the stain turned a dark Red when Aline stuck by Goldman during her two-year incarceration for opposing wartime conscription. Aline also tried her best, financially and otherwise, to prevent her friend's eventual deportation to Russia in 1919.[16]

Further tarnishing her reputation, from a right-wing perspective, was Aline's monetary and moral support for persecuted labor activist Tom Mooney. Mooney had been convicted (falsely, by all accounts) in the Preparedness Day Parade bombing in San Francisco in 1916 that killed ten people and wounded more than forty. Aline worked selflessly on behalf of Mooney, whose case (despite the recanting of eleven jurors and the trial judge's misgivings) dragged on until 1939, when Governor Culbert Olson pardoned Mooney as his first act in office. After the pardon, the FBI continued to hound Aline, and even her death did not remove the hammer-and-sickle smear from the Hollyhock House.[17]

THE WRIGHT STUFF

It took until 1919 for Theodore Barnsdall's estate to be settled, and thus for Aline to finally purchase Olive Hill, at a cost of $300,000. In the interim, fissures began to widen in her relationship with Frank Lloyd Wright, primarily over his design for what remained the overall project's most important element: the theater. The timing had not been propitious to begin with. From 1915 on, the bulk of Wright's time and energy were consumed by his Imperial Hotel commission in Tokyo, Japan. The distraction limited his oversight of the Hollyhock House construction as well, requiring Austrian émigré Rudolph Schindler, who was then apprenticing with Wright in Chicago, to finalize plans for the house and eventually move west to supervise construction.[18] Wright's son, Lloyd Wright, had moved to L.A. in the early 1910s, established his own practice in 1915 and became head of the design department at Paramount Studios a year later. He also worked on Hollyhock House and played a preeminent role in the overall landscaping.[19]

A personality clash between the headstrong Wright and his iron-willed client proved the biggest obstacle to the project's satisfactory completion, an obstacle Aline addressed in a letter she wrote Wright in 1926. "I hope we may…never consider working together again. It can't be done. We are too much of the same mold—egotistical, dictatorial and creative."[20] Wright's arrogance and eccentricity, which in his other work produced some of the century's most original buildings, in Aline's dream theater led to a dead end. His declaiming to her and Norman Bel Geddes early on—"It isn't necessary for me to see other theaters to design better ones"—may have been a perfect formula for Fallingwater, the Johnson Wax Company Building and the Guggenheim Museum. But for the Olive Hill project, it was a recipe for disaster.[21]

The theater was never completed in Wright's or Aline's lifetime. As for Hollyhock House, completed in 1921, Aline had a litany of complaints. The building leaked and was constantly damp. The windows didn't work, and the master bedroom was too small for a proper bed. The dining and living rooms accommodated no more than six people (per Wright's belief that no larger number "could maintain intelligent conversation"). And of the thick concrete doors, Aline decried, "I need three men and two boys to help me get in or out of my own house."[22]

Later, of course, Hollyhock House would become a Los Angeles Historic-Cultural Monument (No. 12), a World Heritage List nominee and be considered one of Wright's greatest achievements. It was the first of his Los Angeles designs and marked a transition between his early Prairie Style and later pre-Columbian-influenced creative phases. Its inspiration, as in all his work, was drawn from the local cultural and physical environment. The building's exterior allusion to Mayan pyramids and the inner courtyard's to a Spanish *casa* reflect the region's Native American and Spanish Colonial roots. The surrounding landscape, in its evocation "of an oasis in a semi-desert climate," incorporates the area's hybridized natural and reconstructed ecology.[23]

Hollyhock House's future accolades and critical esteem were no consolation to Aline at the time, however, and her frustration with the building's discomfort was compounded by Wright's inability to produce a satisfactory design for the theater. He did manage to complete, in 1922, two other facets of the theater complex: the so-called Residence A, intended to house the company's director; and Residence B, which was meant to house other members of the troupe. Wright, however, briefly used the latter building as his offices, and Schindler later redesigned it as an alternative living space for Aline and daughter Betty.[24]

With the theater plans in limbo, Aline took heart in one of her father's oil-drilling adages: "If you come up with a dry hole, walk away and look for a new opportunity."[25] She turned Residence A into a children's center for dance and musical education, using the Dalcroze method developed by Swiss composer and music theorist Émile Jaques-Dalcroze in the late 1890s, emphasizing rhythm for ear-training and body movement. She also became a key patron and cofounder, with Artie Mason Carter and Dr. T. Percival Gerson, of the Hollywood Bowl, whose signature Easter Sunrise Services originated on Olive Hill in the early 1920s. Besides her financial support, Aline helped create the program for the Bowl's first full season in 1924 and participated in the planning of the new bowl shell, designed by Lloyd Wright in 1928, which remains the template for the various earthquake and acoustical upgrades that followed.[26]

THE BATTLE OF BARNSDALL PARK

With Hollyhock House a house in name only and the theater complex a fading prospect, Aline already in 1924 proposed giving the house and grounds to the city of Los Angeles. The house was to be used as a library and the grounds maintained as a newly named Barnsdall Park. Despite support from the Board of Library Commissioners, the Department of Recreation and Parks and the community at large, the city council, bowing to pressure from real estate interests myopically concerned with a decline in property values, nixed the deal in a unanimous vote. A revamped deal passed council muster three years later, with the house now set to be maintained by the California Art Club. Dedicating the house and park to her father, Aline had a bronze plaque placed on the fountain at the entrance to the house. The plaque featured Thede's embossed portrait, symbols of the oil industry he pioneered and a somewhat ambiguous inscription: "Our fathers mined for the gold of this country. We should mine for its beauty." Less equivocal was her pacifist-inspired condition that no war memorials be erected or military-related activities be held on the park's premises.[27]

Aline's battles with Los Angeles were far from over, however. Her decade-long support of Tom Mooney, despite the vindication of his 1938 pardon, still rankled the city's ruling class, as did her continued use of billboards on her property to promote progressive causes that the *L.A. Times* and other major newspapers either avoided or undermined and that tourist guidebooks labeled "leftist propaganda." Turning the other cheek, Aline loaned her artwork collection, featuring multiple works by Monet, Utrillo, Renoir, Picasso, Braque and Gauguin, to the Los Angeles County Museum, significantly enhancing its holdings.[28]

The FBI, which now labeled Aline part of the state's political "lunatic fringe," continued shadowing her every move, including to her new home in Denver, Colorado, in 1942. Maintaining a home in Palos Verdes for her frequent business visits to L.A., she was forced to return the same year when the Board of Park Commissioners voted to raze the badly deteriorated Residence B and Hollyhock House, which the Art Club had already been ordered to vacate. Enlisting Frank Lloyd Wright's and others' assistance, Aline was able to forestall the board's decision, ultimately gaining a full reprieve in 1946, when the city approved plans "to convert Hollyhock House into an exhibition hall for famous artists, lectures, and exhibits."[29] Later that year, while staying at the Roosevelt Hotel, another common stopover on her many city visits, Aline died of coronary thrombosis. She was sixty-four. After a private ceremony in Los Angeles, she was returned to Titusville, Pennsylvania, for interment in the Barnsdall Mausoleum.[30]

The Barnsdall Park Legacy

With Aline out of the fray, the seesaw battle over Barnsdall Park resumed. Violating her condition against anything war-related in the park, the city in 1948 approved plans of Aline's longtime nemesis, Dorothy Murray, for a World Wars I and II memorial. In 1951, daughter Betty sold frontage along Vermont Avenue for a shopping center and along Sunset Boulevard for a branch of the Kaiser Permanente Hospital. In 1954, she authorized the demolition of Residence B and had a Wright-designed house on Edgemont Street replaced by an apartment complex. Over the next twenty years, her fourth husband, developer Harlan Carl Erickson, added a car wash, office buildings, more apartments, markets and retail complexes along Edgemont and Vermont.[31]

Not all of Aline's dreams went for naught. In 1954, the Municipal Art Gallery, partly designed by Frank Lloyd Wright, was completed. In 1956, with Murray's lease expired, the city once more took over Hollyhock House. In 1963, the house was designated a Historic-Cultural Monument, to which the Director's House and the remaining park were added in 1965. In 1967, the Junior Arts Center was built; in 1971, the damaged Municipal Gallery was rebuilt, with a theater on the lower level; and in the mid-1970s, significant renovations were made to Hollyhock House.[32]

But stubborn resistance remained. In 1977, another old nemesis, former Department of Recreation and Parks general manager George Hjelte, filled an official city history of Barnsdall Park full of the old Red-baiting smears. Depicting Aline "as a radical, an eccentric, a Communist," Hjelte ludicrously implicated her in the *L.A. Times* building bombing of 1910, well before her commitment to leftist ideals and six years before her arrival in the city. What was worse, docents conducting tours of Hollyhock House repeated Hjelte's lies.[33]

Such is thankfully no longer the case. Just as Los Angeles broke out of its reactionary funk in the 1970s and '80s to become one of the most progressive cities in the country, so has Barnsdall Park been embraced as one of L.A.'s diamonds in the rough. In 2015, Hollyhock House completed another major renovation, emerging as well heeled and close to its envisioned state as possible.[34] Public tours, free of Hjelte's vitriol, are once more underway, and the rest of the park's multicultural venues are thriving, including the Barnsdall Gallery Theater. Having "lost the battles but won the war," Hollyhock House's place in architectural history is secure, as is Aline Barnsdall's as one of the city's greatest benefactors and, along with Frank Lloyd Wright, as the prime stage-setter for Silver Lake Bohemia.[35]

2

PASSING THE BATON

RUDOLPH SCHINDLER AND RICHARD NEUTRA

Two bluebloods, Aline Barnsdall and Frank Lloyd Wright, brought leftist politics and modernist architecture to the outskirts of Silver Lake. But it took two Austrian Jewish immigrants, Rudolph Schindler and Richard Neutra, to shift the political and cultural epicenter to Silver Lake proper. Neutra was the first important architect of the International Style to put down roots in Silver Lake. For the large inventory of homes (fourteen) he designed and built in the area, he is generally recognized as the Father of Silver Lake Modernism. A street along the Silver Lake Reservoir, where a string of homes designed by him are located, is even named Neutra Place. But the distinction as the first modern architect of note to work in Silver Lake belongs to Schindler, who arrived in the United States in March 1914, a full nine years before Neutra. Together, the celebrated pair's collective contribution to Silver Lake's built environment amounts to twenty-six total buildings, a truly impressive number given the district's small geographical area.

R.M. SCHINDLER

Schindler, who preferred to drop his given names, Rudolf Michael, in favor of the initials R.M., was born to a middle-class Viennese Jewish family in 1887. Although Schindler's ethnicity would later have proved a liability (and even then wasn't an asset), fin de siècle Vienna couldn't have been better suited to a young bohemian's coming of age. At the crux of the modernist revolution in the arts and sciences, the Austrian capital at the turn of the century boasted iconoclastic thinkers and creators in almost every field: Gustav Mahler and Arnold Schoenberg in music; Max Reinhardt and Arthur Schnitzler in theater; Gustav Klimt, Oskar Kokoschka and Egon Schiele in painting; Sigmund Freud and his cohort in psychoanalysis; and not least Otto Wagner, Joseph Hoffman, Joseph Maria Olbrich and Adolf Loos in architecture. These innovators helped found the Vienna Secession, a radical arts movement whose motto—"Der Zeit ihre Kunst. Der Kunst ihre Freiheit." (To every age its art. To every art its freedom.)—capsulized the group's desire to break from tradition and express new styles attuned to the turbulent times.[36]

Adding to the stimulating atmosphere were the talents of Schindler's parents: his father, Rudolf senior, was a skilled cabinetmaker; his mother, Francisca Hertl, was one of the few women awarded the Austrian Golden Cross of Merit in millinery. From an early age, the junior Schindler showed a gift for drawing.[37] At nineteen, he enrolled in the Imperial Institute of Engineering, where architect and scholar Carl König made the greatest impression on him. Although "a conservative in the midst of a tumultuous era," König imparted a flexible understanding of architecture that opened the door to innovative approaches in his students' later work.[38]

A year before graduating, Schindler transferred to the Vienna Academy of Fine Arts, then under the directorship of another giant, Otto Wagner. Wagner, who had designed many of the most famous Viennese landmarks in the historicist style, would break with tradition and become, like many of his contemporaries, a proponent of architectural realism. According to architectural historian David Gebhard, Schindler "fell first under the spell of Wagner and only later under that of Loos." A pioneer and theorist of modern architecture who espoused an approach free from unnecessary ornamentation, "it was Loos who had the lasting effect on him. The religious intensity of the older man's commitment to architecture as 'high art,' and to its relevance for his own existence and for life in general, was fully absorbed by Schindler."[39]

After graduation from the academy in 1913, Schindler was accepted as a draftsman at the firm of Ottenheimer, Stern & Reichel in Chicago and sailed to America in mid-1914. As Gebhard relates, Schindler originally planned to complete his three-year contract with the Chicago firm, "then work for a year or two with Frank Lloyd Wright, before returning to Vienna to work for Loos. Indeed, the sense of being a stranger in a strange land and the desire of eventually returning to Vienna remained with him even after he came to California; but the reality became increasingly remote"—and inconceivable after the Nazi annexation of Austria in 1938.[40]

Schindler had wanted to work for Frank Lloyd Wright ever since the European publication of his Wasmuth Portfolio in 1911, which created a sensation in architectural circles. After unsuccessfully applying for work with "the Master" for several years, Schindler was finally accepted in 1917 after Wright secured the commission for the Imperial Hotel in Tokyo. Hired mainly for his engineering background, Schindler ended up serving as a jack of all trades in Wright's Oak Park studio.[41]

In 1919, Schindler married Sophie Pauline Gibling, a Smith College graduate from an upper-middle-class midwestern family who taught music at Jane Addams's Hull House in Chicago. While Wright was in Japan, Schindler took over his Chicago operations. In 1920, he moved with Pauline to Los Angeles to supervise work on Aline Barnsdall's Hollyhock House.[42]

As with Barnsdall, the egotistical and mercurial Wright had a rocky relationship with Schindler. Though he completely depended on Schindler to keep his American operations functioning while he was abroad, Wright did little to help Schindler advance his career and was particularly stingy in giving credit or praise to anyone but himself. In response to Wright's half-hearted letter of recommendation upon Schindler's applying for an architect's license—"He has built a number of buildings in and around Los Angeles. And I have not heard of any of them falling down"—Schindler fired back: "I'm afraid it will do me more harm than good....Can't you give me two lines, just two lines of recommendation without any hints of 'what a great man the boss is' and what poor fishes they are in comparison?"[43]

Needing to supplement his meager salary and realizing that his "period of study and work for others would have to end," Schindler began branching out on his own in 1922. One of his first independent projects was the Kings Road House in Hollywood (now West Hollywood), which would become Schindler's personal residence for the rest of his life. Pauline's college classmate and Hull House roommate Marian Chace and her husband, Clyde, with whom the Schindlers would live together at Kings Road in quasi-communal fashion, arrived in Los Angeles while the building was under construction.[44] The idea for the house, which was destined to become a landmark of early modern architecture and Los Angeles bohemianism, was partly inspired by Pauline. A composer, educator and arts patron, she

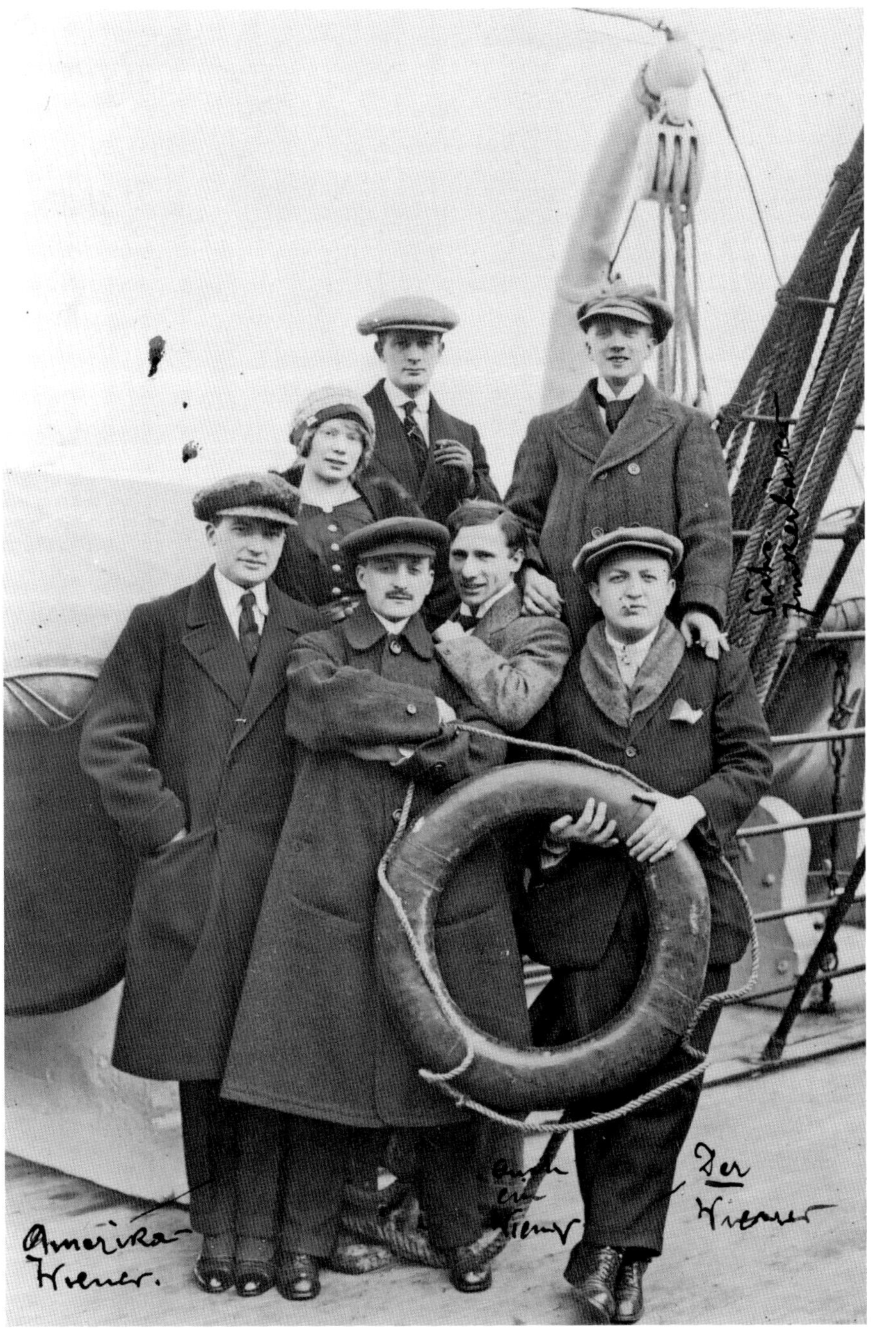

Schindler (front row, second from left) aboard the *Kaiserin August Viktoria* en route to the United States, March 1914. *Courtesy of the Architecture and Design Collection, University Art Museum, UC Santa Barbara.*

had espoused, before meeting Schindler, "an open meeting house…a place of simplicity where people from all walks of life could meet together."[45]

Besides its radical concept, design and construction that "redefined residential architecture and challenged traditional assumptions about domestic space," the house became a focal point for forward-thinking aesthetic, cultural and political activity from the 1920s to the 1950s.[46] Poetry readings, dance performances and concerts attracted American and foreign notables, including photographer Edward Weston; painters Paul Klee, Lyonel Feininger, Wassily Kandinsky and Alexi Jawlensky; composers John Cage and Henry Cowell; and architects J.R. Davidson, Kem Weber and Frank Lloyd Wright. The Kings Road House is widely considered, along with the How House (1925) in Silver Lake and the Lovell Beach House (1926) in Newport Beach, among Schindler's greatest architectural achievements.[47]

By the mid-1920s, due to the influx of political leftists, the proximity of the movie studios and the ramifications of Hollyhock House, Silver Lake became L.A.'s incubator for unorthodox lifestyles and original architecture. Yet while many of his contemporaries hewed to the chic orthodoxy of Internationalism, Schindler carved his own niche, eschewing the International Style's emphasis on outer expression in favor of inner experience. "The sense for the perception of architecture, is not for the eyes," he stated, "but living. Our life is its image."[48]

As architectural critic Carol Arnovici describes his approach:

> *R.M. Schindler's work has the great merit of embracing, instead of enclosing space. The inner part of the enclosure always remained a part of and in harmony with the outer space. Nothing that was within the reach of the vision, from the outer lawn to the distant mountains was left out of the concept and rhythms of his buildings. He never succumbed to the platitudes of internationalism, but was content to interpret his vision of the new humanism in its proper perspective in relation to the nature of the site, the economy of the materials, the personalities of the occupants and the grace of the living…He was one of the few architects of our day who recognized and lived up to the idea that a home is a dwelling place for both the body and the soul.*[49]

As a result of his nonconformity among the nonconformists, Schindler's work went largely unappreciated during his lifetime. He never achieved the international success accorded many of his modernist contemporaries, including compatriot Richard Neutra, and was relegated almost exclusively

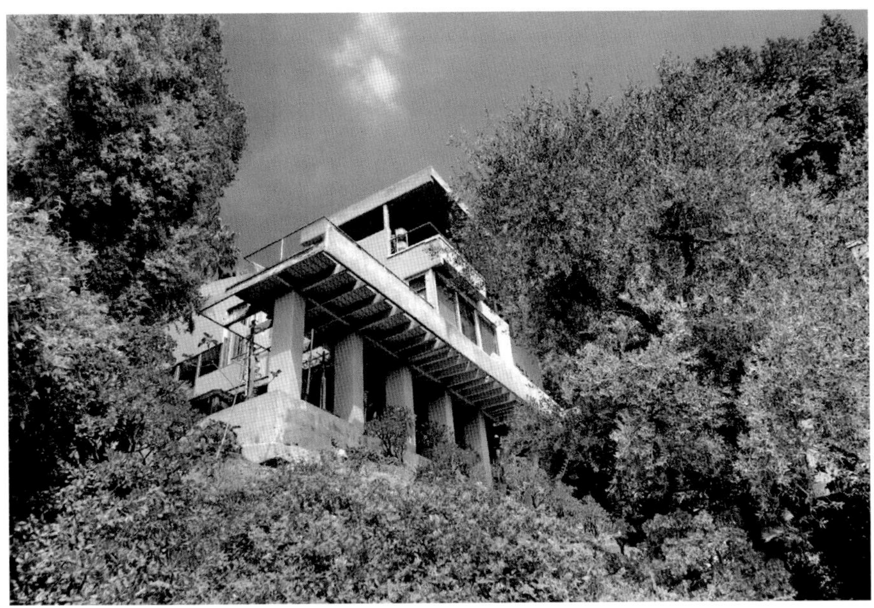

Walker House, R.M. Schindler, 1938.

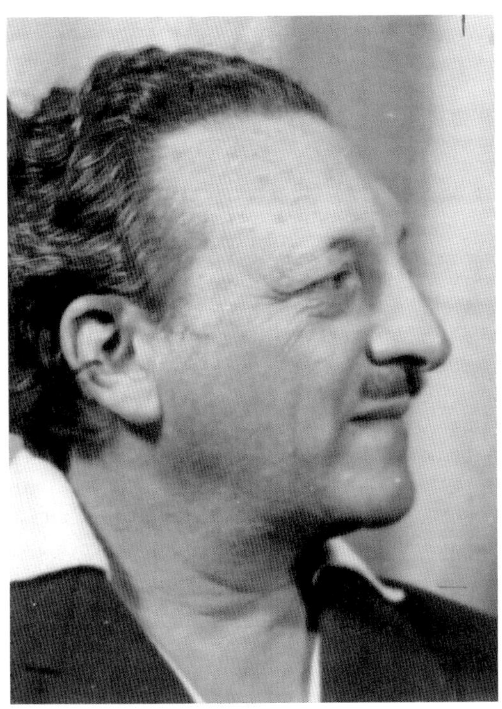

Portrait of R.M. Schindler.
Courtesy of the Architecture and Design Collection, University Art Museum, UC Santa Barbara.

to modest residential commissions. Nevertheless, Schindler had many devoted admirers and followers similarly less beholden to current fashion. He counted among his friends and clients celebrities in film, art and dance, and those, like himself, of a leftist political persuasion.[50]

Between 1923 and 1949, Schindler designed a total of twelve residences and apartment buildings in Silver Lake. One of his earliest and most successful projects was a home for James Eads How, the "Hobo Millionaire," a latter-day St. Francis who renounced a lavish inheritance and spread his fortune to the poor (see Chapter 17).[51] Other noted beneficiaries of his work were the aforementioned Peter Yates and Frances Mullen, whose Evenings on the Roof concerts, held in Schindler's redesigned loft, emulated his and Pauline's Kings Road gatherings and became one of the city's most famous salons (see Chapter 6). Peter "Bart" Yates, who knew Schindler well from his parents' concerts, offered this description:

> *He was a strikingly handsome, animated man. He had the Edwardian type of flashing vigor. He had the Viennese suavity at its best and also the Viennese indifference, in a way, to the ordinary facts of life.…He was not devoted to the arts. He was interested in the people who took part in them, particularly dancers…* [which] *included going off with one person or another to his hideaway in the Palm Springs direction about every weekend. So he had, you might say, a personal attachment to the arts. Apart from that, he was a man almost without ambition, almost without self-interest. He devoted practically all his time to building small residences for people who couldn't afford to pay much money.…He built practically nothing in the way of "show" architecture. He would draw up just sufficient plans to get by the city authorities. Then he would go ahead and improvise on those plans…to accomplish things which perhaps he couldn't account for to the authorities under the building regulations. I think that he had almost as much fun in getting away with violations of the building regulations for the good of architecture as in anything else that he accomplished.*[52]

RICHARD NEUTRA

Richard Neutra, five years younger than Schindler, was born to a wealthy Jewish family in Vienna in 1892. His father, Samuel, the owner of a metal foundry, and his mother, Elizabeth (Betty), a prominent activist in the

Vienna Israelite Community organization, had careers that "straddled the arts and sciences, as Neutra's own work would do."[53] More than merely absorbing the city's cutting-edge cultural environment, the Neutra family actively participated in it. Their friendship with Freud no doubt influenced Richard's older brother Wilhelm to become a psychoanalyst. Younger brother Siegmund, who mingled with Schoenberg and his circle, became a concert violist. And through his sister Josephine's marriage to art curator Arpad Weixlgärtnerart, Richard gained an appreciation for art history and entrée to the likes of Klimt and Kokoschka.[54]

Neutra fell under Adolf Loos's spell right off the bat, studying under him at the Vienna University of Technology beginning in 1911. It was here that he and Schindler also met for the first time and formed, at least for the time being, a mutual admiration society.[55] In Neutra's first year at the school, Schindler noticed him showing great interest in one of Schindler's drawings at an exhibition of the graduating class. "He was the first," Schindler said later, "to understand exactly what I was after."[56]

Neutra's studies were interrupted, his health encumbered and his love life consolidated by World War I. Serving as a cavalry officer in the Balkans, he contracted malaria and, while recovering in Switzerland, met his future wife, Dione Niedermann. The couple married in 1922 and settled in Berlin, where Neutra went to work for Erich Mendelsohn, a pioneer in Expressionist architecture.[57] Having maintained a correspondence with Schindler, and impressed by his Frank Lloyd Wright connections but also by the city and state where Schindler was now ensconced, Neutra wrote his former schoolmate that he, too, "hoped someday to emigrate…to the land of opportunity, and more specifically to California."[58]

With savings set aside from his work with Mendelsohn, augmented by funds from a first prize he shared with Mendelsohn for the design of a project in Haifa, Palestine, Neutra arrived in New York in 1924. Tracing Schindler's American path, he secured a position as a draftsman with Holabird and Roche, a pioneering Chicago firm famed for designing some of the world's first skyscrapers. Contact with Frank Lloyd Wright came soon thereafter, first at Wright's mentor Louis Sullivan's funeral and then with a paying job, and board, at Wright's Taliesin home in Wisconsin.[59]

The Taliesin experience had its delights, especially "being in the presence of a genius," but Wisconsin winters were a far cry from the California sunshine Neutra had envisioned. By spring 1925, the Schindlerian trajectory was completed when his compatriot invited him to join him in Los Angeles. And indeed, without Schindler's support, Neutra may never have made a go of it: Schindler provided encouragement, put a roof over his head and even offered him a business partnership.[60]

Their business and personal relationships, initially, were harmonious. The men's, and their wives', avant-garde artistic and progressive political orientations matched well, and the cooperative living experience of cooking meals and dining together held a certain charm—for a while. The first signs of strain began between the women. Pauline found Dione alternately "cordial and abrasive" and her attitudes on education, nutrition and child-rearing "narrow," while Dione "resented Pauline's intense scrutiny and ridicule, but appreciated her [and Rudolph's] sophisticated social life and avant-garde circle of friends." "It is a tangle like in a Dostoyevsky story," Dione later wrote her mother.[61]

As for the husbands, despite their shared Viennese Jewish backgrounds and aesthetic and political affinities, their personalities were at opposite poles. Neutra biographer Barbara Lamprecht sums up the paradox:

> *Schindler and Neutra were doomed to become Southern California's favorite architectural couple, Schindler playing id to Neutra's superego; Neutra's Apollo to Schindler's Dionysus; the former the verbose go-getter, the latter an articulate hippie; Schindler the collarless shirt, Neutra the wearer of ties; Schindler as shaper of space, Neutra the architect of systems; Schindler finding Eden, Neutra creating Utopia.*[62]

The parting of the ways came when *Los Angeles Times* columnist, physician and naturopath Dr. Philip Lovell (for whom Schindler had designed the aforementioned Lovell Beach House) chose Neutra over Schindler to design a house for him in the city, the Lovell Health House (built in 1929). While the Lovell Beach House is now considered one of Schindler's masterworks, "the building had problems with budget overruns and leaking," and despite "Lovell's professed liberalism in regard to sexual expression," he resented the notoriously libertine Schindler's "growing infatuation with [his wife] Leah."[63]

Besides severing the last strand of their personal relationship, Lowell's dropping Schindler for Neutra marked a turning point in the architects' careers, with Schindler thereafter relegated to small residential projects while Neutra went on to regional and international fame as one of the major contributors to the International Style. Three years after the completion, and instant acclaim, of the Health House, Neutra—with support from Dr. Cornelius Hendrik van der Leeuw, a Dutch psychiatrist, tobacco heir and

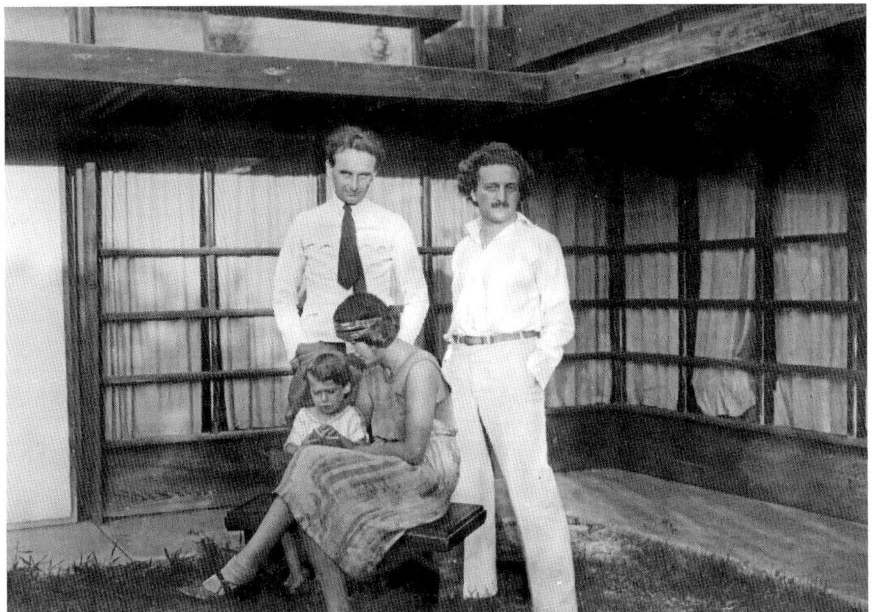

Richard Neutra, Schindler, Dione Neutra and Dion Neutra, Kings Road House, circa 1928. *Courtesy of the Architecture and Design Collection, University Art Museum, UC Santa Barbara.*

modern architecture enthusiast—built a home on Silver Lake Boulevard beside the reservoir for himself, Dione and a family that was growing along with his reputation.[64] A modest dwelling that incorporated innovations of the Health House on a smaller scale, the home served as Neutra's design studio until a separate office, the Neutra Office Building, was completed on nearby Glendale Boulevard in 1950.

Between the building of his house and studio, Neutra purchased other lots on Silver Lake Boulevard and adjoining Argent Place. The several houses the Father of Silver Lake Modernism built there over the years led to the section being dubbed the "Neutra Colony." In 1992, in posthumous celebration of his 100th birthday, Argent Place was officially renamed Neutra Place.[65]

Though a unique amalgam of his body of work, the Neutra Colony constitutes only a small portion of his overall oeuvre. Between 1923 and 1969, he completed an astounding 260 projects, extending across the Unites States, to Europe and, perhaps most prestigiously, to the U.S. Embassy building in Karachi, Pakistan (unfortunately demolished in 2013). The expanded geographical and architectural scope was spurred by Neutra's partnership in 1949 with Robert Alexander, whose firm's emphasis, especially in the

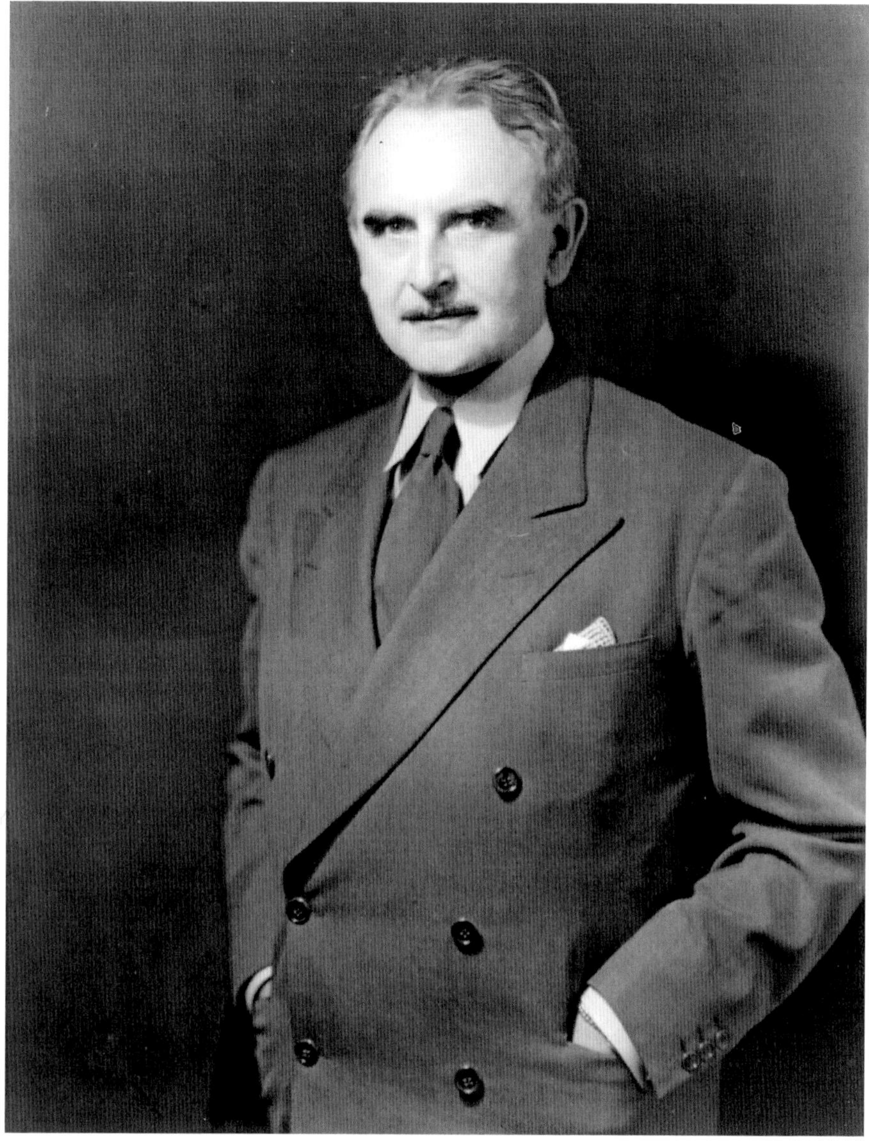

Portrait of Richard Neutra in his prime. *Courtesy of Archives–Special Collections College of Environmental Design, California State Polytechnic University, Pomona, California.*

postwar period, shifted from domestic dwellings to commercial buildings and large public projects.[66]

The most ambitious, and controversial, of the latter was the abortive Elysian Heights public housing complex planned for Chavez Ravine.

Similar to Neutra's Channel Heights project in San Pedro in the early 1940s incorporating a shopping center, schools and community buildings, the Elysian Heights project was infused with utopian idealism. Poised for construction in the early 1950s, the project ran afoul of anti-Communist paranoia and an emergent "corporate modernist" business model that favored Dodger Stadiums and upscale cultural centers to desperately needed affordable housing.[67] Differences of opinion, personality and temperament—unrelated to the Chavez Ravine debacle—led to a dissolution of the Neutra-Alexander partnership in 1958.

By this time, however, Richard Neutra's place in the architectural pantheon was secure. As Lamprecht summarizes:

> *What made Neutra unique was not the endless search for form but the endless search for the human being…Even though his architecture is often construed as being a "machine in the garden," for Neutra the real "machine" in the garden is the human being, whose daily experience could be calibrated through his or her relationship to the environment. The connectedness between the indoors and outdoors of Neutra homes suggested…as Arthur Drexler, the late head of design of the Museum of Modern Art noted, that "it is impossible to sit inside a Neutra living room and still wish that one could get outdoors."*[68]

Another of Neutra's strengths was a knack for making livable use of limited space. John Bertram, principal of Bertram Architects, is a living beneficiary of this ability. Perhaps uniquely among present-day designers, Bertram has gained intimate knowledge of Neutra's work both through his restorations of four historic Neutra homes, among them the Brown House in Bel-Air, and the "more modest and arguably more authentic" McKintosh House he comes home to every day in Silver Lake (designed by Neutra for Mr. and Mrs. Harry G. McIntosh in 1939).[69] The nine-hundred-square-foot house at 1317 Maltman Avenue, consisting of two bedrooms, one tiny bathroom and a hallway-like kitchen, exemplifies the spatial ingenuity also on display at Neutra's own Silver Lake house.

Just as Neutra's achievements must take into account significant mentors and benefactors, notably Adolf Loos, Frank Lloyd Wright and Richard Schindler, among others, his legacy must include the boost he gave future luminaries such as Gregory Ain, Harwell Hamilton Harris, David Hyun and Raphael Soriano, who apprenticed with Neutra before embarking on their own careers (see Chapters 3 and 14). That the Neutra spirit lives on among current Silver Lake designers is no more evident than in the beautiful Silver Lake branch library built in 2009 at the corner of Glendale and Silver Lake Boulevards, a skip and a jump from the Neutra Office Building and a wink and a nod from Neutra's former house. Designed by Barry A. Milofsky and Thomas Michali of M2A Architects, the building, besides its geometric aesthetic and use of industrial materials, is clearly "a nod to Richard Neutra and his indoor/outdoor aesthetic."[70]

The Meeting of the Century

In 1953, Neutra suffered a second heart attack (the first occurred in 1949) and was hospitalized at Cedars of Lebanon Hospital in East Hollywood (now a Scientology center). Remarkably, Rudolph Schindler happened to be recovering from cancer surgery at the same time and place. One day, he looked up from his hospital bed to find none other than Neutra, his bitter rival with whom he hadn't spoken in decades, wheeled into the double room beside him. Biographer Thomas Hines describes the amazing coincidence:

> *Neutra had been given the choice of a double room or a single, but had chosen the former so as to have someone to talk to.... It seemed the epitome of destiny. After recovering from the initial disbelief, the long-estranged friends adjusted to their tragic-comic predicament and attempted to establish old ties.... Friends and family members who visited the room daily recalled a spirited conversation, mostly of Vienna and old times and places.*[71]

Likely left unspoken were the divergent paths their careers had taken. Schindler's stature as a notable modernist wouldn't be fully recognized until Esther McCoy's *Five California Architects*, published in 1960. Renowned since the 1930s, Neutra had been named *Time* magazine's "Man of the Year" in 1949. Not only fame but longevity as well was on Neutra's side. While Schindler would succumb to cancer soon after his hospital-room reunion with Neutra in 1953, Neutra would continue working, with the help of his architect son, Dion, for another two decades. He received an honorary degree from UCLA in 1969.[72]

In the spring of 1970, Neutra and his wife, Dione, departed for an extended European lecture tour. While visiting friends in Germany, he suffered a massive and, this time fatal, heart attack. Dione continued living

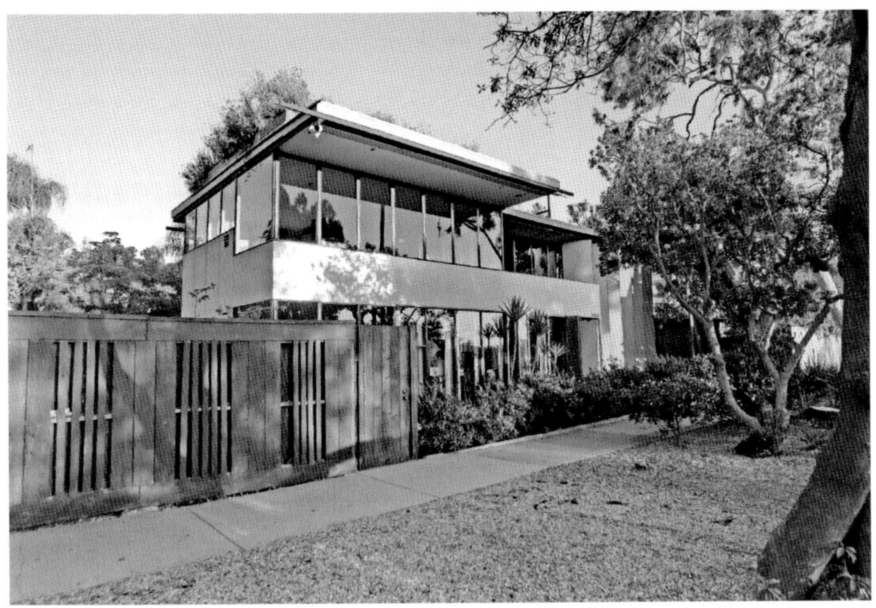

VDL Research House, Richard Neutra, circa 1932; rebuilt by Dion Neutra, 1964.

at their Silver Lake home, named the VDL Research House in honor of its benefactor, Dr. van der Leeuw, for twenty more years, hosting musical and political events and inviting visiting artists to stay for extended periods. Son Dion has carried the Neutra torch to the present, through his own architectural work and promotion of his father's. Upon Dione's death in 1990, the VDL House was bequeathed to the California Polytechnic University Foundation and the College of Environmental Design. Her ashes and those of her husband were scattered under a Chinese elm in the VDL House courtyard.[73]

3

THE SORCERER'S APPRENTICES

GREGORY AIN, HARWELL HAMILTON HARRIS AND RAPHAEL SORIANO

Richard Neutra's inclusion in the 1932 "Modern Architecture" exhibition at the New York Museum of Modern Art confirmed his growing international reputation. The subsequent increase in commissions required taking on assistants. First and perhaps foremost among these was Gregory Ain, who first met Neutra in 1928 while he was still living at Schindler's Kings Road House. Ain came to Southern California in 1911 with his parents, Baer and Chiah (née Weissberg) Ain. Baer, the son of a Polish rabbi, had been exiled to Siberia for his Menshevik socialist activities.[74] When Chiah's prosperous, well-connected family was unable to secure Baer's release, he escaped in 1906 and was reunited with his wife and daughter in Germany, and together they set sail for America, arriving on Christmas Day 1906.[75] The family lived first with Chiah's relatives in Pittsburgh, where Gregory—named after Gregory Gershuny, a Menshevik hero—was born in 1908.[76]

Uncomfortable with his in-laws' middle-class values, Baer moved the family first to Kentucky before settling in the Lincoln Heights section of Los Angeles. Like neighboring Boyle Heights, Lincoln Heights was an ethnically diverse community with a large number of Russian and Eastern European Jews, many of whom shared Baer's leftist beliefs.[77] Taking his socialist ideals to the hilt, Baer next moved the family to Llano Del Rio, a utopian farming commune in the Antelope Valley founded by socialist labor lawyer Job Harriman. Baer had supported Harriman's run for mayor of Los Angeles in 1911, which Harriman had been favored to win until a bomb detonated by union activists shortly before the election destroyed the *L.A. Times* building, killing twenty-one people and, by association, Harriman's chances. Harriman's utopian experiment floundered as well; after a year and a half, the Ains returned to East Los Angeles.[78]

Although Gregory was only eight years old at the time, the taste of communal living would have a significant impact on the architect-to-be, particularly his later achievements in low-income and cooperative housing. Back in Lincoln Heights, Baer insisted on supplementing what he believed was the public school's capitalist-oriented education with progressive home schooling. Gregory admired his father, who "excelled in everything he did, from athletics to mathematics to world literature," but his authoritarianism and perfectionism caused considerable friction between them.[79]

After graduating from Lincoln High School, Gregory, at his father's insistence, enrolled at the University of California, Southern Branch (UCSB), because of its free tuition and public status. The school, soon to be relocated to Westwood and renamed UCLA, was then situated in East Hollywood at the present site of Los Angeles Community College. Though Gregory had preferred USC, UCSB proved a boon in one regard. He was inspired there by a lecture entitled "Space Architecture" delivered by R.M. Schindler, which, besides establishing his future calling, gave Gregory a means of finally rebelling against his father.[80] After a year, he transferred to USC, partly because it was the only local school that offered an architecture program and, mainly, he later stated, because this "was the only field my father knew nothing about."[81]

As it turns out, USC's department didn't know much about it, either. Unlike the grounding in modernist principles Schindler and Neutra had gleaned in state-of-the-art Vienna, USC's program remained tied to the neoclassical Beaux-Arts tradition. This proved only a momentary detour, however, for in 1928, recalling the UCSB lecture, Gregory visited the Kings Road House, where he met both Schindler and Neutra.[82]

The meeting was decisive both personally and professionally. In addition to introducing him to the pioneering modernists, one of whom would give Gregory his first apprenticeship in the field, the two older men's creative and political orientations offered another partial resolution to the Oedipal conflict with his father. As Schindler biographer Esther McCoy observes, "Because of the Schindlers' [and Neutras'] involvement in left-wing politics, Ain accepted modern architecture as an agent of social change."[83]

During their initial encounter, Ain commented to Neutra how wonderful it must be to live in such a modern house, to which Neutra replied that only by using industrial technology could houses be truly modern. The remark so impressed Ain that he immediately enrolled at the Academy of Modern Art in Hollywood, where Neutra was lecturing.[84] Of even greater benefit than the coursework, Neutra's Lovell Health House, then under construction in the Los Feliz hills, served as a laboratory for the students. Practicing what he had preached to Ain, Neutra, in the Health House, designed the first steel-frame house built in the United States and one of the first to utilize sprayed-on concrete. Ain even contributed to the building's innovations by donating the headlights from his Ford Model A, which were incorporated into the staircase.[85]

Neutra's apprenticeship program grew out of the students' collaboration. The Academy classes were held at night, allowing students to work on Neutra's projects during the day. Among the student apprentices was Harwell Hamilton Harris, another future modernist, and Ain's first wife, Agnes Budin. To make ends meet, Ain hired on with other architects, including M. Marcus Priteca, best known for designing ornate theater palaces for Alexander Pantages, and Schindler, for whom he worked on low-cost housing projects and a "revolutionary" Standard Oil service station.[86]

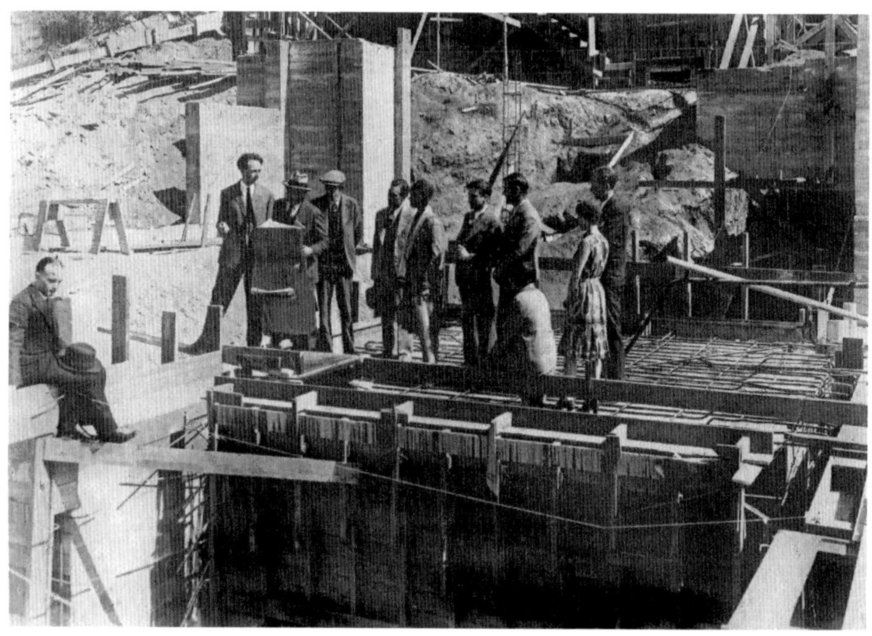

Neutra (standing far left) with students from Academy of Modern Art at Lovell House site including Harwell Hamilton Harris (third from Neutra's left) and Gregory Ain (fifth to left of Neutra). *Courtesy of Thomas S. Hines.*

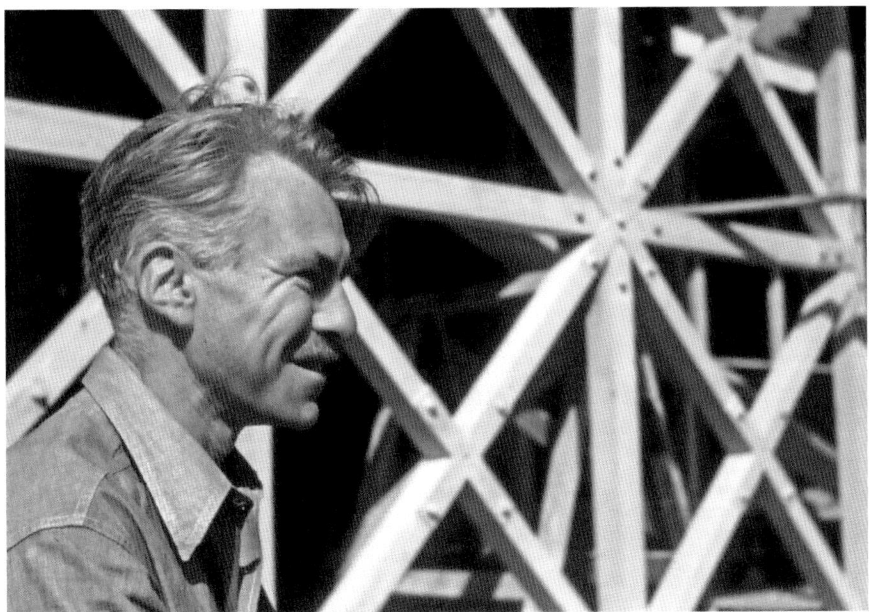

Portrait of Gregory Ain. *Courtesy of Eames Office LLC.*

In 1932, Neutra solidified his celebrity with the completion of his Silver Lake home, the later-named VDL House. Ain not only helped engineer the structure; he and Agnes also lived in the house, along with the Neutras, for the first two years. Paralleling problems the Schindlers and Neutras had experienced at Kings Road, cohabitation at VDL created a strain, here prompted not by the wives' mutual hostility but by Oedipal conflict between Ain and Neutra. As McCoy describes, the interaction at VDL produced "a claustrophobic interdependence and complex paternalistic associations; Neutra seems to have fully inhabited his role as a father figure, and Ain became the resentful and rebellious son."[87]

In 1935, in another Schindler-Neutra parallel, this time with their break over the Lovell Health House commission, Ain severed relations with Neutra over his failure to pay Ain's agreed-upon salary of ten dollars a week. Rather than struggling to find his footing, Ain's solo practice quickly found a niche—one that unfortunately would come back to haunt him in the postwar period. For the moment, with his father's Menshevik ideals and the Llano del Rio experience having returned from the repressed, Ain was more committed than ever to using modern architecture for social change.[88]

Although he apparently never officially joined the Communist Party (CP), during the Depression Ain was the most visible architect at gatherings with groups labeled as Communist fronts, including the John Reed Club. Over his comparatively short career, he designed numerous important structures in the Greater Los Angeles area, mostly for clients committed to progressive, some would say radical, causes, including at least twenty-five known Communists.[89] These included gay rights pioneer Harry Hay (see Chapter 7), for whose mother Ain built a home in the Hollywood Hills in the early 1950s.[90] For the CP homes, Ain's designs served a dual purpose, as living spaces and gathering places for secret political activity—secrecy being of vital importance in the heyday of the LAPD's notorious Red Squad, not to mention the FBI. The Silver Lake house Ain designed for CP members Samuel and Cecilia Tierman is a good example. Architecturally bold, with a unique interior highlighted by a pyramidal skylight giving it an almost monumental feel, the home's exterior appears to be an "unassuming tract house."[91]

Ain pioneered the democratic "open floor plan," in which living room, dining room and kitchen are all open to one another, the direct opposite of the standard for wealthy clients, including many of Neutra's, in which

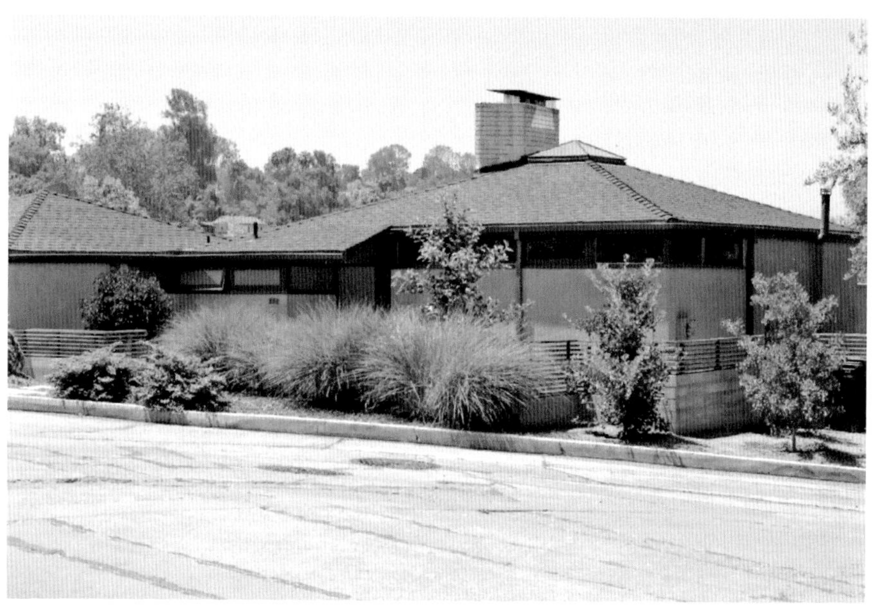

Tierman House, 2323 Micheltorena Street, Gregory Ain, 1940.

the kitchen, intended for use by servants, was closed off and isolated. For Russian-born Communist Alice Orans, Ain designed a house with folding partition walls between the children's bedrooms that "allowed children greater independence and responsibility."[92] For radical feminist Urcel Daniel, secretary of the Los Angeles Newspaper Guild, Ain's design, in this case borrowing directly from Schindler, embraced the needs of the newly emancipated single woman by striving to "liberate [the occupant] from the incessant household rhythm."[93] During World War II, Ain was chief engineer on Charles Eames's famous plywood chairs, and in 1952, he moved into offices on Hyperion Avenue in Silver Lake, which he built and occupied together with African American architect James "Jimmy" Garrott (see Chapter 11). Bringing *Silver Lake Bohemia*'s interconnective chain full circle, while working at his Hyperion office, Ain was living at the Schindler-designed Bubeshko Apartments a few blocks away.[94]

In the wake of the city's housing shortage caused by the influx of wartime veterans, Ain's attention shifted from single-family homes to multi-family housing projects. The first of these, conceived at a meeting in 1946 between Ain, ten left-wing veterans and their attorney, Matthew Richman, would become one of the great success stories in cooperative housing and a prototype for future innovation.[95] The now legendary Avenal Cooperative Housing Project, located at 2939–49 Avenal Avenue in Silver Lake, was listed in 2005 in the National Register of Historic Places.

During the McCarthy era, the Avenal project, its founding members and Ain himself, were less highly regarded. Tainted by his Communist affiliations, Ain's practice declined. Among his greatest disappointments, and greatest losses for Los Angeles architecture, was his exclusion, due to his politics, from the prestigious Case Study House program. He did some lecturing at USC, built his last Los Angeles house in 1963 and, the same year, with the anti-Communist cloud finally lifting, was appointed dean of the Pennsylvania State University School of Architecture, where he served until 1967. Ain died in 1988 at Sunset Hall, a Unitarian retirement home for leftists in Los Angeles.[96]

As a final tribute, we offer the testimony of architect Antony Unruh, who has the good fortune of working in Ain's Silver Lake studio on Hyperion Avenue, which he purchased in 1993:

> *Ain's office building is a beautiful example of the early modernist ideal of a "machine for living"—light, simple, stripped of decoration and built on a practical post and beam format. My partner, Trish Boyer, sometimes*

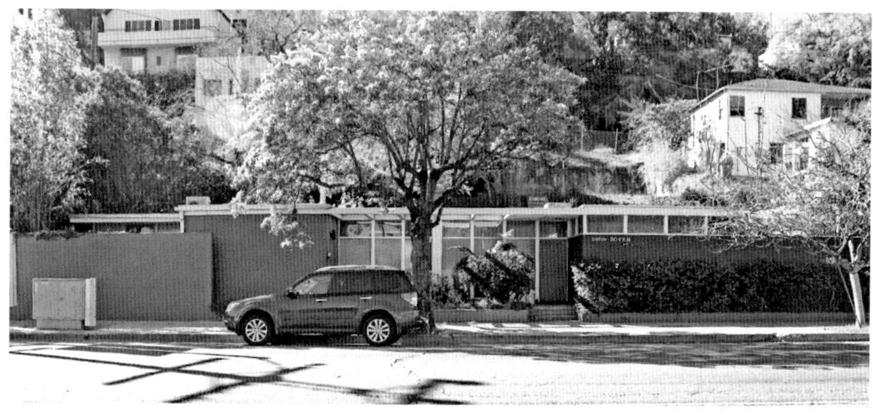

Ain, Johnson, Day and Garrott Office, Ain, Johnson & Day, 1947–48.

> *explains her appreciation for Ain's thoughtfully functional and peaceful design by stating that even when she doesn't feel like working, she always wants to come to the office. What has been interesting for us has been to adapt the new materials, technologies and lifestyles to the renewed enthusiasm for the spare modern aesthetic promoted by Ain and his peers. Having met a few Ain clients, I have gained some insight into his eccentric personality, his interest in cars, politics, social awareness, music and his interest in yoga. On several occasions I was told of his having office meetings while he did a yoga headstand. I have had the privilege of remodeling and restoring two Ain-designed houses in Silver Lake, the Daniels and Oran houses, originally built in 1939 and 1941 respectively. Being in his office surrounded by his spirit has afforded me the ability to tackle the projects with a clearer understanding of his intent for the buildings he built.*[97]

Harris and Soriano

Harwell Hamilton Harris and Raphael Soriano neither lived nor maintained offices in Silver Lake. Both, however, like Ain, trained with Richard Neutra and achieved international fame partly for the buildings they designed here. Of the two, Soriano more readily fits the bohemian bill, having engaged in an openly artistic lifestyle with little interest in wealth or status.[98] Harris, if more conventional in outlook and behavior, rubbed shoulders with many of the iconoclasts featured so far, including the woman, and building, that got the local avant-garde ball rolling: Aline Barnsdall and the Hollyhock House.

While a sculpture student at Otis Art Institute (now Otis College of Art and Design), the Redlands-born Harris was invited to Barnsdall's Olive Hill home. Overawed by the experience, as he later described, he "abandoned thoughts of becoming a sculptor…this was sculpture on a grand scale and I simply couldn't stand still."[99] Following the seemingly obligatory initiation rite for Silver Lake modernists, Harris next visited the Kings Road House and met both Schindler and Neutra, the latter shocking the neophyte by offering him a job on the spot. Though he wouldn't live at Neutra's Silver Lake residence, as Ain and his wife briefly did, Harris spent part of his apprenticeship at the VDL House.[100]

Harris's marriage to Jean Murray Bangs, whose earlier marriage to union organizer Abe Portif had given her entrée to left-wing intellectual circles, expanded Harris's horizons. Although he apparently steered clear of political engagement himself, the Harris-Bangs relationship, as Thomas Hines describes, intertwined "Jean's interest in art, life and politics into a symbiotic personal and professional partnership."[101]

Like Schindler and Ain, Harris, too, would "break" with Neutra, not over personal issues but over aesthetics. His mature work veered from his mentor's "machine" style toward Frank Lloyd Wright's "organic" approach.[102] Several of the seven homes Harris designed in Silver Lake reflect this shift, with his own residence, the Fellowship Park House in adjoining Echo Park, providing the crowning example. Built on a steep hillside, the house was constructed mostly of wood, with a dramatic stone path curling in and around the perimeters of the rooms. The building won the House Beautiful Small House Competition in 1937 and first prize at the Pittsburgh Glass Institution, besting two of Neutra's submissions.[103]

Harris was also involved in one of the most eclectic of all Silver Lake homes, a 1906 bungalow purchased in 1942 by Edward Albert Adams, founder and first president of the Los Angeles Art Center School. Not a licensed architect himself, Adams collaborated over many years with several professionals on the home's redesign. Harris prepared the initial drawings in 1951, after which Adams engaged John Lautner's one-time partner Douglas Honnold (see Chapter 13) and John Rex in 1955 to build a garage, grill and masonry deck. In 1966, A. Albert Cooling, an instructor at the Art Center School, refashioned the house into the form it retains today, with the final phase completed, after Cooling's death, by Taliesin Fellow James Delong. The house, located at 2331 Cove Avenue, was designated Los Angeles Historic-Cultural Monument No. 922 in 2008.[104]

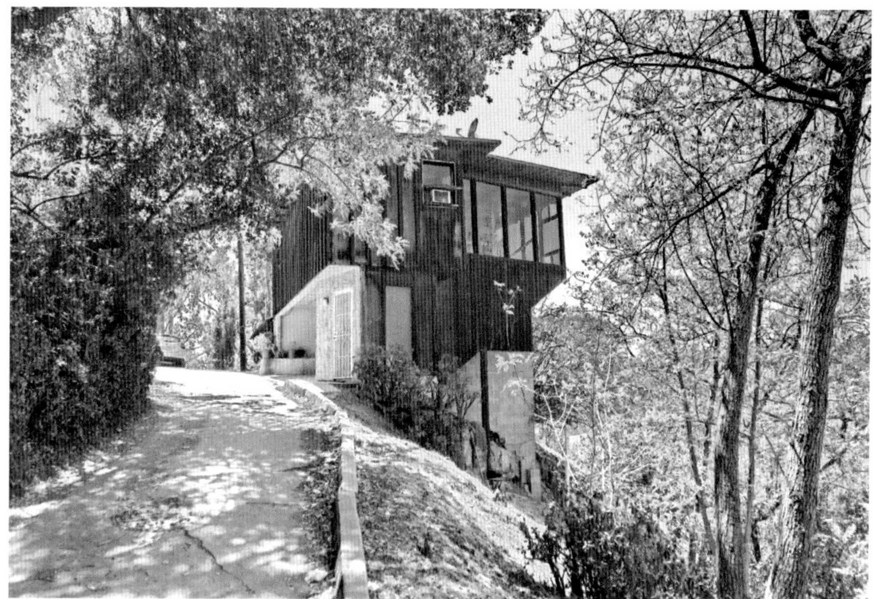

Fellowship Parkway House, Harwell Hamilton Harris, 1935.

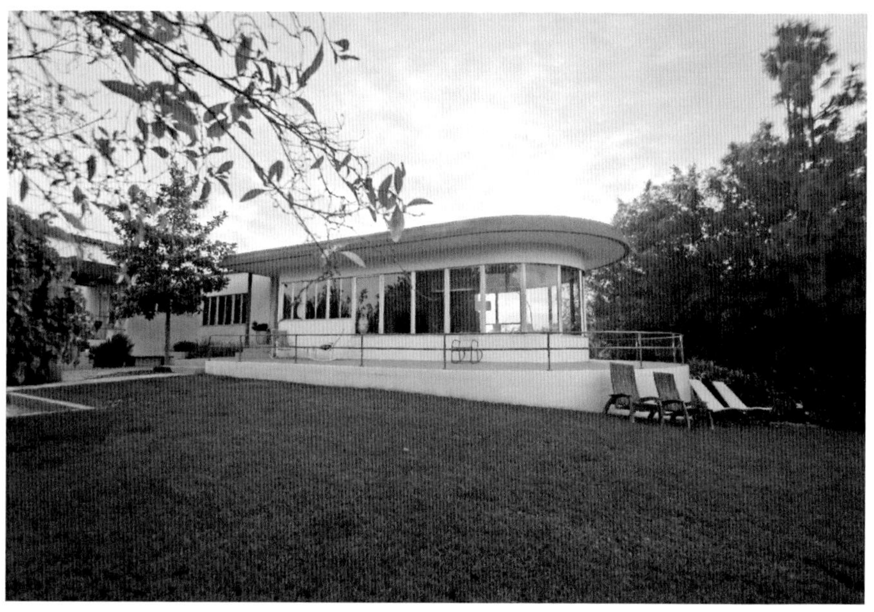

Lipetz House, Raphael Soriano, 1936.

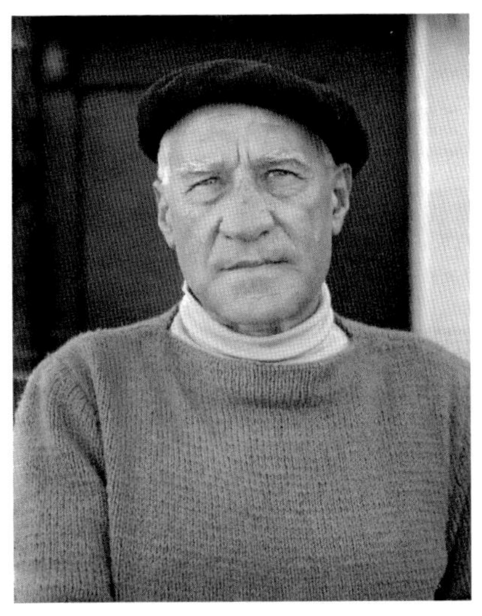

Portrait of Raphael Soriano. *Courtesy of Getty Archives.*

Although Raphael Soriano designed only three structures in Silver Lake, one of them, the Lipetz House, created a sensation as one of three buildings presented at the American Pavilion at the Paris Exposition in 1937, winning the prestigious Prix de Rome. The success of the Paris show secured for Soriano "visibility and prominence… as the strongest Modern purist in the International Style."[105]

Soriano was born in 1904 on the Greek island of Rhodes, where his Sephardic Jewish ancestors had immigrated during the Spanish Inquisition. In addition to the island's chiefly spoken modern Greek, as a boy he learned classical Greek and Latin and became fluent in French and later Italian after Italy wrested control of Rhodes from Turkey in 1912. To escape the island's isolation and his demanding father, Soriano seized the opportunity to move to Southern California after World War I, courtesy of financial backing from his grandfather and a welcome mat provided by three of his mother's sisters living in Los Angeles.[106]

With an affable, outgoing personality coupled with his gift for languages, Soriano easily established relationships in his adopted city. Influential friends helped him gain admission to the USC School of Architecture, though, as with Ain, the stodgy Beaux-Arts program left him uninspired and frustrated. As with Ain and Harris, Soriano's creative and career breakthroughs came through contact with Richard Neutra. He was introduced to Neutra's modernist ideas, as well as to Frank Lloyd Wright's, at lectures the two men gave at the Philharmonic Auditorium. While he found the more-famous Wright's remarks "rhetorically florid, empty and self-important," Neutra's, which he found "full of rational and inspirational exhortation… so inspired Soriano that he asked Neutra to accept him as an intern without compensation."[107]

Happenstance is often as important as talent to success in any field, and the manner in which Soriano secured his first independent commission, the career-making Lipetz House, is a noteworthy example. At a screening of a French art film at the left-wing John Reed Club in the early 1930s, he helped translate its essence for a woman seated beside him. As Thomas Hines describes the encounter:

> *In their conversation following the movie, the woman was impressed by the architect's knowledge of film and music, and invited him the following month to a concert to be performed by her sister, concert pianist Helen Lipetz. Moved by the same qualities that impressed her sister, Helen and her husband Manuel commissioned the young unknown architect to design their house.*[108]

But there's more to the story. Though not quite on a par with Schindler's shenanigans, Soriano's relationship with Helen Lipetz was more than just professional. Though it would take him fifty years to come clean, Soriano admitted in a 1985 interview for the UCLA Oral History Project that he and Helen had fallen "madly in love the first time our eyes met." She was, he recalled, "my first beautiful love." Soriano "declined to elaborate on the duration of the affair" with his female patron, Hines confides, "but had no trouble acknowledging their mutual satisfaction with the house."[109]

An Apprentice at Heart

Although he never worked for or even met Richard Neutra, Michael Lehrer, perhaps more than any living architect, exemplifies the profound influence Neutra, as well as Schindler, Wright and other major modernists, continue to exert on present-day designers—especially those fortunate enough, as was Lehrer, to have grown up in his heroes' stomping grounds and to maintain offices directly in Silver Lake. Opened in 1985, after his graduation from college and an apprenticeship with Frank Gehry & Associates, Lehrer's firm has won over sixty local, state, national and international design awards since 1996. His Water + Life Museum in Hemet, a renowned environmental showcase, was honored as the first LEED Platinum museum in the world. He was elected president of the Los Angeles branch of the American Institute of Architects (AIA) in 1999 and, in 2004, was elevated to AIA's College of Fellows. Despite all his accolades, Lehrer has never forgotten the pioneers that paved the way, as he expressed in an interview with one of the authors:

Growing up next to Griffith Park, as a child, I was surrounded by great landscapes and spectacular architecture. Neutra's Lovell House was just over the ridge behind our house. Wright's Ennis House lined a ridge one canyon over, and Schindler's Schrage House, with a garden by Neutra, was atop a hill on the other side of our canyon. A great Soriano house was just up the street at the edge of Griffith Park, and Barnsdall Park was a mile away. Growing up, architecture, landscape, native flora, and joy were givens to my day-to-day existence. I decided to be an architect when I was eight. I was in love with a girl whose father (S. Kenneth Johnson, the J in DMJM) was an architect. By the age of ten, I was entranced by Frank Lloyd Wright's drawings and seduced by his line: how the line of the building would become the line of foliage, and then extend to become the line of the topography, and continue as the picture frame. This sublime integration was the font of my sensibility about architecture and landscape. While I was an undergraduate at Berkeley, this sensibility incubated organically within me. At Harvard's Graduate School of Design, this integration would become a way of life.[110]

4

AVATAR OF THE AVANT-GARDE

Anaïs Nin

Not only was Anaïs (Ah-na-EEs) Nin arguably the most famous literary artist to reside in Silver Lake, but her enmeshment in the area's various avant-garde and bohemian strands rivals if not surpasses that of Peter Yates as well. It's as if every cultural or political aspect of the place conjoined with Nin in some way, recalling—in their tendril-like intertwining—her 1936 novel *House of Incest.*

Nin's actual hilltop house stood on Hidalgo Avenue to the east of Silver Lake Reservoir, where she lived from the early 1960s until her death at seventy-three in 1977. It was designed by Eric Lloyd Wright, grandson of Frank Lloyd Wright, son of Lloyd Wright and half-brother of Nin's second "husband" Rupert Pole (more on the cause for the quotes later). Her best friend and confidant, *Midnight Cowboy* author James Leo Herlihy (see Chapter 5), spent his last twenty years in a house he was drawn to because of Nin, on a hill just across the way from hers. On her same hill, Mexican revolutionary Ricardo Flores Magón (see Chapter 10) had established an anarchist commune in the 1910s, and the pioneering Rose Scharlin Cooperative Nursery School (see Chapter 12) still offered progressive education. Nin could be glimpsed at Yates's Evenings on the Roof salons (see Chapter 6), whose other guests included the likes of Igor Stravinsky and Arnold Schoenberg and whose eponymous addition to Yates's Micheltorena Street bungalow was designed by Rudolph Schindler.[111] Regular musical gatherings were held at Nin's home as well, organized and participated in by Rupert Pole, who played viola in the monthly chamber concerts. More intimate tête-à-têtes at Casa

Hidalgo included prominent feminists Deena Metzger and Judy Chicago. As close friend Ruth Ross (whose own Eric Lloyd Wright–redesigned house lay across from Herlihy's and Nin's and down the street from Harry Hay's) summarizes, "Anaïs knew them all."[112]

Nin's life, both personally and creatively, was an uncommonly tumultuous one, partly from circumstance, partly by her own doing. Her itinerant nature and artistic leanings were bequeathed from birth. She was born in 1903 in Neuilly, France, to Joaquin Nin, a Cuban pianist/composer (of Spanish/French descent), and Rosa Culmell, a Cuban classically trained singer (of Danish/French descent).[113] The nomadic lineage expanded geographically when, in 1914, upon separation from Joaquin, Rosa moved ten-year-old Anais and her two brothers, Thorvald Nin and Joaquin Nin-Culmell, briefly to Barcelona and then to New York City. There, Anaïs became fluent in English, dropped out of school at sixteen and worked as an artist's model. Cuba and France reentered the picture when she married her first husband, American Hugo Guiler, in Havana in 1923 and moved with him to Paris the following year.[114]

Nin's libertine sexual proclivities were affirmed, in print, in her first published work, *D.H. Lawrence: An Unprofessional Study* (1932).[115] The proclivities in practice, though edited out of her first published diaries in 1966, sprang from the bohemian lifestyle she plunged into, marriage notwithstanding, in Paris. This included a torrid affair with Henry Miller and with his wife, June, the former leading to one of several abortions she would have over the years. The lesbian side of the ménage à trois, featured in the 1990 Hollywood film *Henry and June*, never blossomed into full-fledged bisexuality, as Nin explained in a later diary: "My love of woman…was never answered because June did not initiate me at the time when I might have been awakened. It has remained like a small area unlived in my life, in fact the only one." Her sexual identity, rather, took on a Jungian cast, as described in a quote in the same diary from Dr. Esther Harding: "No individual is entirely male or female. Each is made up of a composite of both elements."[116]

Poles Apart

Though she had no direct contact with Jung, Nin would undergo lifelong psychoanalysis, including with another of Freud's protégés, Otto Rank, whom she added to her list of lovers and who crucially influenced her

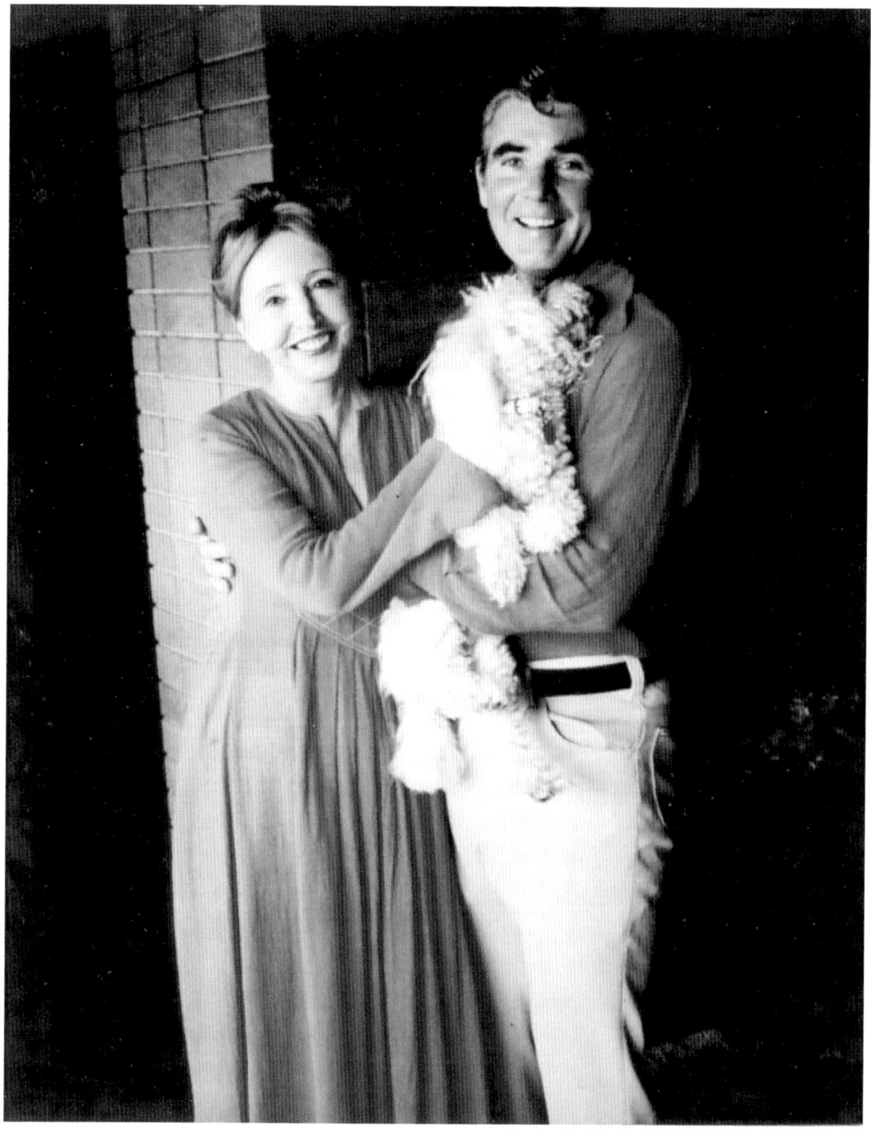

Anaïs Nin with Rupert Pole. *Courtesy of Anaïs Nin Trust.*

improvisatory, surrealistic writing style. The blending of fact and fiction extended to her diaries, which infamously played fast and loose with the truth, and to her own day-to-day life. The crowning dissimulation began after she and Guiler moved to New York to escape the impending war in Europe, and where she met Rupert Pole, in 1947. Her affair with and eventual "marriage" to Pole, a man sixteen years her junior (Guiler was five years her senior), began Nin's "bicoastal trapeze," as she called the bigamous relationships and cross-continental homes she would secretively maintain, with the abetment of friends—until the publication of her diaries, and the tax implications this entailed, forced her to annul the marriage to Pole.[117]

A key supporting player in the elaborate ruse was Nin's self-christened "Lie Box": a small folder with file cards, subdivided into New York and Los Angeles sections. Post office boxes in both locations, and an endless string of alibis—meetings with New York publishers, confabs with Hollywood producers—propped up her Janus-faced shuttling between "the pillar [Hugo] and the tree [Rupert]."[118]

That the hoax ever completely fooled the dual swains is doubtful. Nin biographer Deirdre Bair describes Pole as "seeing only what he wanted to believe," which included her lies, "or, like Hugo, he pretended that he did."[119] But Nin's pillar-tree metaphors for her twin spouses are apt. Guiler, himself a schizoid mix of banker and eventual avant-garde filmmaker (under the pseudonym Ian Hugo), had enabled Nin's writing and comparatively lavish lifestyle through his financial dealings in Paris and New York. Pole's "green" streak, meanwhile, signaled a yen for nature, not money. Related by his mother's marriage to the illustrious Wrights, and by blood to Shakespearean actor Reginald Pole, Pole the younger boasted a degree in music from Harvard, played guitar as well as viola, performed in USO shows and on cruise ships and had just finished a turn in a Broadway play when he met Nin on an elevator going to a party hosted by one of the heirs to the Guggenheim fortune. Back on the West Coast, he earned a second degree in natural science and landed a job as a forest ranger in Sierra Madre, where he lived in a mountain cabin, on and off with Nin, from 1950 to 1955. Pole's next career turn, as a biology teacher at Thomas Star King Junior High (now Middle) School on Fountain Avenue, brought him and Nin, for the first time, to Silver Lake.[120]

Notes from the Underground

"Life got a little more glamorous," Nin wrote in her diary about the now (bigamously) married couple's move to an area more compatible with her cosmopolitan sensibility and avant-garde spirit.[121] Silver Lake fit the bill on both scores. It was situated between Hollywood and downtown, with nicknames such as Bohemian Hill, the Swish Alps and, if neighboring Echo Park was factored in, Red Hill and Mount Moscow.

As she had in New York's Greenwich Village, Nin reveled in the stimulating milieu. She championed the Beats and attended a reading of *Howl* by Allen Ginsberg, at which he ripped off all his clothes and threw them at the audience.[122] She took LSD (once, in a doctor-controlled setting); though she felt that an imaginatively blocked America could benefit from the drug's "dynamiting" effect, she also rued having "to pack LSD with each [of my books]" so that people could "transcend outer events and read their meaning."[123] She befriended L.A.-based British writers Aldous Huxley and Christopher Isherwood and maintained close contact with experimental filmmakers Curtis Harrington and Kenneth Anger, in whose *Inauguration of the Pleasure Dome* (1954) she had performed, as well as in Maya Deren's *Ritual in Transfigured Time* (1946) and Ian Hugo's *Bells of Atlantis* (1952). "I was created by the underground," she summed up her fringe orientation and appeal. "I belong to the underground."[124]

If the people and surroundings were glamorous, her initial Silver Lake residences were not. The "Poles'" first abode was a small apartment, owned by the Pacific Palisades–residing Isherwood, above the current Alimento restaurant and Modem Salon at 1710/1712 Silver Lake Boulevard. In 1959, they moved to a basement apartment at 1729 Occidental Boulevard, but the seesaw would swing back up in the new decade—residentially and in Nin's career.[125]

Although she initially referred to their newly built Swish Alps chalet as lying on "the wrong side of Silver Lake," before long it had become not only "conducive to writing" but also her very own "small paradise just five minutes from downtown."[126] The sparkling waters ringed by verdant hills and rugged mountains reminded her of Italian alpine lakes, the swimming pool in which she swam in the buff every morning "heals me" and the secluded yet open Eric Lloyd Wright–designed house with its basic materials and simple lines were "where my peace and happiness is."[127]

The favors the house bestowed, Nin partly returned in kind. According to Ruth Ross, Nin was responsible for Eric Lloyd Wright's emerging from his father's shadow and asserting his architectural independence. When Eric's name surfaced as a candidate to redesign Ross's Spanish-style bungalow in the mid-1970s, Pole advised against his half-brother. "Eric had been working for his father," Ross explained. "When Lloyd fell ill, Rupert, who (like me) was a child of the Depression, wanted Eric to join a

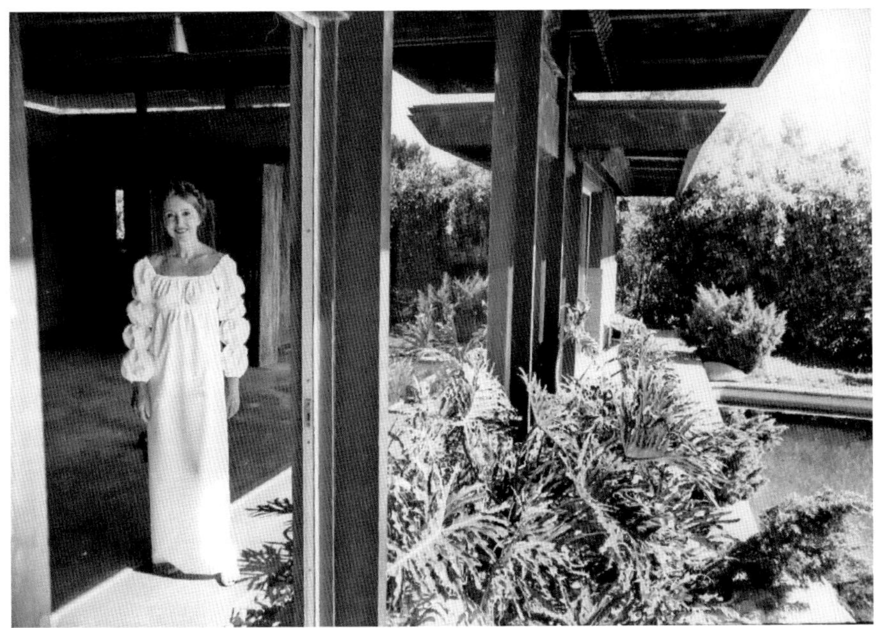

Anaïs Nin at home in Silver Lake. Portrait by Marianne Greenwood. *Courtesy of Anaïs Nin Trust.*

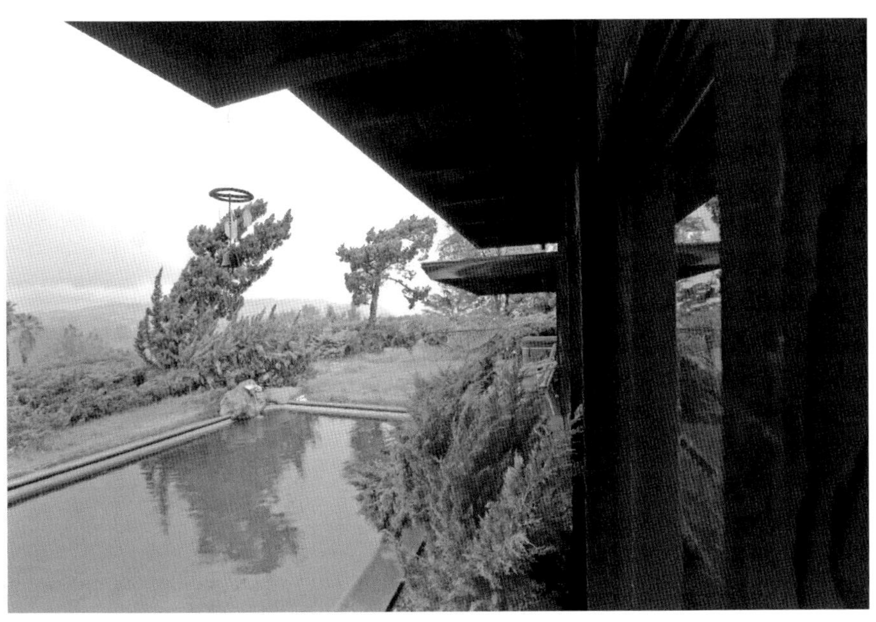

Nin-Pole Residence, Eric Lloyd Wright, 1962.

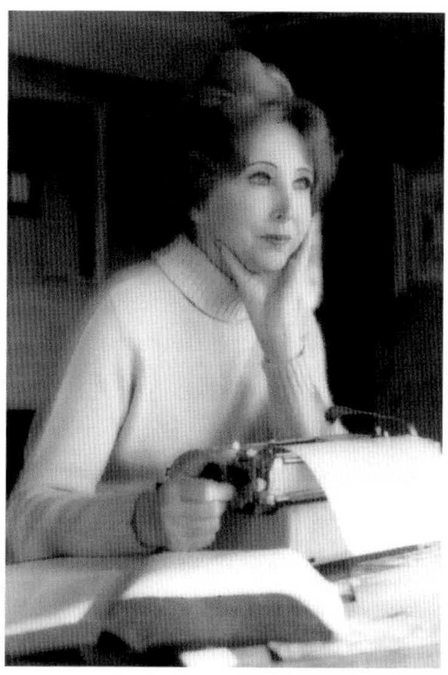

Anaïs Nin Portrait by Christian du Bois Larson. *Courtesy of Anaïs Nin Trust.*

firm for financial security. Anaïs wanted him to develop his own personality as an artist. She was the one who got him to start working on his own."[128]

Nin's counsel was a projection of her personal philosophy, reinforced by the recent acclaim she had achieved. Seemingly destined to remain a literary footnote, her latest novels relegated to self-publishing (with Guilder's aid), the publication of her six volumes of diaries by Harcourt Brace Jovanovich in 1966 turned her into an overnight sensation—"a myth in her own time, the Scheherazade of the diary genre."[129] Timing was key to the lightning success. As Barbara Kraft, one of a select group of tutorial students Nin took on in her last years, explained: "The publication of the diaries coincided with the women's movement, which catapulted her into the status of an icon. She was thought to possess an authentic feminine voice, free of male influence....It was an unbeatable combination in those idealistic days."[130]

The erotica Nin had written with Henry Miller in Paris in the 1940s, which she personally scorned but finally allowed to be published in the 1970s, also sold well and further boosted Nin's liberated woman's reputation through its "striking expression of female sexuality."[131] Nin's exotic appearance further enhanced her popularity, as a writer and media celebrity. "There were not many sixty-three year-old women," biographer Bair describes,

> *who walked around in broad daylight with hair entwined with ribbons and flowers and piled high on their heads, who wore long flowing gowns of white cashmere or silver lame covered with dramatic capes that once belonged to parish priests or French policemen, and who painted their faces and lips dead white...and darkened their eyes so heavily they were startling when glimpsed unexpectedly on a sunny afternoon.*[132]

Whether so intended or not, the dead white lips and darkened eyes proved an omen, as Nin's experience of her newfound adulation was short-lived.

The cancer first diagnosed and surgically removed in the 1950s reappeared in 1970, taking her life seven excruciating years later. Befitting her flair for drama and theatrics, Nin's ashes were scattered from a plane across Mermaid Cove near Catalina Island in deference to her birth sign of Pisces, "ruled by the planet Neptune, the planet of illusion," under whose influence she felt she had lived all her life.[133]

And Pisces may have been on to something. When the veil of illusion was removed from her heavily edited diaries in two 1990s biographies (one by Bair, the other by Noël Riley Finch), Nin's account of her life was revealed to be "all smoke and veils…a labyrinth of lies." While the omission or altering of names, done at the behest of the people involved, could be forgiven, many found the failure to disclose her bicoastal husbands, multiple abortions and an incestuous relationship with her father, not to mention the acts themselves, unconscionable. Beyond the unsavory details, others found Nin's character, especially as presented in the diaries' unexpurgated version posthumously edited by Pole (he died in 2010), "a monstrous narcissist if not a pathological personality."[134]

Nin had anticipated and owned up to the narcissism charge, defending this trait as a necessary adjunct and spur to self-realization—as artist and human being. "I want to contribute to the world one fulfilled person—myself," she told Herlihy.[135] As for the diaries' disingenuousness, this too she confronted, more mysteriously, in "Story of the Diary, Editing and Publishing," written the year before the diaries' publication: "I believed every word I wrote. They were written by another self."[136] And though this may have seemed an obfuscation at the time, for a postmodern generation attuned to fluid rather than fixed identity and relative rather than absolute truth, Nin's "polymorphous perversity" has made her relevant once again. "She is still on the tongues of young people today," Katya Meyer, whose parents socialized with Nin in the 1970s, observed. "She seems to still hold the bar for female erotic writing."[137]

Nin and Me

My (Vincent Brook's) personal association with Nin is threefold: extending to her work, her physical presence and her Silver Lake abode. A child of the 1960s who attended UC Berkeley during the heyday of the Free Speech movement, I instantly fell under the thrall of her diaries and could almost

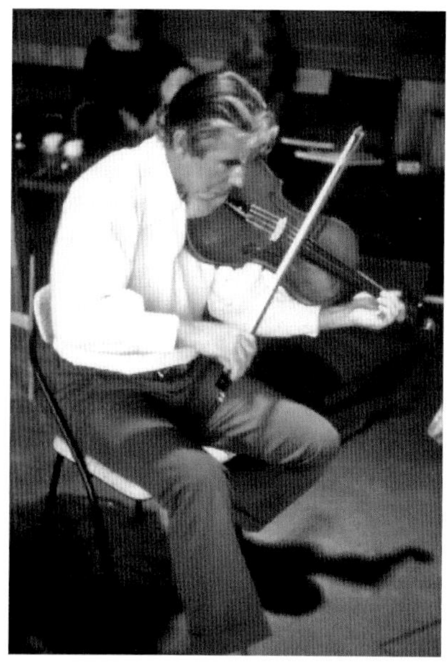

Rupert Pole performing at the monthly string concerts. *Courtesy of Anaïs Nin Trust.*

count myself among the "Ninnies" (as her groupies were called). I also happened upon my idol once in the flesh in the early 1970s as she exited the Los Feliz Theater on Vermont (which then showed mainly art films), looking not quite as exotic as Bair described but striking enough in a long, flowing, Indian-style gown "of the kind popular among the counterculture in those days," as Barbara Kraft relates, "but one which she wore regally."[138]

The Casa Hidalgo connection I owe to my cousin Mike Meyer, who joined Rupert Pole's monthly chamber concerts as a regular violinist in the early 1970s. Mike's younger brother Tommi also occasionally played violin or second viola to Pole, with Harriet Katz, wife of former California state senator Howard Berman, rounding out the group on cello. Audience members included the musicians' spouses, other relatives and assorted neighbors and friends. My wife, Karen, and I attended a few of the concerts, though after Nin's death.

When Nin was alive, she generally remained in another room writing during the concerts but would emerge during the post-concert schmoozing, where, as Mike's wife, Miriam, recalled, "She held court....She was delicate, pretty, floated in her long skirts, and was fairly self-centered, but I was fascinated nevertheless."[139] As was Nin by the concerts, despite the long-distance listening, as is evident from this excerpt from one of the last diary entries, titled "The Book of Music":

> *The quartet played Debussy. It unleashed a flood of tears. I did not want to die. This music was a parting from the world. Music was always the music of exile. There existed another world I had been exiled from, the possibility that music was an expression of a better world.*[140]

5

SILVER LAKE'S SPIRITUAL SON

JAMES LEO HERLIHY

"My spiritual Son" is how Anaïs Nin referred to James Leo Herlihy, whom she met in 1947 at Black Mountain College in South Carolina, where he was a student twenty-four years her junior and she was an invited speaker.[141] The two famed authors-to-be went on to form a lifelong personal and artistic friendship, in which one can't help but read—given her childless "marriages" and the fraught familial relationships in much of his writing—a strong Oedipal current. When he ended up moving in 1974 to a home at 3527 Landa Street, above Silver Lake Reservoir across the hills from Nin, geographical propinquity was added to the special bond they shared.

For the openly gay, countercultural Herlihy, his Swish Alps/Bohemian Hill house was a far cry and welcome contrast from the working-class milieu of his Detroit, Michigan childhood and the Catholic upbringing of his alcoholic father and overbearing mother—circumstances and character types that would figure prominently in his subsequent plays, short stories and novels.[142] The comparatively idyllic surroundings could not cure his chronic depression, however, which—exacerbated by Nin's death in 1977, the falling away of friends from AIDS in the 1980s and the death from cancer of his partner, James Kirkwood, in 1989—drove him to take his own life, in 1993 at age sixty-six, from an overdose of sleeping pills.[143]

Unlike Nin, who kept writing, despite her terminal cancer, to the bitter end, Herlihy had all but ceased writing by the early 1970s. Three short plays, collectively (and tellingly) titled *Stop, You're Killing Me,* were published in 1970; his last novel, *The Season of the Witch*, came out one year later.[144]

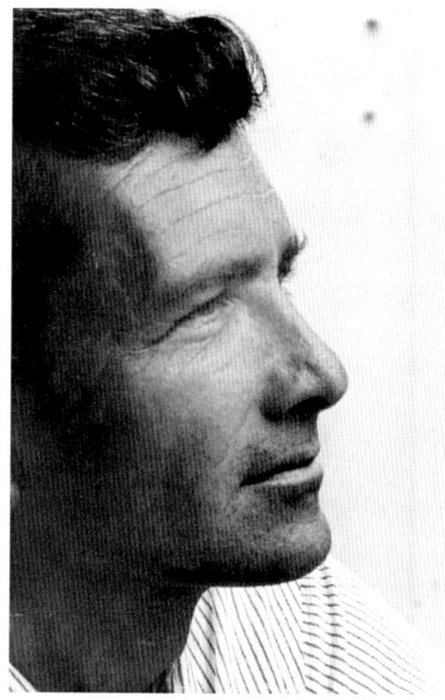

James Leo Herlihy portrait. *Courtesy of Special Collections, University of Delaware Library.*

Far from becoming a recluse, however, he corresponded avidly; remained active in the peace and gay rights movements; traveled extensively to Europe, North Africa and South America; taught writing for two years at City College in New York; and enjoyed socializing with literary friends such as Nin, Tennessee Williams and Christopher Isherwood. As one of his correspondents, photographer Lyle Bonge, related: "Even though he gave up writing—he was still a letter writer. It was all very personal and intimate. About sex and death but also about his joys...on working on his garden, on cooking, with often a whole page devoted to a supper he had had the night before; how he had fixed the meal; something new he had learnt."[145]

Herlihy hinted at two possible reasons for the abandonment of his literary career: the smash critical and financial success of the Hollywood film adaptation of his 1965 novel *Midnight Cowboy* and an early conversation with his dear friend and muse Anais Nin. Shortly after *Midnight Cowboy* won the Academy Award for Best Picture of 1969, Herlihy complained in a letter to friend and poet M.C. Richards: "*Midnight Cowboy* has made me too well known for my own comfort and has put some things off balance. I'm not writing well and that hurts my vanity....I do hope and pray that after this book [*The Season of the Witch*] I will be delivered forever from the horrors of fiction writing."[146]

The conversation with Nin, during their time together at Black Mountain College, concerned what they each hoped to achieve with their writing. Herlihy said his main aim was to improve the world through socially conscious novels like those of Upton Sinclair. Hers (cited in a different context in Chapter 4) was "to contribute to the world one fulfilled person—myself." "And that was the beginning," he later recalled, "of—for me—a life-long double-mindedness. There was this part of me that wanted to do something for the world and part of me that wanted to understand what it meant to be a fulfilled individual." Most of all, he learned from Nin, "If you want to affect the world, first of all you have to affect yourself."[147]

The "double-mindedness" admission is telling, as it underscores a key difference between Herlihy and Nin. For the more spiritually than socially minded Nin, there was no dichotomy between writing and self-fulfillment. To the contrary, the two aspirations were of a piece, and the adulation her writing produced, especially the diaries, only further validated their commensurability. For Herlihy, the reconciliation of art and life was one he strove mightily to achieve, obviously with mixed results.

Playing the Game

Herlihy's first serious writing was for the stage. It emerged organically from his stint as an actor with the Pasadena Playhouse from 1948 to 1950. His first staged play, *Streetlight Sonata: A Modern Tragedy*, was performed at the Playhouse in 1950, and the second, *Moon in Capricorn*, premiered at the Theatre de Lys in New York in 1953.[148] Nin facilitated Herlihy's artistic growth when she observed in his writing, and urged him to further develop, a transcendence of "direct action [through] the equivalent of jazz…[its] rhythm and flashes of insight."[149] His more self-conscious adoption of a "jazzy" approach in a subsequent short story, "The Sleep of Baby Filbertson" (1953), paid off; the story was picked up by *Paris Review* in 1953 and "marked the beginning of his career as a published writer." Another short story, "Jazz of Angels" (1953), was loosely adapted into an experimental film by Nin's husband, Ian Hugo (aka Hugo Guiler).[150]

A fellowship with the Yale Drama School in 1956, combined with hard knocks on a series of dead-end jobs, furthered the merging of Herlihy's background, life experience and social conscience in two new Broadway plays: *Crazy October: A Comedy* (1958), starring Tallulah Bankhead, and especially *Blue Denim* (also 1958). The latter not only became Herlihy's first commercial success but also, though not a box-office hit, was adapted for the big screen in 1959, with screenplay and direction by Philip Dunne and a top-flight cast, including Carol Lynley, Brandon De Wilde and MacDonald Carey.[151]

Blue Denim owed much to the "southern gothic" of writers Carson McCullers, Flannery O'Connor and Tennessee Williams and to 1950s teen angst movies such as *The Wild One* (1953) and *Rebel Without a Cause* (1955). It also uniquely reflected the "lives of quiet desperation" of the "tranquilized 50s" (the play was originally titled *Sleepwalker's Children*) and

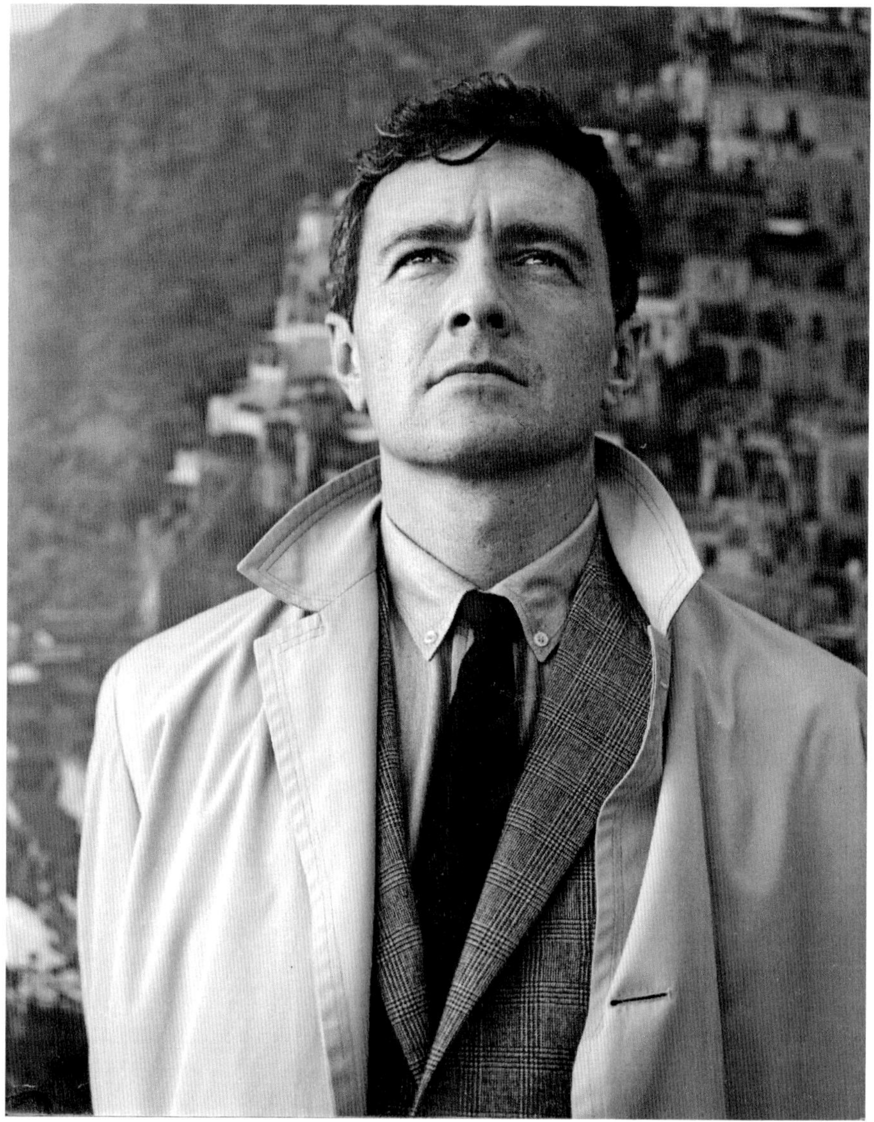

James Leo Herlihy portrait. *Courtesy of Special Collections, University of Delaware Library.*

was, in what would become a pattern, distinctly semiautobiographical.[152] In this and succeeding work, Herlihy transmuted his dysfunctional family, struggles with sexual identity and peripatetic meanderings (Nin called him a "chronic hitchhiker") into lonesome, alienated, restless misfits seeking to escape "the decay of the suburban family," the clutches of booze-ridden fathers and smothering mothers and the overall oppressiveness of American society.[153] A tortured gay subtext increasingly permeated his writing ("a semi-hidden homosexual world of young men" who seemed "to be suffering some nameless common loss"). But the work also began suggesting that the protagonists' psychological damage wasn't necessarily a dead-end street, but offered at least the possibility of a "pilgrimage of self-discovery" and "a deeper reconnection with the world."[154]

Suicide lingered as a motif in Herlihy's first two novels. Teenage Cliff's mock suicide note and his secret, much older lover Echo's actual self-propelled death in a car crash punctuate the first novel, *All Fall Down* (1960), which became his second Hollywood movie in 1962 (directed by John Frankenheimer and starring Warren Beatty, Brandon De Wilde, Angela Lansbury, Karl Malden and Eva Marie Saint). Cliff's older brother Berry-Berry's declamation, "I hate life!" (Berry-Berry itself a homonym for "bury-bury") also rhymes with *Midnight Cowboy*'s lonely eccentric Townsend Locke's motto, "I loathe life, I loathe every minute of it!" But just as Cliff's life-affirming "I love life!" at the end of *All Fall Down* suggests the titular "All" is overstated, protagonist Joe Buck's bus ride from New York City to Florida at the end of *Midnight Cowboy*, burdened with the sickly, crippled Ratso Rizzo but also with a newfound, other-directed spirit, represents "death at the same time as it symbolizes the promise of a new life."[155]

Joe Buck's move to Florida mirrored Herlihy's own odyssey from New York to Key West in the mid-1950s. And in its fusing of psychological alienation and the social inequality of America's big cities, the novel nudged the author closer to the resolution of his double-sidedness. Indeed, in his "personal engagement with his subject" and the emotional plumbing of past experience, Herlihy matured, with *Midnight Cowboy*, into what one might call (in a nod to the Stanislavsky technique he surely encountered in his acting/playwriting days) a "Method writer."[156] The preparation he undertook for his next novel, *The Season of the Witch* (the title an homage to Donovan's 1966 song "Season of the Witch"), reinforces this notion.

Bent on reflecting the social and spiritual upheaval of the 1960s in which he avidly participated, Herlihy set out with his friend Evan Rhodes on a cross-country hitchhiking trip "to document the new phenomenon." Caught up in the flower-child optimism and consciousness-raising of the period, Herlihy "felt reborn and invigorated" by what he observed and directly experienced, including group meditation and antiwar protests. The conjoining of his personal experience with the countercultural current

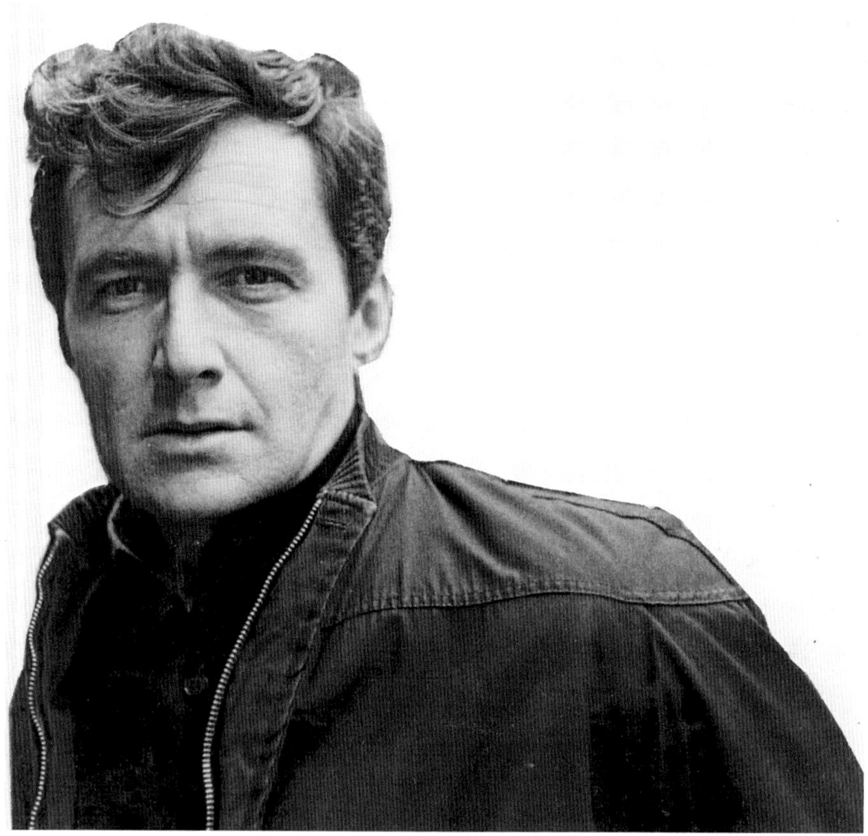

James Leo Herlihy portrait. *Courtesy of Special Collections, University of Delaware Library.*

resulted, for literary critic Robert Ward, in "an autobiographical fragment" that marked "his growth as a political writer."[157]

The journey of reinvention for *Season of the Witch*'s protagonist Gloria Random can be taken as an allegory for "the genesis of a golden age."[158] As another character in the novel, aptly named Peter Friedman, described the process: "We'll learn to be aware, we'll learn to watch ourselves in such a way that when the ghosts of our parents show themselves in our behavior, we'll be free to pick what's life-affirming, and simply reject what's ugly and dark."[159]

Calling It Quits

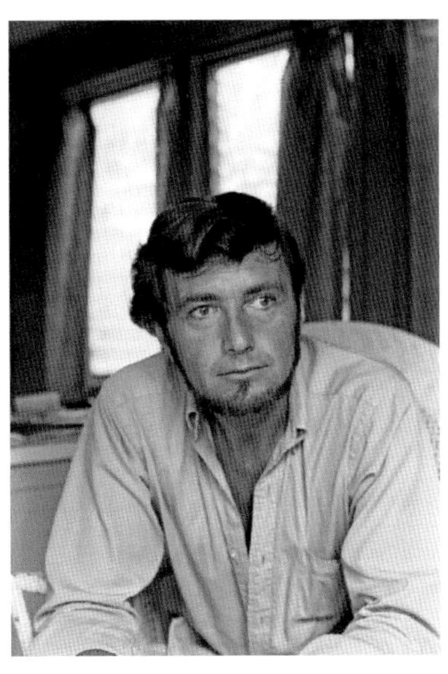

James Leo Herlihy portrait.

By the early to mid-1970s, for Herlihy, such rejection included "the horrors of fiction writing." He turned instead, at least for a time in his Silver Lake abode near Anaïs Nin's, to becoming what she had called "a self-fulfilled person." He accomplished the feat on his own terms, with "cooking, teaching, and gardening" becoming "extensions of his creativity, not an end to it."[160] And while his approach clearly differed from Nin's, she acknowledged his success by noting, upon visits to his house in the mid-1970s, that it "fused with fantasy and beauty" and that "he was happy."[161]

This was not the case for long. Not entirely giving up writing, he worked on abortive projects, including a historical novel of the Midwest and a biography of eccentric artist Henry Faulkner. He also had a bit part in the film *Four Friends* (1981), aptly about the ups and downs of the 1960s and '70s, directed by his Black Mountain College classmate Arthur Penn. Despite sharing in the disillusionment that followed that idealistic epoch, and unlike many who deserted their countercultural ideals in its wake, Herlihy, in perhaps the most meaningful expression of his "self-fulfillment," remained devoted to "the misfit types who peopled his novels and plays." As friend Lyle Bonge recalled, "He often filled his home with them and protected them from the police. The total over the years probably numbered over a hundred. After his death a young man huddled all night on the curb in front of his house."[162]

6

SALON, AMERICAN STYLE

PETER YATES AND EVENINGS ON THE ROOF

The flight of artists and intellectuals from Nazi Germany and World War II led to a flourishing of Europe-style salons in Los Angeles in the 1930s and '40s. Held on weekends in the émigrés' homes, generally on the Westside and hosted by women, the gatherings combined kaffeeklatsch schmoozing and social networking (often for jobs in Hollywood) with occasional readings and musical performance.[163] Toronto-born Peter Yates's "Evenings on the Roof" concerts, held on Sundays at his home in Silver Lake from 1939 to 1941 (and at other venues until 1954), built on the European salon tradition, with some added wrinkles.

One of these additions was to the house itself, "a typical Los Angeles–style bungalow" erected in the 1890s, which Yates and his wife, pianist Frances Mullen, had rented in 1936. In 1938, with the help of a gift from Yates's great-aunt Ella, the couple was able to purchase the dilapidated building at 1735 Micheltorena Street and hire Rudolph Schindler to renovate it. Rather than construct a separate studio for the concerts in the back, as Yates and Mullen had envisioned, Schindler mounted the studio atop the existing structure and, voila—the name and location of the music series were established.[164]

The structure of the Evenings on the Roof events—indeed, that they were structured at all—differed significantly from the émigré salons. These predominantly German-speaking gatherings (both in terms of their hosts and participants) were rather un-Germanic in their comparatively casual, drop-in format. And while music was often played, it was largely an added

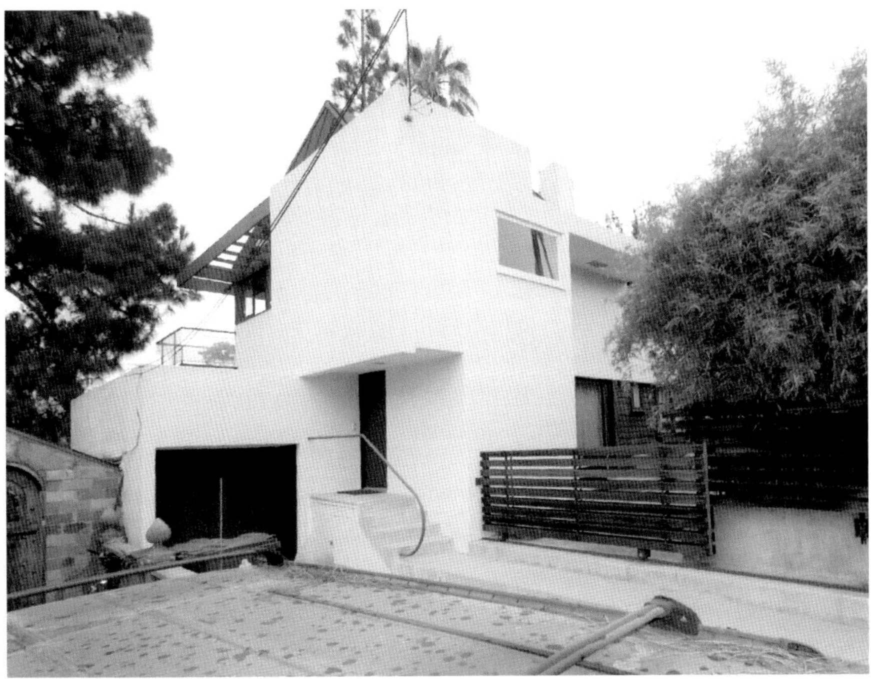

Yates Studio, R.M. Schindler, 1938–47.

attraction, depending more on the mood and makeup of the guest list (if there was one) than on any preordained plan. Yates painstakingly prepared in advance and publicized his musical programs; the concerts were held the fourth Sunday of the month year-round, with admission "scaled to second-run movie prices" (with receipts going to the musicians).[165]

The disparate structures reflected disparate purposes. As salons "in exile," the European-style affairs offered both a comforting simulacrum of a cultural practice left behind and a useful support group for strangers in a strange land. And while, even in their homelands, salons had operated on the margins as a kind of "underground high culture," in their diasporic formation, particularly in hedonistic Southern California, "the circle around and within the salon grew tighter, the sense of difference more acute, and the survivalist angst more urgent."[166] Austrian-born Hollywood screenwriter and producer Gottfried Reinhardt, son of Max Reinhardt, captured the ambivalence in calling the Los Angeles émigré community "a Ghetto under Pacific Palms."[167]

Ambivalence, American Style

Yates's ambivalence came from his feeling himself a stranger in his *own* land—La-La Land, in particular. Though born in Canada in 1909, Yates's parents were U.S. citizens, and he earned a BA from Princeton, moved to Southern California in 1931 and married Redlands-born and -bred Frances Mullen the following year.[168] Once he began devoting himself to his wife's concert career, "music itself became his life."[169] But the seeds of music's transformative potential had been planted in the aspiring poet, who conceived his writing in musical terms, a few years before.

On the verge of the Great Crash, Yates was transported by successive radio concerts featuring Toscanini and Stokowski. "I think the change symbolized by that pair," he later wrote, "went as deep into our culture as the Depression."[170] His musical ambitions broadened in 1933 at a Hollywood Bowl concert, whose program of modern art music seemed to him "an exact musical parallel to cubism and Gertrude Stein," his favorite poet.[171] The eventual Evenings on the Roof would synthesize the broadcast and Hollywood Bowl experiences and transcend them as well: balancing the classical and the modern, showcasing established and emerging talent (including his wife) and creating a community of composers, musicians and audiences in an environment of possibility and exploration.[172]

Where the European-style salons and Evenings on the Roof most overlap is in the émigré connection. The flood of foreign composers and musicians to Los Angeles in the 1930s and '40s was not only a boon to the Hollywood film industry; in turning the city into "the capital of the world of art music," it also drastically altered what had been a conservative and insular musical scene. Otto Klemperer's arrival in 1933 (he served as L.A. Philharmonic music director) and Bruno Walter's arrival in 1939 (he also conducted there) "elevated performance standards and musical understanding to new heights."[173] Other European musical giants, several of whom attended and/or performed at the émigré salons and/or Evenings on the Roof, included conductor Ingolf Dahl; composers Arnold Schoenberg, Igor Stravinsky, Ernst Toch and Ernst Krenek; cellists Emanuel Feuerman and Gregor Piatigorsky; violinist Jascha Heifetz; and pianists Artur Rubinstein, Artur Schnabel and Josef Szigeti.

Then there were the émigré Hollywood composers—Max Steiner, Erich Wolfgang Korngold, Friedrich Hollander, Franz Waxman and Miklos Rosza, among others—without whom there would have been no "Golden Age" of American movie music. Here the European/Hollywood connection worked both ways; besides the promise of work in the studios, the pool of talented performers "proved a magnet to the émigré composers fleeing Hitler." As for American composers, the Depression spurred their migration to the movie capital, as "the film studios' pay was better and steadier."[174] The Evenings on the Roof took both the émigré and Hollywood aspects into account by recognizing "the genius of neglected resident émigré composers" and encouraging "performers of highest quality whose identity had been obscured by orchestral or studio work."[175]

Ojai Moment

Yates's notion of the concerts had gestated by 1934, but many obstacles to its realization remained. The first was money. Already struggling financially on his low-paying public relations job while his wife pursued her musical career, the couple lost all their belongings in a fire that year. When Mullen fell ill with her first pregnancy and moved in with her parents in Redlands to recover, Yates, left alone in their San Bernardino apartment, "reached a crisis of despair."[176] His solution was to seek spiritual guidance from renowned Indian guru Krishnamurti, who, despite renouncing his followers, was thought to still be in the area.

Setting out on foot with a knapsack, a few books and a slab of bread, Yates trekked up to a Vedantist ashram in the San Bernardino Mountains. Rather than Krishnamurti, he found a swami "in white topee, white polo shirt, riding breeches, boots, and cane," he later wrote, "a thorough imposter, like most but not all of their kind."[177] Undeterred in his spiritual odyssey and driven by "a terrible and intimate realization of aloneness," Yates hiked on to Ojai—a "blessed haven" where again he failed to meet Krishnamurti. What he did come upon, while recovering from his strenuous journey at a Theosophists' cooperative community, was "the solution to the musical and communal problems he had been pondering."[178]

Yates now conceived the concerts along the lines of the modernist architects: as breaking down barriers, for musicians and audience alike, between performance and pleasure. As he wrote college friend and fellow poet Peyton Houston at the time, the music, rather than in a concert hall, should take place "in a house or studio, once or twice a week, free or at local movie prices." Informality would be the order of the day, enhanced by having recitals proceed "without bows, entrances, or exits." Variety in the repertoire would result from programming "not only unusual music but such things as Bartók children's pieces," and edification from "often repeating a big work in an evening or in successive evenings...until both audience and performer have digested it. Outside artists should be invited to perform works not ordinarily allowed them in recital, their fee being the evening's take."[179] Finally, in total opposition to "art for money's sake...it should be impressed on the mind of each player that the primary reason for his performance is his own pleasure in it, that if the audience is small or absent that is no reason for personal disappointment or loss of pleasure....Such is the community idea."[180]

The manifesto for the concerts had been written. But six years would pass before it would (or could) be translated into action. In the interim, Yates and Mullen's first two sons, Peter "Bart" Yates and George Yates, were born in 1934 and 1936, respectively. Yates changed jobs twice: working for the Civilian Conservation Corps as an English teacher to troubled youth in the San Bernardino Mountains from 1934 to 1936 and with the California Department of Employment in downtown Los Angeles as a job placement interviewer from 1937 through the early 1960s. In 1938, the Micheltorena Street house was purchased and Schindler's rooftop studio constructed for a whopping total cost, of the property and remodeling combined, of $4,900.[181]

On the musical front, the couple's befriending Viennese pianist Richard Buhlig in 1935 proved "inspiring and stimulating" to them both. The studio performances Buhlig gave at his Los Feliz home "of modern programs he was preparing for New York concerts" clearly meshed with Yates's community idea. Mullen's musical development was boosted by her studying with a pianist who, as Yates put it, "makes modern speech of modern music."[182] And Buhlig's connections to the cream of the émigré community led to contact with the likes of Klemperer and Schoenberg. The latter especially, for Yates, "embodied the 'spiritual integration' he searched for in all art," and by March 1939 he was meeting regularly with the father of atonal music. Nor was Schoenberg the only composer or musician with whom Yates would form a bond. Along with his deep passion for and broad knowledge about music, his "gift for gathering artists and gaining their trust and respect" played a key role in the launching and longevity of the series.[183]

Yates had drawn up initial plans for the Evenings on the Roof in October 1938, with the first series of concerts set to run from April 1939 to November 1941. Though it may not have seemed so, several factors made the timing propitious. As early as 1925, Henry Cowell, "the apostle of musical modernism," had attempted events similar to the Evenings on the Roof with his New Music Society of California concerts held at the Biltmore Hotel.

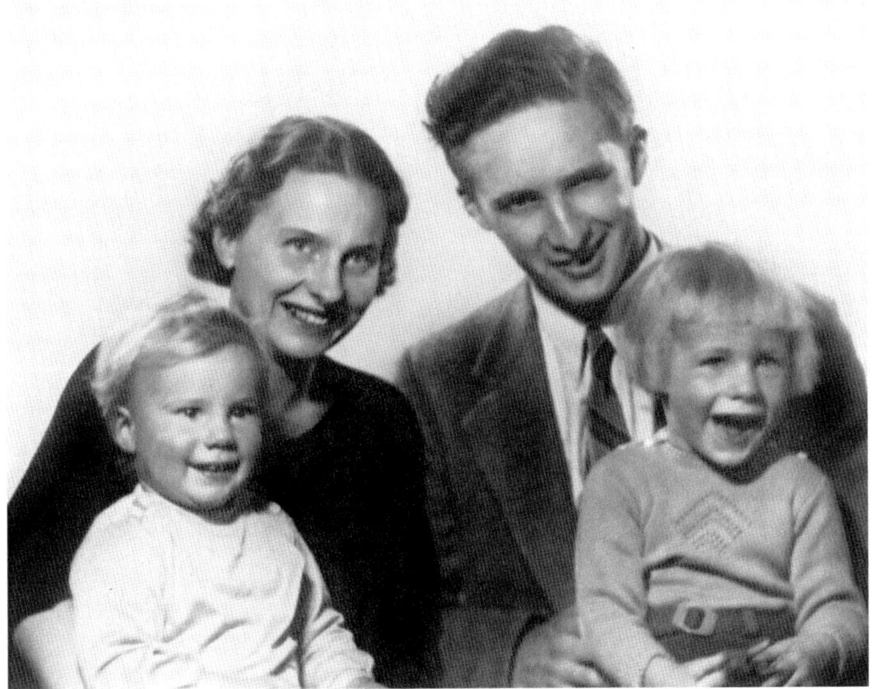

The Yates family sits for a formal portrait by Jose Reyes, circa 1938. *From left to right*: George C. "Cochran" Yates, Francis Mullen Yates, Peter Yates and Peter B. "Bart" Yates. *Courtesy of Peter B. "Bart" Yates.*

Cowell's aim, "to present musical works embodying the most progressive tendencies of the age, and to disseminate the new musical ideals," struck a chord with local critics, but he soon moved to more conducive cultural climes in San Francisco.[184] And the Depression didn't improve L.A.'s cultural, or political, climes. Fresh from the city's racist deportation of thousands of Mexican immigrants and Mexican American citizens in 1932, in the mid-1930s, Dorothy Lamb Crawford reports,

> *local composers' organizations were formed to resist the European influence. They soon widened into the national Society of Native American Composers, which promoted "Americanism" in music until the society's demise in 1944. The new voices of twentieth-century rebellion, called "Ultramoderns" in music, were perceived by California composers as a threat and a danger to human sanity.*[185]

Mullen had confronted a similar aversion to the new and non-American at one of her programs at the Biltmore Hotel in 1934. Her choice of material (Schoenberg and Bartók), one critic wrote, must have seemed "like the language of Lapland to the majority of hearers."[186] The Bartók sonata, in particular, Yates later recalled, caused "as close to an uproar as our decorous audience has ever created." As for his wife's avant-garde concerts in general,

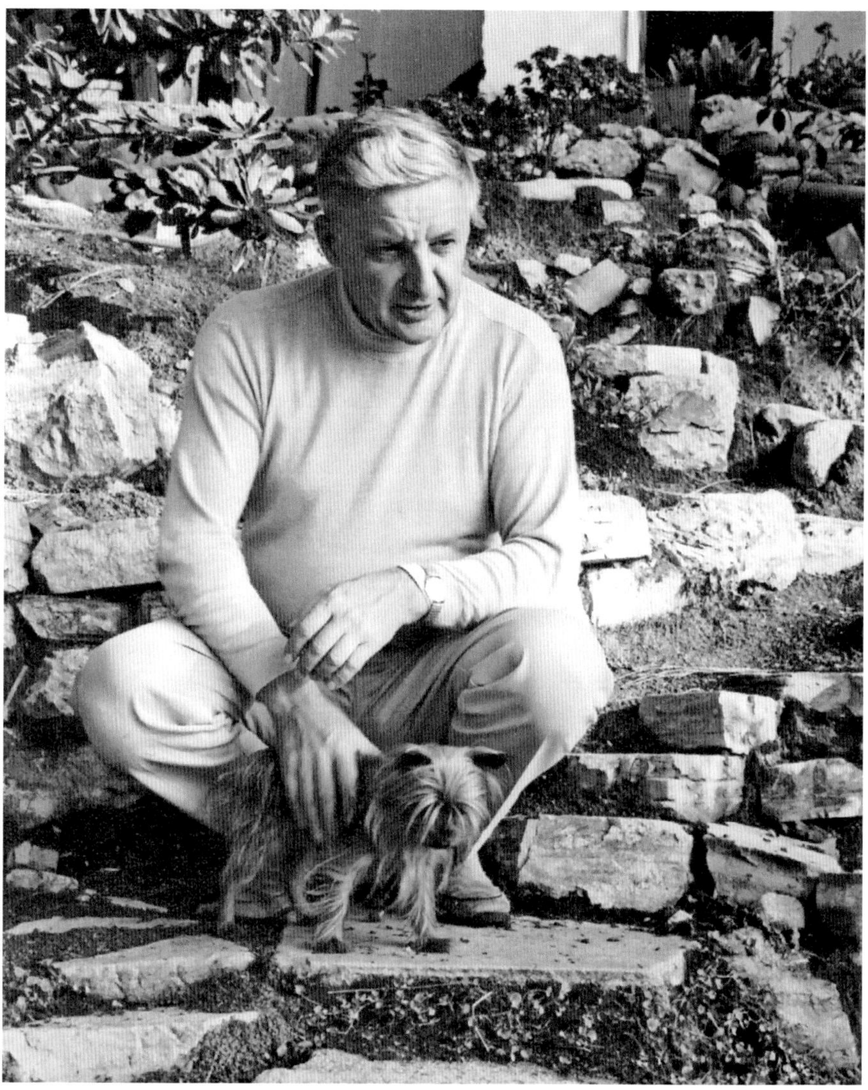

Peter Yates with Timmy, the family's toy Yorkshire terrier, 1960s. *Courtesy of Peter B. "Bart" Yates.*

he added, "there was always fury. There was reproach in the family, from friends, and so on."[187] The combination of nativism and provincialism led, by the late 1930s, to an atrophy of challenging music of all sorts. Despite the embarrassment of riches in musical talent, Crawford observes, "Los Angeles in 1938 not only lacked any performances of chamber music but had no consistent introduction to modern music."[188]

Though a detriment to the city's overall music scene, the "hostile cultural surroundings" offered Evenings on the Roof a golden opportunity. Yates may have recalled Los Angeles in the 1930s as a "veritable Sahara of artistic incomprehension" consisting of "small cultural centers surrounded by vacant parking lots." But Hollywood, for all its commercialism, and L.A., because of its bent for reinvention, "imparted to the atmosphere of the young city a free-wheeling creative spirit."[189]

Another seeming downside that worked in Evenings on the Roof's favor was Klemperer's departure from the L.A. Philharmonic in 1940. While the post-Klemperer philharmonic ignored émigré composers and performers, and other established institutions exploited them, "Yates gave them special recognition." His concerts "became the steadiest performance forum for émigré composers in Los Angeles," while "drawing a substantial émigré audience, hungry for the challenging fare they had known in their homelands."[190] The craving for alternative fare from musicians and aficionados alike, plus a talent pool to die for, made Evenings on the Roof's timing especially ripe.

What Evenings on the Roof ultimately accomplished, Crawford summarizes, was "to summon from the area's unfocused conglomerate of performers, composers, and potential audiences a unique synthesis."[191] For music critic Lawrence Morton, whose "Monday Evening Concerts" at the Los Angeles County Museum of Art (LACMA) were an extension of Yates's series, Evenings on the Roof "inaugurated an age of musical enlightenment" in Los Angeles.[192] And music historians have gone Morton one better, hailing the concerts (ongoing in revised format) as "the oldest new-music series in the world."[193]

Rise and Fall

The first Evenings on the Roof concert, held on April 23, 1939, underscored the series' intentions. Although (or because) Yates knew from his wife's Biltmore experience that Bartók was "unacceptable" to Los Angeles audiences, the first program consisted entirely of chamber works by the Hungarian composer.[194] Nineteen people attended the opening, and another twenty came to its reprise the following Tuesday. Such repeat performances, as Yates's manifesto had proposed five years before, became an integral and well-received facet of the series' first three seasons. A particular programming coup was exposing audiences to neglected American composer Charles Ives in a three-program festival in 1940. On the performance side, Yates created some controversy by sprinkling in accomplished amateur musicians with the professionals—"a bone of contention with some players," Crawford reports, "and often a point of criticism from reviewers." But Yates held firm to his philosophy that "amateurism in the best sense—is essential to art."[195]

An all-Schoenberg program in 1941 marked the end of the Micheltorena-based concerts. Having grown too popular to accommodate standing room–only audiences in the rooftop studio, the series, still under the Evenings on the Roof banner, moved to more spacious locales, including two Hollywood venues: the social service–oriented Assistance League Playhouse on St. Andrews Place and a KFWB radio station studio (on the Warner Bros. lot) on Sunset Boulevard. Evenings on the Roof had been broadcast as early 1940, and a regular radio series, featuring Los Angeles composers, premiered in 1948.[196] By that time, the concerts had moved again, to Wilshire Ebell Theater in Mid-City; in 1951, County Supervisor John Anson Ford secured, free of charge, the West Hollywood Park auditorium on San Vicente Boulevard.[197]

Throughout the series, Yates battled nervous exhaustion and physical illness caused by the immense strain of organizing the concerts and resuming his writing—of poetry, children's stories and magazine articles on music—on top of his grueling and frustrating nine-to-five office job, which became literally intolerable during World War II. Besides the expansion of his workweek to forty-eight hours and the curtailment of holidays and vacations, his supervisor, in flagrant violation of the recently passed Fair Employment Practices Act, instructed Yates to hire neither African Americans nor Jews. His refusal to discriminate (much less break the law) led, Yates believes, to his being passed over for promotion.[198]

Adding to his health and employment woes, growing pains threatened the Evenings on the Roof's artistic integrity and very survival in the mid-1940s. Though the Music Guild offered to foot the bill for the burgeoning series' 1945–46 season, the guild's establishment orientation and paltry funding put "our ambition, our idealism…in deep debt," Yates bemoaned. The crisis was thankfully resolved through contributions from Max Laemmle (head of the like-named theater chain and a cousin of Universal founder Carl

Laemmle), Artie Mason Carter (cofounder of the Hollywood Bowl) and other wealthy donors, allowing Evenings on the Roof to regain financial footing and artistic independence.[199]

An added attraction of the series had always been the attendance of noted composers—especially at concerts featuring their own works, which they often performed. Appearances by celebrated writers and other non-musical artists further enhanced Evenings on the Roof's prestige. Aldous Huxley, a frequent attendee, even participated in a special event, reading a short essay at a memorial concert for Dylan Thomas, for which Stravinsky had written some of the music.[200] Others in the avant-garde circle who attended concerts and/or social gatherings at the original Micheltorena Street venue included Anaïs Nin and Rupert Pole.[201] Susan Sontag, who defied her parents by attending the recitals as a teenager in the late 1940s, recalled Evenings on the Roof, in tandem with the émigré cultural wave, as "an essential part of Los Angeles' golden age."[202]

Writer Phyl van Ammers, a high school student of Rupert Pole's who took piano lessons with Frances Mullen in the late 1950s, recalls seeing Stravinsky and John Cage at the Yates home.[203] Filmmaker Baylis Glascock, who as a college student was a live-in caretaker for Yates and Mullen's youngest, polio-stricken son, John, and lived at the house for two years after John's death from pneumonia in 1962, remembers Cage and Peggy Guggenheim once staying overnight there. Besides their performing, composer Harry Parch, conductor Michael Tilson Thomas and soprano Marni Nixon also were frequent guests.[204] Peter "knew everything and knew everyone," van Ammers summarizes. "Everyone in Bohemian Los Angeles went through the Yates house."[205]

Beyond the high-end socializing, remarkable enough given their taxing schedules, Yates and Mullen went out of their way to help those on the way up. Yates arranged a screening of Glascock's film on the Watts Towers for Cage and Guggenheim, and the couple's influence on van Ammers was life-altering: "They transformed my life when I was a teenager....Peter took me to the Ojai music festival, to art exhibits...and when I was grown up, he got my poetry published."[206]

By 1954, mounting physical and emotional strain (including from John's onset of polio and confinement to an iron lung) forced Yates to relinquish the concerts' day-to-day operations. Having shed some administrative duties in the late 1940s, he now passed full control of the series to longtime confidant Lawrence Morton. Morton moved the newly named "Monday Evening Concerts" to the L.A. County Museum of History, Science and

Art in Exposition Park and in 1965 relocated it to the newly constructed LACMA on Wilshire Boulevard, where the concerts remained up to and beyond Morton's retirement in 1987.[207]

POST-MORTON

Yates's involvement with the concerts and the arts in general by no means ceased with his passing the Evenings on the Roof baton to Morton. In the late 1950s, he took the Monday Evening Concerts to the radio airwaves, on public station KPFK, and began another salon-like series, Poetry Los Angeles, "for the benefit of local poets."[208] In 1964, he received a Ford Foundation grant that enabled the research and writing of two books, *An Amateur at the Keyboard* (1964) and the now classic compendium *Twentieth Century Music* (1967). In 1968, with only a bachelor's degree, he was appointed chair of the music department at Buffalo State College (later State University of New York at Buffalo). Not about to play Ivory Tower, he continued championing contemporary music, organizing concerts for contemporary composers and presenting weekly musical programs on the campus radio station.[209] A bundle of energy to the very end, Yates succumbed to a heart attack in 1976 at age sixty-six. But his trailblazing spirit has lived on.

After Morton's departure, the Monday Evening Concerts resumed under the auspices of composer and LACMA music director Dorrance Stalvey, until his death in 2005, when the museum severed its ties. The series refused to go quietly into that good night, however. An ardent group of supporters, including L.A. Philharmonic music director Esa-Pekka Salonen, L.A. Opera music director Kent Nagano and Philharmonic Society of Orange County artistic coordinator Justin Urcis, kept the program running.[210] Performances were held at the REDCAT (Roy and Edna Disney Cal-Arts Theater), part of Walt Disney Concert Hall downtown, and at Zipper Hall in the adjacent Colburn School—where, after a brief hiatus, they continue to run.[211] That the series' saviors were aware of Evenings on the Roof and its esteemed place in Los Angeles music history is reflected in a 2007 statement on the group's website, which not only references the path-breaking concerts but also almost seems to be channeling its founding father.

"In its new, independent configuration," mondayeveningconcertsla.org declared, *the series harkens back to its grass roots, when concerts were given on the roof of the home of the series' founder, Peter Yates. "What happened with LACMA is a curse and a blessing," says Urcis. "We lost our institutional support, but it's a liberation of sorts—now anything's possible! What's exciting is that we have an opportunity not just to have x amount of concerts on Mondays, but to be a force for contemporary and unusual music throughout the city. This isn't just any series.... We're continuing an important legacy."*[212]

7

SCALING THE SWISH ALPS

HARRY HAY AND THE MATTACHINE SOCIETY

Well before West Hollywood became the high-profile LGBT hub of Los Angeles in the 1970s, Silver Lake reigned supreme as the city's gay and lesbian mecca.[213] The area's hilly terrain, combined with its same-sex demography, even inspired its in-joke nickname, the Swish Alps. More than just L.A.'s residential center for homosexuals since the 1920s, Silver Lake is where the first sustained gay rights organization in the United States, the Mattachine Society, was formed. Named after a medieval French theater troupe, the group's founding came about through an uncanny convergence of place (Silver Lake and environs), time (early post–World War II period) and person (Harry Hay).

Together with his lover, Rudi Gernreich, and three other gay men—Dale Jennings, Bob Hull and Chuck Rowland—Harry Hay held Mattachine's first meetings in November 1950 at his 2328 Cove Avenue home overlooking the Silver Lake Reservoir. That all the original society members were leftists as well as gay, and three of the five, including Harry, were Communists, would play a key, if counterintuitive, role in the group's formation during the McCarthy era. Harry Hay himself seemed destined, from the cradle, to serve as Mattachine's founding father.

Making Hay

"He was born a sissy," Stuart Timmons begins his biography of Henry "Harry" Hay, "with a delicately imperious streak that surfaced when he was two."[214] Though his birthplace is listed as Worthing, England, Harry's "preferred heritage" was to the individualism, egalitarianism and clan devotion of his Scottish Highlander ancestors—counterbalanced with the cosmopolitanism of forebears who had settled in New Zealand, South Africa and several American states (including California) before Harry's birth in 1912.[215]

By no means a "Red diaper baby" (child of radical leftists), Harry grew up in the lap of luxury afforded by his father Big Harry's (named for his size and imperious manner) mining engineer posts, first with Cecil Rhodes's operations in South Africa and Ghana and then with the Guggenheim family's in Chile. A mining accident Big Harry suffered in Chile, resulting in a partial leg amputation, motivated the family's move in 1916 to Los Angeles for the better medical treatment and business prospects the burgeoning metropolis provided. Undeterred by his peg leg, Big Harry jumped into the fray, padding the family coffers via citrus farming and real estate before establishing a stable residence in 1919 in the mid-Wilshire area (now Koreatown), a short distance from Silver Lake.[216]

Though Harry inherited his father's name and physical stature (he'd shot up to six-foot-two by age twelve), the macho, uber-capitalist, increasingly authoritarian Big Harry was an unlikely model for a future Communist gay activist whose main personality traits were "flamboyance and sensitivity."[217] These qualities would prove his saving grace, however, not because of the beatings by Big Harry they induced, but because of the independence of mind they encouraged.[218]

High intelligence reinforced Harry's independent spirit. Possessed of a photographic memory and, at age nine, among the first students to be tested "gifted," he entered Virgil Junior High at ten years old and Los Angeles High at twelve. A book Harry came across at the school library, of all places, both crystalized and helped him cope with his emergent gay sensibility. At a time when psychologists considered homosexuality a mental disorder and its practice was a crime in all fifty states, Edward Carpenter's *The Intermediate Sex*, written in 1906, proposed same-sex identity as not only normal and healthy but "a valuable social force."[219] The book produced an "'earth-shaking revelation' and lasting change in Harry's life," prodding him to look at his gayness not as deviant or perverse but as something "essential" about him.[220]

Harry's communist worldview was actually aided, if inadvertently, by his father. To shift his son's attention "away from music and literature and that sort of thing," Big Harry sent the thirteen-year-old to work on a relative's ranch in western Nevada during the summer. Harry's fellow field hands, it turns out, included members of the Industrial Workers of the World (IWW, called "Wobblies"), a radical leftist union. They introduced Harry to Marx, and their slogans, "One big union" and "One for all and all for one," enthralled him. Their homophobic epithets, however, foreshadowed a similar conflict he would later encounter as a Communist Party member.[221]

Harry's subsequent activism was more wholeheartedly influenced at the ranch by an old, blind Paiute Indian he met at a tribal encampment. The old man drew Harry near, ran his hands across Harry's face and spoke a few words in Paiute, which Harry was told meant the man wished him well "because someday you will be a friend." Only when he was working in the American Indian movement in the late 1960s did Harry learn that these words and gestures were a formal blessing from none other than Wovoka (aka "the Ghost Dance Messiah" and "Red Man's Christ"), considered "the greatest mystic and prophet of his people."[222]

The homophobic Wobblies also inadvertently furthered young Harry's gay education. To help pay for his trip back to L.A. the following summer, they gave him an IWW card to help him get work on a steamer heading south. On a stopover in Monterey, a drunken Harry had his first gay encounter with a twenty-five-year-old sailor, who was unaware, and later aghast, that he'd had sex with a fourteen-year-old (who, at six-foot-three and 175 pounds, easily passed for twenty-one). Harry himself hadn't felt abused and later jokingly alluded to his having "molested" the older man.[223]

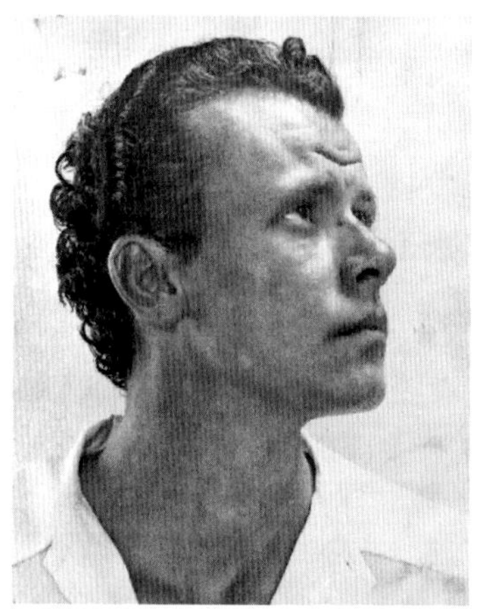

Harry Hay the young activist. *Courtesy of ONE Archives at USC Libraries.*

Though qualified to enter college at fifteen, Harry opted to remain at L.A. High for two more years, during which his leadership skills came to the fore as president of the California Scholarship Federation and head of the school's debating and dramatics societies. In studying for (and eventually winning) the Southern California Oratorical Contest,

Harry also befriended the previous year's winner, John Cage, in whose early musical experiments Harry would later participate.[224]

Harry's post–high school education began not in college but in Pershing Square, when a menial job at a downtown law office brought him in contact with L.A.'s main outdoor gay hangout. And it was there in 1929, on furtive late-night trysts, that seventeen-year-old Harry experienced his first longer-term same-sex relationship—for a half year, with a thirtysomething man from St. Louis, Champ Simmons. Besides introducing Harry to the city's underground gay scene, Champ planted the idea of gay organizing through the story of Henry Gerber's pioneering (but short-lived) efforts in Chicago a few years before. Gerber, a German immigrant, drawing on a gay-oriented group begun in Berlin in the 1890s, had formed the Society for Human Rights in 1925, which showed promise until its "members were arrested and subjected to lurid headlines naming them homosexuals and thus criminals."[225]

Harry's brief Stanford University education, beginning in 1930, also came more from extracurricular activities than his classes. Except for a theater course that would resonate both with the Mattachine Society and his eventual acting career, Harry picked up the most pointers from San Francisco's lively gay scene and bisexual student romances. His latent gay activist side also began to surface when he shocked gays and straights alike by "coming out" queer early in his sophomore year. He dropped out of school soon thereafter, partly due to a sinus infection, though his "daring declaration" was the more likely cause.[226] While recuperating from the infection with the Wobblies on the Nevada ranch, Harry—à la Peter Yates's Ojai Moment—hatched the idea of a gay communal utopia that would bridge the socialist/homosexual divide and become a founding principle of the Mattachine Society.[227]

Back in Los Angeles in 1932, renewed contact with John Cage led to Harry's joining Cage's avant-garde circle, from which his own performing, and Cage's music career, would spring. Besides engaging in private "merry drag performances" with Cage's gay coterie, Harry's excellent singing voice led to his doing the vocals in one of Cage's early concerts. His cultural horizons were further expanded through Cage and company's tours of Silver Lake's emerging treasure trove of modernist architecture.[228]

JOINING THE PARTY

Gay, bohemian and communist elements fused, courtesy of another gay avant-gardist, Will Geer, a Communist Party (CP) member ten years Harry's senior whose ideological bent more closely matched Harry's than the Zen-inclined Cage. He began an affair with Geer while performing agitprop theater around the city in the 1930s and, following his mentor-lover's lead, joined the CP in 1934.[229] Geer, meanwhile, became a prominent character actor in Hollywood films of the 1940s, was blacklisted in the 1950s and rebounded in the 1970s through his star turn as Papa Walton on *The Waltons* TV series (1971–81).

The radical political commitment had its downside for Harry as well, not from McCarthyism but from the CP itself. Party doctrine, by the 1930s, had incorporated the Wobblies' working-class machismo. Initially countenanced in the Soviet Union, homosexuality by 1928 was deemed a "social peril" and by 1934 was formally criminalized by Stalin.[230] Thus, as did Geer and other gay Commies, Harry was forced to mask his sexual identity (and secrete his activity) for what, at the moment, seemed a more urgent cause.

Ever a bundle of energy, Harry, on top of his leftwing activism and acting gigs, worked as a movie stunt rider and dialogue coach, ghostwrote screenplays, collaborated on an avant-garde film (*Even—As You and I)* and coauthored a political novel, *Tide Rises*, with Viennese film director Reginald Le Borg. Though the novel was never published, a script they partnered on, *Heavenly Music* (about Mozart and other famous composers meeting in the hereafter), went on to win the Academy Award for Best Short Subject in 1943 (albeit minus Harry's name in the credits).[231]

Harry's immersion in the leftist and Hollywood worlds naturally brought him in contact with many Jews, with whom he empathized, especially during the Nazi period, as members of a fellow oppressed minority. Philo-Semitism and Communist homophobia, the latter which he began to internalize and sought Jungian therapy to control, converged in 1938 in Harry's marriage to a Jewish Communist, Anita Platky. Harry confessed his homosexuality as a thing of the past, and the couple set its sights on "the higher purpose of 'building the movement.'"[232]

Outside the conjugal bedroom, heterosexual vows ran afoul of natural instinct.[233] By 1939, Harry was back to nighttime "quickies" in Lafayette Park and other gay meeting grounds. Nor did the couple's two-year move to New York City in an (ultimately unsuccessful) search for more lucrative employment help suppress the primal urges Harry continued to satisfy on the sly in Central Park and which briefly blossomed into a romance with a Frank Lloyd Wright architectural protégé, William Alexander. Besides performing with and becoming interim head of the leftist New Theatre League during the New York sojourn, Harry also found time to take part in Alfred Kinsey's groundbreaking sexual research.[234]

Harry's breakup with Alexander and job opportunities in the defense industry after America's entry into World War II sent him and Anita back to Los Angeles in early 1942. Their rented cottage on Lake Shore Drive in Echo Park—along with Silver Lake and Boyle Heights, the city's primary leftist residential and organizational base—nudged Harry closer to Mattachine's place of origin. And in 1943, requiring more spacious quarters after the adoption of their first daughter, Hannah, the Hays rented a three-story house at 2328 Cove Avenue, where the gay group's first meetings would be held.[235]

For the next seven years, Harry continued to "play it straight," living in what he later called "an exile world." To their CP comrades, he and Anita seemed "a model Communist couple."[236] They adopted a second child, Kate, in 1945, helped form a cooperative nursery school (see Chapter 12) and even joined a church—the politically progressive First Unitarian Church on 8th Street.[237] Harry began teaching classes on Marxism and folk music, which he saw as a grass-roots "weapon against oppression," and as theoretician of the People's Songs organization, he befriended folk legends Woody Guthrie and Pete Seeger.[238]

Steady work remained hard to come by (not helped by Harry's firings for attempted union organizing), until a job in a manufacturing plant in 1948 brought in a regular salary.[239] Ironically, just when financial stability was achieved, Harry's warring Communist and gay identities would be realigned, then torn asunder again, by outside forces that, for all the inner turmoil they caused, would help Harry reclaim his sexual identity and re-channel his social activism.

Communists had never been the most virulent institutional homophobes. Indeed, a perceived conspiratorial bond between Communists and homosexuals compounded the dread of both among right-wing moralizers, whose numbers were legion in still quite conservative Los Angeles. No surprise, then, that a Lavender Scare arose along with the Red Scare in the early Cold War period. The increased risk of exposure this posed to the CP, given gays' greater vulnerability to arrest in the McCarthy era, induced the party, however reluctantly, to expel its known homosexual members. Although he managed to maintain his cover, even with Anita, for a few more years, the double whammy of state-sanctioned oppression and Communist Party antipathy pushed Harry closer to realizing his long-held dream of a sexuality-based identity politics.[240]

Harry was not alone in sensing the time was ripening for bolder action. Already in early 1947, an RKO studios secretary named Edythe Eyde (later changed to "Lisa Ben," an anagram of "Lesbian") self-typed and hand-stapled—on the sly in her studio office—the first homosexual publication in the United States, *Vice Versa: The Gayest American Magazine*.[241] *Vice Versa* folded after nine issues in early 1948, but the first Kinsey Report, released in June 1948, offered further incentive. The report's findings of a sizeable proportion of homosexuals among the general U.S. population (up to 10 percent for men and 2–3 percent for women), while it exacerbated the crackdown on gays by magnifying the alleged security threat they posed, reinforced the practicality of gay organizing by demonstrating, as Harry put it, that "rather than a few isolated misfits lurking about the red-light districts of the largest cities, there were, in fact, millions of homosexuals—everywhere."[242]

Shortly after the Kinsey Report's release, Harry proposed a new gay group, called Bachelors Anonymous, based on the principle that homosexuals, like blacks and Jews, were an "oppressed minority."[243] Unable to muster support for this then-radical notion, two years later Harry finally found the ideological and sexual inspiration to push the project through. In 1950, at a Lester Horton dance class in Hollywood, he met and fell in love with twenty-eight-year-old Austrian émigré Rudi Gernreich. His relationship with the avant-garde designer—who would go on to pioneer unisex fashion and "anti-clothing" with the shaved head, monokini and thong—"changed everything." Together, the couple created, as Harry put it, "'a society of two' that became Mattachine."[244]

PERSEVERANCE

On November 11, 1950, Harry and Rudi convened the inaugural meeting of the Mattachine Society at Harry's Cove Avenue home with fellow founding "Mattachinos" (as they called themselves) Dale Jennings and two CP members, Bob Hull and Chuck Rowland. The name Mattachine, which Harry discovered in his music research, derived from a medieval French, all-male, politically oriented theater troupe, *Societe Mattachine*, whose members wore masks and whose leader dressed as a woman.[245] As Harry later explained, "The Mattachines conveyed vital information to the oppressed in the countryside of 13th–15th century France, and perhaps I hoped that such a society of modern homosexual men, living in disguise in 20th century America, could do similarly for us oppressed Queers."[246]

Communist principles and organizational strategies infused Mattachine's "preliminary concept," in calling for "androgynes of the world" to unite and in the group's secretive, underground, cell-like structure, to maintain anonymity.[247] The group's mission statement capsulized its threefold purposes: "TO UNIFY" homosexuals and give them "a feeling of belonging"; "TO EDUCATE," through dissemination of information and further research, "all interested homosexuals" and "the public at large"; and "TO LEAD… the whole mass of social deviates" to achieve the above-expressed unification and education.[248]

Harry's fascination with homosexuality in Native American culture, on which he would later write extensively, is evident in his calling Mattachine the fulfillment of "a vision-quest more important than life."[249] Los Angeles's indigenous queer roots, specifically, were tapped as well. The Tongva Indians, who had dominated the basin for thousands of years and up to the

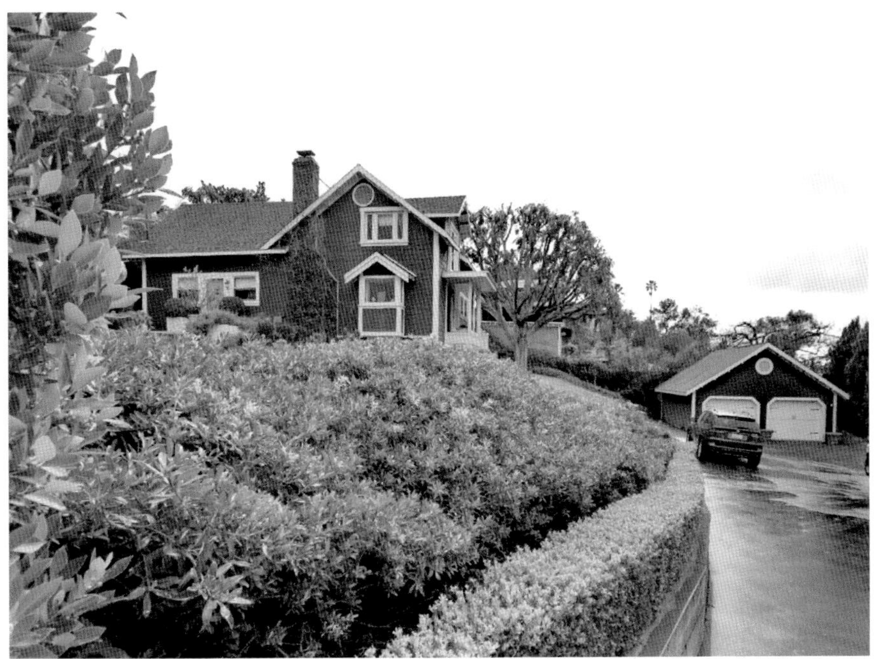

Harry Hay House in Silver Lake, 2328 Cove Avenue.

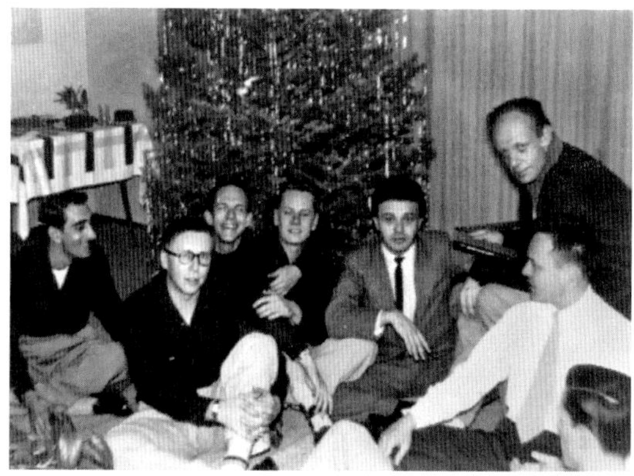

Right to left: Mattachine Society founders Harry Hay (looming above), Dale Jennings (light tie), Rudi Gernreich (dark tie), Stan Witt, Bob Hull (laughing), Chuck Rowland (glasses) and Paul Bernard. *Courtesy of ONE Archives at USC Libraries.*

Spanish pueblo's founding in 1781, not only were tolerant of homosexuals but often revered those who "wore clothing of the opposite gender." These *berdaches* (or "two-spirit people," in anthropological parlance) "took on a variety of magic social roles," including that of shaman or spiritual healer. The Native American influence is palpable in Mattachine's inclusion, early on, of ceremonial rituals—"performances of identity, sanctified at the level of myth…bordering on the transcendental or sacred"—which "the Mattachinos often referred to as 'magic.'"[250]

Whatever magic spells the Mattachinos may have invoked, they offered little protection from the outside world. Harry's disclosure of Mattachine's founding and his homosexuality—to a shocked Anita and disappointed but less surprised CP district supervisor Miriam Brooks Sherman—led to divorce from his wife in 1951 and an "honorable discharge" from the party the same year. Though estranged from his wife, he maintained visitation rights with his children, to whom his new place on Fargo Street in Echo Park kept him in proximity. Mattachine meetings moved there and to other locations, including Harry's widowed mother's new Gregory Ain–designed house on Oakcrest Drive in the Hollywood Hills.[251]

Mattachine's initial organizational success helped salve the familial and political wounds. The society became a state-registered nonprofit corporation in 1953, and following Dale Jennings's landmark victory in a lewd conduct case that year, in which Mattachine played a proactive role, membership exploded. Though no official lists were compiled (secrecy was still deemed necessary), the original five-member cell (self-named the "Fifth Order") had burgeoned by mid-1953 into a multi-pronged association with two dozen guilds throughout California and an estimated combined membership of five thousand. The influx of more politically moderate members proved a double-edged sword, however. With McCarthyism at its peak, Harry's and the other CP members' politics, so crucial to Mattachine's raison d'etre, became a liability. When Harry was identified in a local paper as a Marxist, and *L.A. Mirror* columnist Paul Coates painted the entire group Red, the Mattachine's core contingent was forced out of the organization.[252]

As if divorce from Anita, detachment from his children, discharge from the CP and being dumped from his dream organization wasn't traumatic enough, the end of Harry's affair with Rudi Gernreich, the same year as his ousting from Mattachine, "was a dreadful heartbreak from which it took me years to get over." Unsurprisingly, Harry "went into an emotional tailspin," which a new relationship with a clinging, manic-depressive young Dane, Jorn Kamgren, scarcely ameliorated. An appearance in 1955 before the House Committee on UnAmerican Activities (HUAC)—based on testimony from FBI informants who had attended his music classes in the 1940s—added further insult to injury.[253]

Harry's meeting his life's partner, John Burnside, in 1963 (Harry was fifty-one, John forty-seven) happily turned things around, both personally and politically. A former staff scientist at Lockheed, John's claim to fame, and a comfortable living, came from the invention of the teleidoscope—a lens-based variation on the kaleidoscope that struck a hallucinogenic chord with the 1960s generation. The couple plunged body and soul into the Flower Child and political facets of the counterculture, adding their own personal touch with the founding of the Circle of Loving Companions (a more modest and mellower version of Mattachine) in their Angelino Heights home on Edgeware Road in 1965. Harry became involved with the American Indian movement and, after the Stonewall riots of 1969, became the first chair of the California Gay Liberation Front.[254]

The couple's "back to nature" move to San Juan Pueblo in the early 1970s brought "gay activism to northern New Mexico."[255] But the big coup, for Harry and gay activism, came in 1979 with his cofounding, with Don Kilhefner and Mitch Walker, of the Radical Faeries. A gay-centered political, ecological and spiritual movement, the Radical Faeries combined Harry's affinity for nature and Native American culture with the dream of a gay brotherhood his Nevada ranch interlude had sparked and Mattachine had briefly kindled. Surpassing even Mattachine in the rapidity and breadth of its growth, the Radical Faeries spread like wildfire and, by the end of the decade, had branches throughout the United States and Canada and in Great Britain and Australia as well.[256]

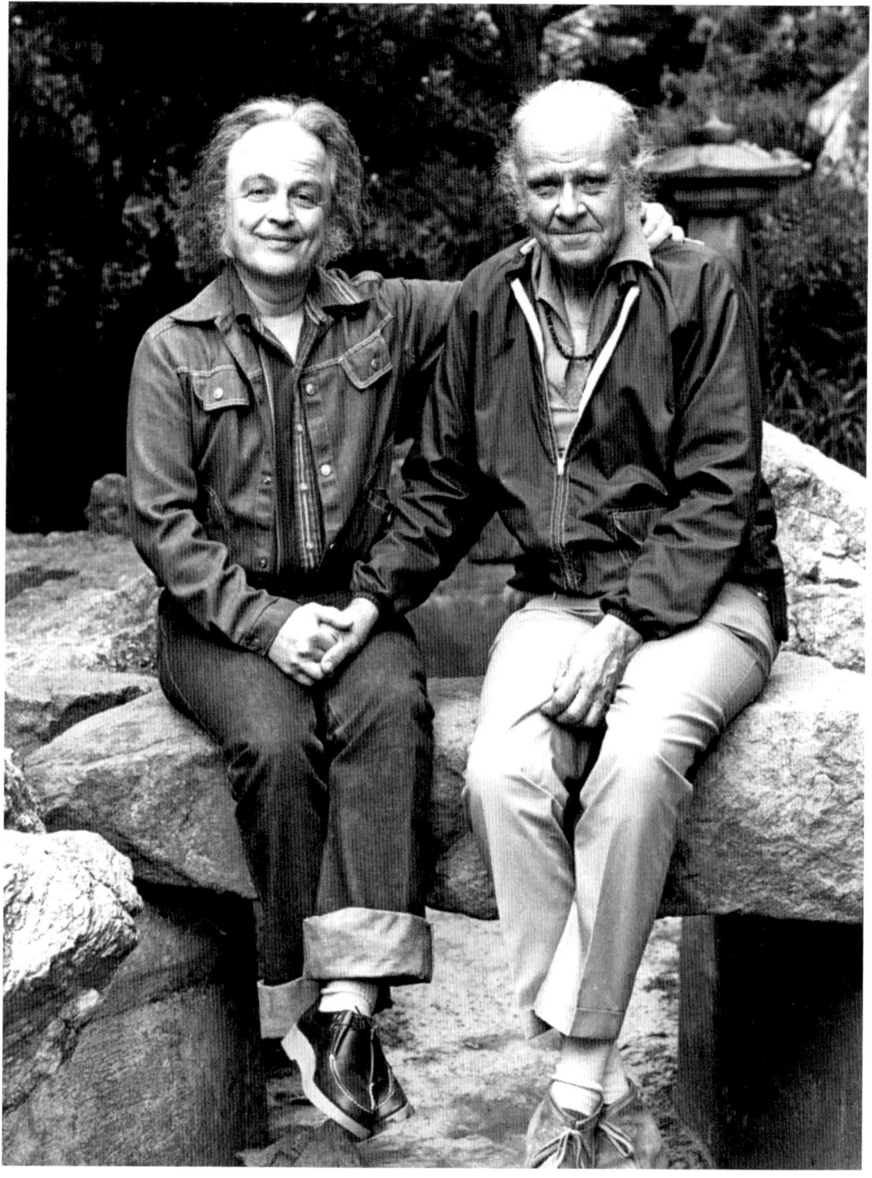

Life partners Harry Hay and John Burnside, 1960s. *Courtesy of ONE Archives at USC Libraries.*

Mirroring Mattachine on the downside, personality and political conflict, this time not with latecomers but with Kilhefner and Walker, led to Harry's separation from the Faeries' leadership in late 1980. Kilhefner and Walker also split off from the group, but Harry, though heartbroken at having once more "built up the dream…only to see it torn down," continued to attend the nature retreats that formed the Faeries' backbone and remained as engaged as ever with gay and other progressive political causes.[257]

Just as it seemed Harry's troubles were behind him, he became embroiled in the greatest controversy of his career. Marching in the 1986 Gay Pride Parade in West Hollywood, Harry, ever the provocateur, carried a sign in support of NAMBLA (North American Man/Boy Love Association), a group held in disrepute by most gay organizations, including the Radical Faeries, for advocating elimination of age-of-consent laws. Harry barely avoided arrest for refusing to remove the unauthorized sign, but the incident was photographed and reported in local and national media, and he was reprimanded by the parade sponsors. Harry defended his brazen action in political and personal terms. On the one hand, he was outraged at "the hypocrisy of a self-appointed gay establishment that would declare a section of the gay community unrespectable." On the other hand, from "having molested an adult when I was a child until I found out what I needed to know" (referring to his sexual initiation with the sailor), he believed that so-called underage sex had value.[258]

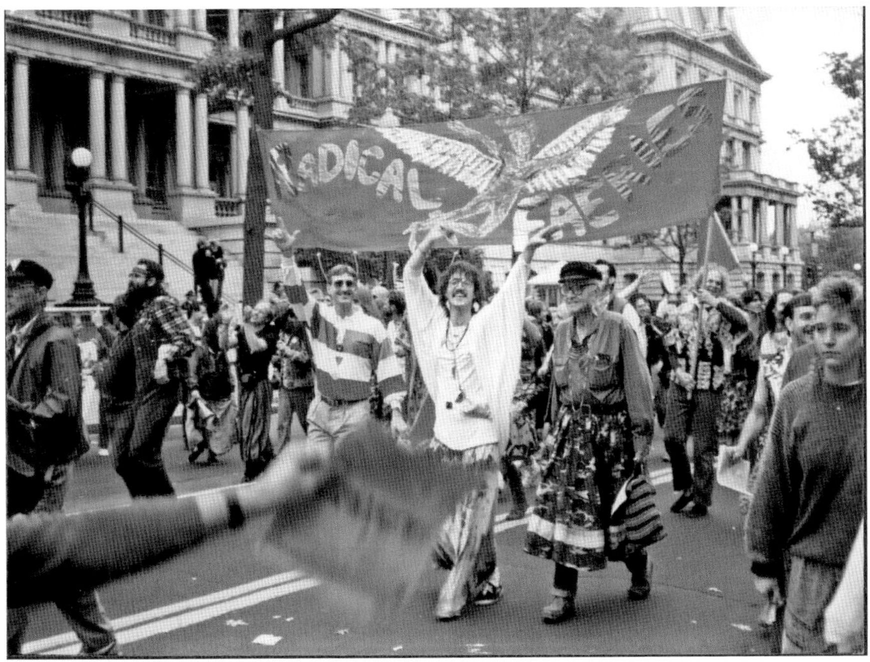

Harry Hay with Radical Faeries, Gay Pride Parade. *Courtesy of ONE Archives at USC Libraries.*

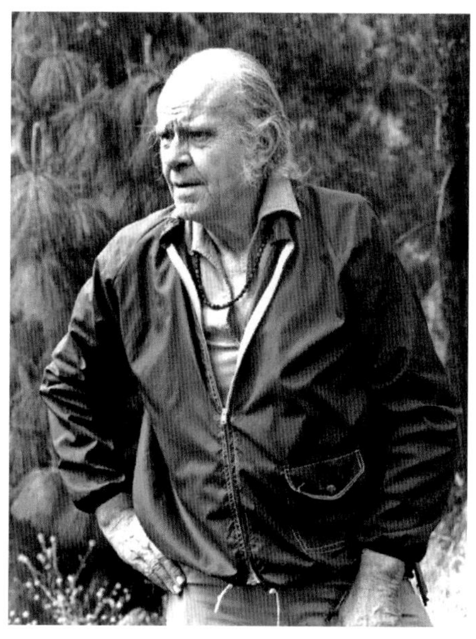

Harry Hay portrait. *Courtesy of ONE Archives at USC Libraries.*

Balancing the latest blow to his reputation and spirit, Harry could take comfort in his long-overdue recognition as the founder of the modern gay rights movement. John D'Emilio's landmark history of the movement, *Sexual Politics, Sexual Communities* (1983), featured the Mattachine Society; Judy Bacha included him in her Los Angeles history mural in North Hollywood's Tujunga Wash; Mitch Tuchman interviewed him as part of UCLA's Oral History Program in 1987; Stuart Timmons wrote an authorized biography in 1990; and among his many university speaking engagements was an address delivered at the Sorbonne in Paris.[259]

A legendary figure by the late 1990s, Harry was chosen grand marshal of the 1999 Gay Pride parade in San Francisco, where he'd moved a few years before for treatment of lung cancer and where he died in 2002 at age ninety. Closer to "home," through the efforts of Silver Lake activist Wes Joe, the L.A. City Council in 2011 officially designated the Cove Avenue staircase, below Harry's former hilltop residence, the Mattachine Steps; and on April 8, 2012, the centennial of his birth, a "Mattachine Steps" plaque was unveiled at the base of the steps. Attended by Radical Faerie members and officiated by California assemblymember Mike Gatto and then L.A. city councilmember and current mayor Eric Garcetti, Harry Hay was honored with full regalia, a stone's throw from where "true history was made."[260]

8

THE ESPRESSO PRIEST AND THE ADVOCATE

Malcolm Boyd and Mark Thompson

Though born a decade and an ocean apart, Harry Hay (born in 1912 in southern England) and Malcom Boyd (born in 1923 in New York City) were brothers under the skin. Just as a shared deep commitment to social justice and gay liberation marked their life's journeys, so did their disparate institutional affiliations—Harry's to the Communist Party and Malcolm's to the Episcopal Church—nurture but also hamper their respective radical callings. When fellow gay activist and author Mark Thompson (born in 1952 in Northern California) is added to the mix—through his bonding with Harry as a charter member of the Radical Faeries and with Malcolm as life partner and eventual spouse—a triumvirate of extraordinary Silver Lake soulmates ensues.

To the Manor Born

Harry and Malcolm's kinship begins with their wealthy upbringings, Malcolm's courtesy of his father heading a corporate accounting firm in Manhattan. Though he was raised in a mansion with servants, class privilege couldn't forestall—indeed, exacerbated, along with his father's alcoholism—a childhood filled with loneliness and alienation.[261] The two men's gayness overlapped as well in its seeming foretelling early on: Harry's with the observation of his "otherness" at age two; Malcolm's with the imprimatur, and caveat, of Evangeline Adams, "the high priestess of astrology," who prepared his natal horoscope. "Be sure he is not made to feel that he is 'queer,'" Evangeline cautioned, "but rather that he has gifts and possibilities, which, if used to advantage, will make him a very superior person."[262]

Harry's and Malcolm's adolescences were matched, as Mark's would be decades later, in the fatherly rejection they suffered from their perceived "unmanliness." Malcolm's separation from his father at age twelve, when his parents divorced, caused additional trauma. "For years afterwards," he recalled, "my father's absence was a void in my life."[263] As for the decline in living and cultural standards caused by the Depression and Malcolm's mother's move, first to a small farm in Texas and then to provincial Colorado Springs, he recalls: "I was always conscious of myself as a young prince who had gone into exile as a pauper."[264] Religious piety proved a partial saving grace. Unlike Harry, whose leftist politics broke with family tradition, Malcolm's eventual seminary studies and ordainment as an Episcopal priest not only resonated with his mother's religiosity but also perpetuated the legacy, one generation removed, of his grandfather's Episcopalian priesthood.[265]

All three men demonstrated precocious intellectual and artistic abilities. Harry's "gifted" testing, grade-skipping and chairing of the high school debating and dramatic societies rhymed with Malcolm's voracious early reading, poetry and essay writing and junior high newspaper reporting that included interviews with noted opera singer Lotte Lehman and writers John Gunther, Carl Van Doren and Harold Laski.[266] Not to be outdone, Mark started his junior high newspaper, edited the high school paper, contributed to the hometown weekly and joined the drama club—the latter less for the acting training than for the "kindred group of non-conformist types: girls with beatnik aspirations and boys with decidedly queer leanings."[267]

Limelight

Harry and Malcolm's Hollywood periods offer another fascinating comparison. While Harry's acting and screenwriting, though not eschewing the mainstream, tended toward the indie and avant-garde, Malcolm had his eye on the brass ring from the start. Fresh out of the University of Arizona in 1943, his stint at a radio workshop run by NBC led to a junior executive position with one of the largest advertising agencies in Hollywood. Before long he was producing his own daily radio program and soon advanced to "director of radio exploitation" (they made no bones about it then) for another prominent firm.[268]

Climbing the show-biz ladder at breakneck speed, Malcolm started his own company, Mal Boyd & Associates, shortly after the war and, by 1948, became one of the first producers for the fledgling medium of television. It wasn't all about "making it," however. In 1948, the same year Harry was forming Bachelor's Anonymous, Malcolm was working to combat racial stereotyping as the first president of the Television Producers Association of Hollywood.[269]

Malcolm's biggest coup came in 1949, when a budding business and personal relationship with legendary actress Mary Pickford and her actor husband, Charles "Buddy" Rogers, culminated in their starting a joint production company, Pickford, Rogers and Boyd (PRB). Despite his lightning rise in the industry and a warm friendship with Pickford, Tinseltown's "selfish, empty, arrogant, and quite loveless" aspect—partly a projection of his own homosexual repression—began to gnaw at his soul.[270]

By 1951, at the peak of his show-biz career, Malcolm began "to escape every so often," taking trips into the Arizona desert and bringing only one book: the Bible. Before the end of the year, he bade farewell to Hollywood and enrolled in the Church of the Divinity School of the Pacific in Berkeley. The *Los Angeles Times* reported his departure, and he was given a lavish going-away party at Ciro's on the Sunset Strip. Although the irony would only surface after he was ordained, one can't help but see a (self-fulfilling) prophesy in Malcolm's having resided, throughout his Hollywood odyssey, in a modest bungalow apartment on Padre Terrace.[271]

Malcolm's abrupt escape from Sin City did not signify a wholesale dismissal of the place. Like Harry, who to the bitter end held fast to Marxist, if not to Communist Party, precepts, Malcolm refused to rationalize his stint in the Dream Factory as either a frivolous interlude or a baneful detour from the path to the Lord. He steadfastly maintained contact with his celebrity friends after reentering the Christian fold and considered "the years in Hollywood…a splendid, warm, painful, alive, real part of my life. I am grateful for them."[272]

Biographical convergence with Harry Hay reached its apex in 1951, as Malcolm's defection from the industry and prodigal return to the church mirrored, almost to the day, Harry's divorce from his wife, expulsion from the Communist Party and founding of the Mattachine Society. The tripartite connection began to gel as well when Mark Thompson entered the world in 1952 in Pacific Grove, just down the coast from Berkeley Divinity School.

Malcolm's skill set held fast during his seminary years—becoming president of the student body, starting a school newspaper, contributing to the *Episcopal Church News*—but so did his homosexual repression. Whereas Harry's lip-service renunciation of his gayness was dictated by the party and abetted by the "talking cure," Malcolm, while in Berkeley, bought into the church's homosexual aversion therapy: guiltily confessing his gayness, hating himself "as a closeted homosexual" and feeling "crucified" for his "affliction."[273]

True love finally broke the homophobic spell. During a year's stay at New York's Union Theological Seminary after his ordainment in 1955, Malcolm began an eight-month affair with a visiting German monk that proved revelatory. "I have found the capacity to love," he later wrote. "I do not believe that it is sin. I do not believe I should be cut off from [God's] love because of it."[274] Yet he still could not muster the courage to openly disclose his orientation, nor was his sexual liberation complete. Resorting to occasional flings and brief affairs, he mainly sublimated his taboo desires in unconventional church practices and social activism.

Juke-Joint Jesus

Malcolm first gained notoriety in 1957 on his first parish assignment in Indianapolis, where he shocked the all-white membership by inviting an African American pastor to speak. Controversy around him widened in 1959, when as a chaplain at Colorado State University he began hosting poetry readings in a local coffeehouse. Not amused by the "jarring blend of Luther and Lenny Bruce," the local bishop denounced the "espresso" and "beatnik priest," as the media gleefully anointed Malcolm.[275] At odds for some time with the church's self-righteous separation of sacred and secular, Malcolm resigned his post in protest, proclaiming, "Jesus Christ is the Lord of the whole of life or none of it."[276]

While on a new assignment at Wayne State University in Detroit in the early 1960s, Malcolm joined the larger civil rights movement, went on the Freedom Rides in the Deep South and was "one of the first white ministers to work the voter registration drives."[277] He remained an ally of Martin Luther King through his anti–Vietnam War period, sympathized with

Black Power and was arrested at an antiwar demonstration at the Pentagon in 1967. Once again echoing Harry Hay, whose radical politics alienated assimilationist-oriented members of the Mattachine Society, as Malcolm's "rebel priest" and "angry young man" images grew, so did opposition from "various rich and socially conservative church members."[278]

The rise of the counterculture in the mid-1960s tilted momentum in Malcolm's favor. *Mademoiselle* magazine sympathetically included him with Federico Fellini, James Baldwin, Jules Feiffer and Norman Mailer as a "Disturber of the Peace." *Life* named him one of "the 100 most important young people in the United States" and a member of "the Take-Over Generation." Most ironically, for a closeted gay priest, he was photographed, duly frocked, for *Playboy*.[279]

Amid the maelstrom of political protests, priestly duties and media attention, Malcolm managed to publish at a prolific pace. Declaring to the *New York Times* "that the most powerful sermons of our times and culture are to be found in the theater, the novel and occasionally in the medium of film," he became the church's regular film reviewer and wrote a series of plays—*Boy* (1961) and a trilogy: *Study in Color*, *They Aren't Real to Me* and *The Job* (1962)—in which he also costarred. Most impressive, already by 1965 he had edited one book and authored six others, starting with *Crisis in Communication* in 1957 and culminating with the smash bestseller *Are You Running with Me, Jesus?*[280]

Building on his bestseller celebrity, Malcolm began reading his religious poetry to the accompaniment of Charlie Byrd's jazz guitar, in clubs in New York and at the 1966 Newport Jazz Festival. An even bigger hullabaloo grew from his appearances at the "hungry i" in San Francisco, where his "standup sermons," fronting for the likes of Dick Gregory and performed with clerical collar, were featured on network television and earned him a new nickname: the "nightclub priest."[281] Reviews were decidedly mixed. *Playboy* called his routine a "slang-packed monolog to the Almighty." *Look* deemed the Episcopal pundit "part Old Testament prophet, part stool-straddling entertainer." Others saw the latest foray into offbeat evangelism as courting controversy for its own sake, and Malcolm himself admitted to becoming a "commodity on tour."[282]

What troubled Malcolm most was his *not* admitting his sexual orientation while insisting that the church "return from formality to actuality."[283] Fittingly, his formal coming out, in a keynote speech in June 1976 at a San Francisco convention of the Episcopal gay and lesbian group Integrity, was headlined first by *The Advocate*, the gay "paper of record," which

Mark Thompson had joined as a staff writer the year before.[284] Malcolm professed his gayness to the straight world a few months later in an interview in the *Chicago Sun-Times*.[285]

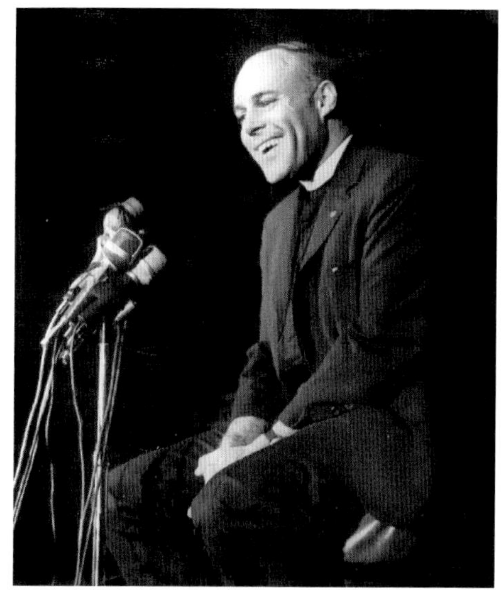

Malcolm Boyd at the hungry i, San Francisco, September 13, 1967.

Malcolm's previous problems with the church were child's play compared to what "came crashing down" after the public disclosure.[286] He was dismissed from his current clerical post and denied other appointments for several years. One former admirer burned his books, and even some of his activist friends—not considering gay rights worthy of the same attention—criticized him for undermining his utility on other social justice issues.[287] Playing favorites on social causes was not a game Malcolm was prepared to play, especially on a cause that affected him personally and that he had so long neglected. The main benefit of "taking off the mask"—as his 1984 memoir described his outing—was its finally allowing him to openly express and fully experience the deepest core of his being.

Malcolm and Mark

Coming of age in the 1960s, reaching adulthood in the post-Stonewall era and with less religious baggage to combat, Mark Thompson had an easier, if by no means fraught-free, entry into gay awareness and activism. Good fortune also helped pave, and pay, the way. Having helped start a gay support group in 1973 while studying journalism at San Francisco State University, Mark's passage into professional gay advocacy, upon graduation in 1975, occurred serendipitously.

Wealthy financier David Goldstein, following his outing and subsequent ousting from Wells Fargo Bank, had just purchased *The Advocate* from its original Los Angeles owners (see Chapter 9) and moved operations to the Bay Area. After viewing a sample of Mark's work, Goldstein offered the twenty-three-year-old a golden opportunity, suggesting he combine a post-graduation backpack trip to Europe with some reporting for *The Advocate.* Mark ended up interviewing David Hockney in Paris, surveying the growing gay scene in Amsterdam and doing an investigative piece in Barcelona on the Spanish Movement for Gay Liberation (MELH), most of whose members had been imprisoned or otherwise silenced by the Franco regime, then in its final throes.[288] Thus began Mark's "Advocate Days," the main title of his 2009 memoir about his twenty-year stint at the paper, eventually as arts and culture editor and senior editor of what can rightly be called "the greatest chronicle of one of the most significant social movements of all time."[289]

Besides jump-starting his journalistic career, *The Advocate* instigated Mark's first contact, and ultimate close relationship, with both Harry Hay and Malcolm Boyd. The meeting with Harry at his Hollywood home in 1979, ostensibly solely for an interview, corresponded with Harry and his partner John Burnside's formation of the Radical Faeries. "The first thing Harry Hay ever told me," Mark recalled, "was to pull off my green frog skin of heterosexual conformity."[290] At first taken aback, Mark—as curious reporter, gay activist and spiritual seeker—also was taken in, and then along, on the first Radical Faeries gathering in the Arizona desert. The experience was life-altering and consciousness-expanding. Mark became an active Radical Faerie member and remains affiliated with the group to the present. He also became (as Malcolm would as well) fast friends with Harry and John.[291]

Mark's interview with Malcolm was even more propitious. On the cusp of *The Advocate*'s relocation back to Los Angeles in 1984, Mark came down to case the joint and interview writer Christopher Isherwood and his longtime partner, artist Don Bachardy, in the bargain. While staying at a Hollywood hotel notably hospitable to gays, Mark found a note from a colleague alerting him to Malcolm's staying at the same hotel (apparently licking his wounds from a breakup). "Mal-colm… Mal-colm Boyd?" Mark muttered to himself, not immediately registering the name. Then it dawned on him: "Oh damn, I had to read *Are You Running with Me, Jesus?* in high school!" To be polite, he went to Malcolm's room for what he thought would be a brief chat; it turned into a four-hour rapt conversation and—after a certain issue was resolved—a thirty-one-year loving relationship.[292]

The sticking point wasn't the two men's thirty-year age and generational differences—which could be worked out, Mark told Malcolm after they'd been seeing each other about a month. "But there's one more

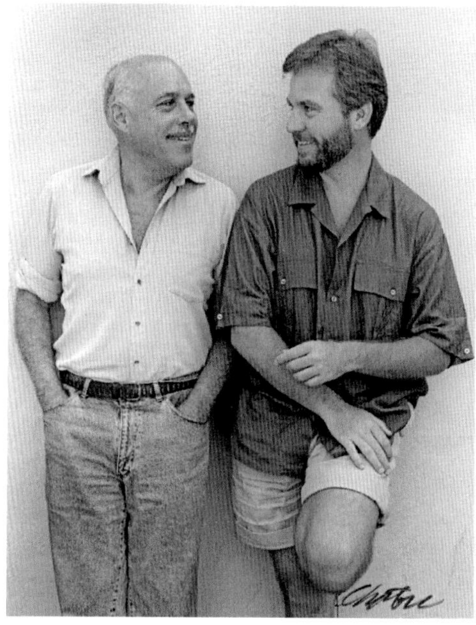

Malcolm Boyd and Mark Thompson, portrait by Crawford Barton. *Courtesy of Mark Thompson.*

thing," he added. "You're an Episcopalian! And a priest!" So they courted, and after a year and a half, with Mark having warmed to Malcolm's church circle and becoming a "cultural Episcopalian," Malcolm descended to one knee at the much-beloved (and sadly missed) Pierre's Los Feliz Inn on Hillhurst Avenue and proposed.[293]

The couple's house search drew them magnetically to nearby Silver Lake, partly for its gay history and sizeable gay population, partly for the lush, hilly landscape and namesake waters that reminded Mark of Northern California. Finding a lovely hilltop, Spanish-style home at 2517 Hyperion Avenue in which two generations of gay men had previously resided, they moved into the place in 1986 and never looked back.[294]

Malcolm had since regained his clerical footing, thanks to his longtime friend, the Reverend Frederick Fenton, who invited him to serve at St. Augustine by-the-Sea Episcopal Church in Santa Monica in 1982. Undeterred by residual hostility in the church community ("We lost some of our members but those who stayed loved Malcolm dearly," Fenton said), neither Malcolm's social activism, increasingly directed at the AIDS crisis, nor his writing flagged.[295]

He held the nation's first "AIDS mass" in 1985. He was elected president of PEN USA Center West (a branch of the international writer's association) from 1984 to 1987. In 1991, he was arrested, shackled and refused water after a "kneel-in" for increased AIDS research funding before the Los Angeles County Board of Supervisors.[296] During his tenure, starting in 1997, as writer-and-poet-in-residence at the Cathedral Center of St. Paul in Echo Park, he also worked as a chaplain for AIDS patients and joined a community-wide effort to turn gay activist and writer Jim Kepner's vast collection into the ONE National Gay & Lesbian Archives at USC Libraries, the largest repository of LGBTQ materials in the world.[297] Along the way, he authored or edited thirteen more books (for a grand total of thirty-three) before his death in 2015.

Encouraged by his fireball partner, Mark flexed his own literary muscles shortly after their Silver Lake life began. Besides his now-classic trilogy—*Gay Spirit: Myth and Meaning*, (1987), *Gay Soul: The Heart of Gay Spirit and Nature* (1994) and *Gay Body: A Journey through Shadow to Self* (1997)—Mark authored or edited five other books, including the highly acclaimed anthology on sexuality and identity, *Leatherfolk: Radical Sex, People, Politics, and Practice* (1991). His gay activism took on new form as well. Two years after leaving *The Advocate* in 1994, Mark earned a master's degree in clinical psychology and became a mental health counselor, working mainly with gay and lesbian youth and people living with AIDS.

Mark and Malcolm exchanged marriage vows in 2004 in a church service at the Cathedral Center of St. Paul. It was the first gay wedding in the United States to be performed by a sitting bishop, J. Jon Bruno. "It was

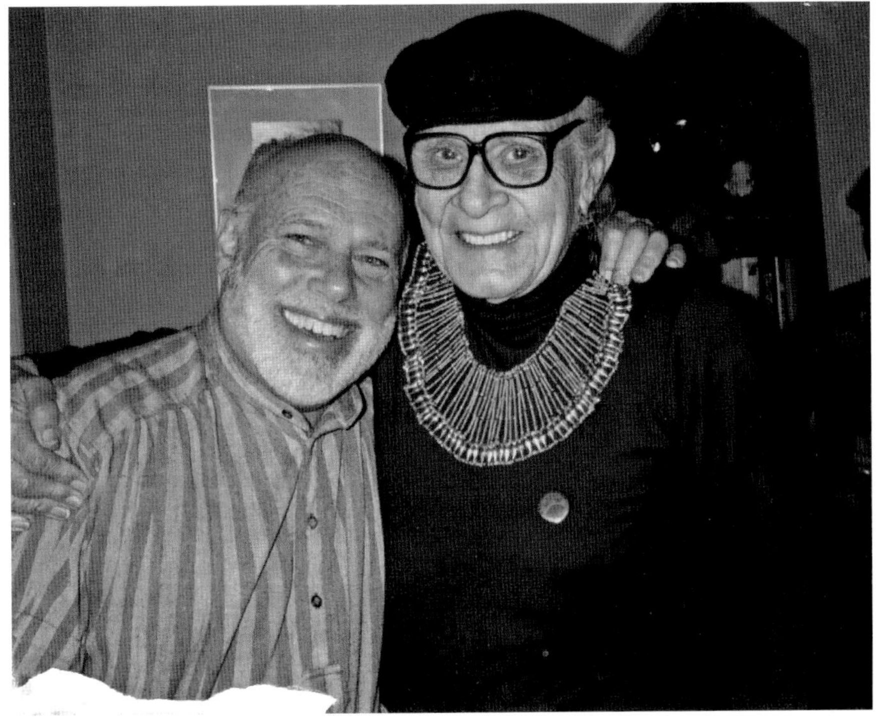

Malcolm Boyd and Harry Hay. *Courtesy of ONE Archives at USC Libraries.*

a huge affair, a real to-do," Mark recalls, though, as seemingly everything involving Malcolm, "it was also controversial. It contributed to the breakaway of several churches in the Los Angeles Episcopal Dioceses, one of the largest in the country."[298] In July 2013, after Proposition 8, California's anti-same-sex-marriage initiative, was overturned by the California Supreme Court, Mark and Malcolm were legally married as well.

On top of all their political, creative and work-related activity, the couple maintained an active social life. They were frequent guests at James Leo Herlihy's Silver Lake soirees and hosted Harry Hay's eightieth birthday at their home in 1992. Both Mark and Malcolm also spoke at the 2013 Mattachine Steps sign unveiling posthumously honoring Harry. "One of the seminal gay figures of the twentieth century," Mark called him. "One of the greatest of all civil rights leaders," Malcolm went further, then added sadly, "but also one of the least known."[299] That Assemblymember Mike Gatto and City Councilmember Eric Garcetti also spoke at the event points to a partial corrective of the ignorance. And when newly elected mayor Garcetti spoke at Malcolm's memorial service at the Cathedral Center of St. Paul in March 2015, a final synchronous touch was added to this tale of two (if not three) brothers under the skin.

9

WHERE IT'S AT

The Black Cat Tavern and A Different Light Bookstore

Although their proud place in Silver Lake history has only recently been recognized, The Black Cat tavern and A Different Light bookstore belong with Harry Hay, Malcolm Boyd and Mark Thompson on the list of local heroes of the LGBT cause.[300] Anyone with some awareness of gay history has heard of the Stonewall Inn in Greenwich Village, where a rebellion against police harassment on June 28, 1969, is credited with triggering the gay rights movement. Surprisingly few, even in Silver Lake, have heard of The Black Cat tavern, at 3909 Sunset Boulevard, where two and a half years prior, on February 11, 1967, "possibly the largest gay protest to be held in this country up to that time" took place.[301]

The historic event's inciting incident occurred a month earlier, in the early morning hours of January 1, 1967, starting at The Black Cat and spilling over onto the neighboring New Faces gay bar (now Circus of Books) at Sunset and Sanborn.[302] Foreshadowing the trouble to come, a dozen undercover vice officers, their "bad coats" (drab suit jackets) a dead giveaway and their presence already a form of intimidation, mingled among The Black Cat's festive New Year's Eve crowd.[303] Shortly before midnight, a gaggle of men in drag swished into the place after a costume contest at New Faces. At zero hour, jubilation erupted. The Rhythm Queens, a black women's trio, broke into a rock version of "Auld Lang Syne." Balloons dropped from the ceiling, confetti was strewn and gay men did what people throughout the Pacific time zone were doing that very moment and people around the world had been doing since time immemorial: they embraced and exchanged New Year's kisses.

Pandemonium of a nastier sort instantly ensued. The bad coats, joined by men in blue, burst into the crowd swinging nightsticks and beating people willy-nilly. Some patrons and bartenders fought back, injuring two officers seriously enough to require hospitalization. Thirteen customers and three bartenders were arrested and forced to lie down in the parking lot until squad cars came to haul them away. Two customers attempting to flee to New Faces were chased down by police. Inside the bar, the cops pummeled the woman owner, Lee Roy (mistaking her for a drag queen named Leroy), breaking her collar bone, and beat two New Faces bartenders unconscious. One of the bartenders, Robert Haas, who suffered a cracked rib, fractured skull and ruptured spleen, was charged with felony assault on a police officer.

Adding further insult to the bloodied and broken bodies, six of those arrested were charged with "lewd or dissolute conduct." Their felonious offense: deigning to hold their celebratory New Year's kisses longer than the LAPD's three-second limit. Ironically, Hollywood had just dropped its three-second limit for kissing on the silver screen (by straights, that is—LGBTs were taboo altogether). The Black Cat Six weren't so lucky: they were found guilty for the "temerity of a kiss," and the U.S. Supreme Court refused to hear their case.[304]

Ample grounds for the protest that followed the New Year's crackdown existed well before that grisly event. Abhorrent treatment of gays existed around the country, but since the formation of LAPD's Sex Squad in the 1930s and under notoriously bigoted Police Chief William S. Parker from the 1950s through the mid-1960s, L.A.'s finest were especially hostile to the city's sizable gay population. Mattachine Society cofounder Dale Jennings's landmark anti-entrapment case of the early 1950s notwithstanding, gays had to walk a tripwire of secrecy and dissimulation. Gay bars were obligatorily windowless and unfamiliar patrons necessarily suspect, lest they turn out to be working undercover.

Alexei Romanoff, a gay Silver Lake resident at the time of the raid and one of the founders of New Faces, who had avoided the raid but participated in the protest, reports a friend and his partner being arrested at a gay bar because one man brushed some spilt beer off the other's shirt.[305] The injustice, aggravation and humiliation of being punished for behavior straight men, and even lesbian women, could engage in with impunity was bad enough. Far worse, and used to coerce gays into pleading guilty to a lesser infraction, was the lewd conduct charge, which added a lifelong stigma of being registered as a sex offender.[306]

Romanoff recalls a more amusing double standard at the time also involving lesbians. At the Canyon Club in Topanga Canyon, a gay and lesbian resort a safer distance from Chief Parker's watchful eye, gay men and women more openly cavorted and danced same-sex-style. Women dancing together and otherwise showing affection had long been sanctioned by society. Gay men had to be protected with an alarm system. The Canyon Club's consisted of two juke boxes, one playing when the coast was clear and another switched to as soon as the police or suspicious-looking characters were seen approaching. The new tune signaled the dancers to switch as well, to opposite-sex partners.[307]

The melee at The Black Cat was no joke—it was the last straw. Enraged by mistreatment and inspired by the civil rights and identity politics movements, a group of gay men began meeting in early January at the Hub, a gay bar in West Hollywood, to plan a response. Spearheading the meetings was a new gay organization called PRIDE ("probably the first application of the word to gay politics").[308] Founded in 1966 by Steve Ginsberg, PRIDE (Personal Rights in Defense and Education) differentiated itself both from the assimilationist gay groups derided by Harry Hay and his own that focused on gay self-realization. Presaging the militant gay groups that would emerge from Stonewall, PRIDE, according to historians Lillian Faderman and Stuart Timmons, "was far more radical in rhetoric and action than any of the earlier homophile organizations had dared to be."[309]

Starting in mid-1966, PRIDE had begun mimeographing an underground newsletter, called the *PRIDE Advocate*, distributed surreptitiously in gay bars.[310] The paper helped promote a series of smaller protests at The Black Cat in early January, culminating in the historic demonstration on February 12. An estimated two hundred to four hundred people from a broad spectrum participated: men and women, young and old, gay and straight. One group paraded along the sidewalk in front of the bar, hoisting placards, shouting slogans and handing out leaflets to passing motorists and pedestrians; another group lent support from the adjoining parking lot.[311]

As common as such protests have become, "at a time when few would dare to publicly identify themselves as homosexual for fear of intimidation and arrest," Jim Burroway reminds us, "this first openly-gay rights protest in Los Angeles was a very bold step."[312] The boldness was compounded by the overall countercultural tension of the time, demonstrated three months prior in the brutal police response to an anti-Vietnam protest on the Sunset Strip, leading to other non-gay, anti-police brutality protests planned for the same day as the one at The Black Cat. Romanoff recalls how fearful he and

CRISIS

FOR INFORMATION

CALL

666-5312
or
936-7809

POLICE LAWLESSNESS MUST BE STOPPED!!

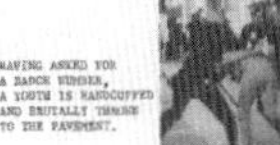

HAVING ASKED FOR
A BADGE NUMBER,
A YOUTH IS HANDCUFFED
AND BRUTALLY THROWN
TO THE PAVEMENT.

THIS HAS HAPPENED IN
COUNTLESS STREETS, BARS,
AND RESTAURANTS IN ALL
SECTIONS OF OUR CITY.

Because Police Lawlessness is not just a problem of the Sunset Strip
but a problem that exists throughout the City of Los Angeles,
there will be:

SIMULTANEOUS
DEMONSTRATIONS
in
Silverlake

Sunset & Hyperion
3900 Sunset Blvd.
&

Sunset Strip · Watts · East L.A. · Pacoima · Venice

Arbitrary Arrests ·
Illegal Search & Seizure
Police Perjury in Courts
ENTRAPMENT

ABUSE of OUR RIGHTS & DIGNITY
must
stop!

SATURDAY FEB 11 9:00 P.M.

Left: Flyer calling for simultaneous anti–police brutality demonstrations around the city on February 11, 1967. *Courtesy of ONE Archives at USC Libraries.*

Below: Protesters at The Black Cat, February 11, 1967. *Courtesy of ONE Archives at USC Libraries.*

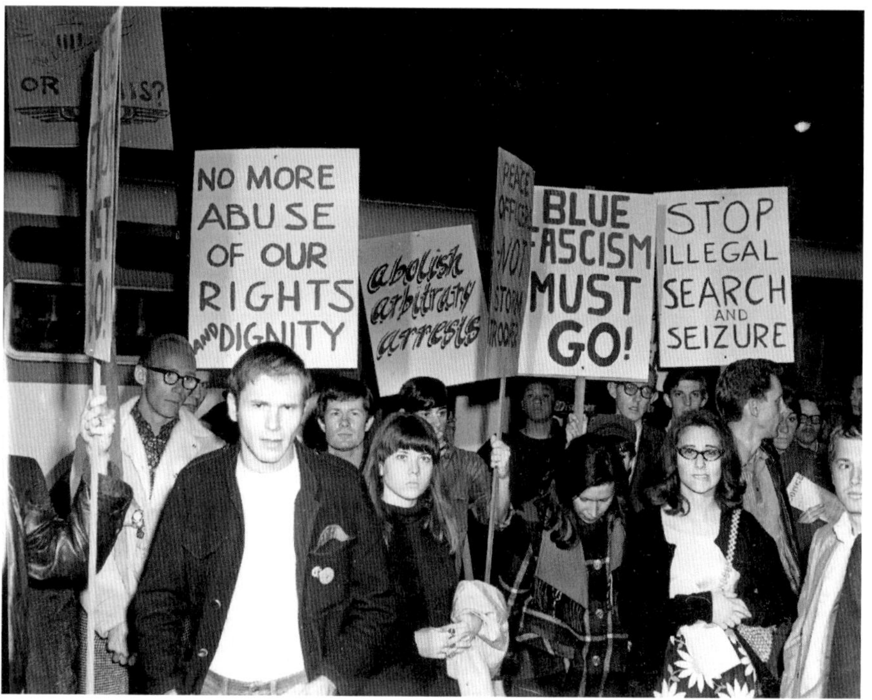

other Black Cat protesters were of the phalanx of officers ringing the area, ready to pounce, even for something as trivial, and trumped up, as littering, should a leaflet happen to fall to the ground.[313] On this occasion, the officers remained on the sidelines—in spite, or because, of the provocative protest signs: "ABOLISH ARBITRARY ARREST," "NO MORE ILLEGAL SEARCH AND SEIZURE," "BLUE FASCISM MUST GO."[314]

Pride and Prejudice

The mainstream media ignored both the New Year's raid and the historic protest; only the *PRIDE Advocate* and *L.A. Free Press*, an alternative weekly, gave them any mention. Partly due to the lack of publicity, no Stonewall-like rebellion resulted. "But a new activism had begun in gay L.A," Faderman and Timmons report. Perhaps most enduringly, The Black Cat episode would lead to a reincarnation of the *PRIDE Advocate* in a form that would play an even greater, and ongoing, role in the gay liberation movement.[315]

Starting in the summer of 1967, Richard Mitch, the force behind the original newsletter, and his lover, Bill Rau, decided to upgrade the mimeographed sheet into a full-fledged newspaper. Professional printing equipment was provided, unknowingly, by ABC studios on Talmadge Avenue (now Prospect Studios, owned by Disney). Rau and two other gay men, Sam Allen and Aristide Laurent, printed television scripts in the day and—à la Edythe Eyde at RKO in the 1940s—printed the gay paper clandestinely in the wee hours. The name was shortened to the now iconic *The Advocate*, and the first issue's front-page headline, echoing Black Power and other militant minority groups, "was the first use on record of the slogan 'Gay Power.'" Ironically, power politics and sagging fortunes within the PRIDE organization allowed Mitch, by the end of the year and for the princely sum of one dollar, to purchase the rights to what would become "the first national gay news publication."[316]

Gay activism may have been up and running, but government-sanctioned homophobia was alive and well. Reenergized by Ronald Reagan's conservative governorship (starting in 1967), and with the LAPD still riding shotgun, harassment of gay bars (estimated at eighty strong in L.A. at the time) intensified.[317] The Black Cat and New Faces became prime targets. Buckling to the pressure even before The Black Cat protest, New Faces closed on January 21, 1967. The Black Cat, which had only opened the

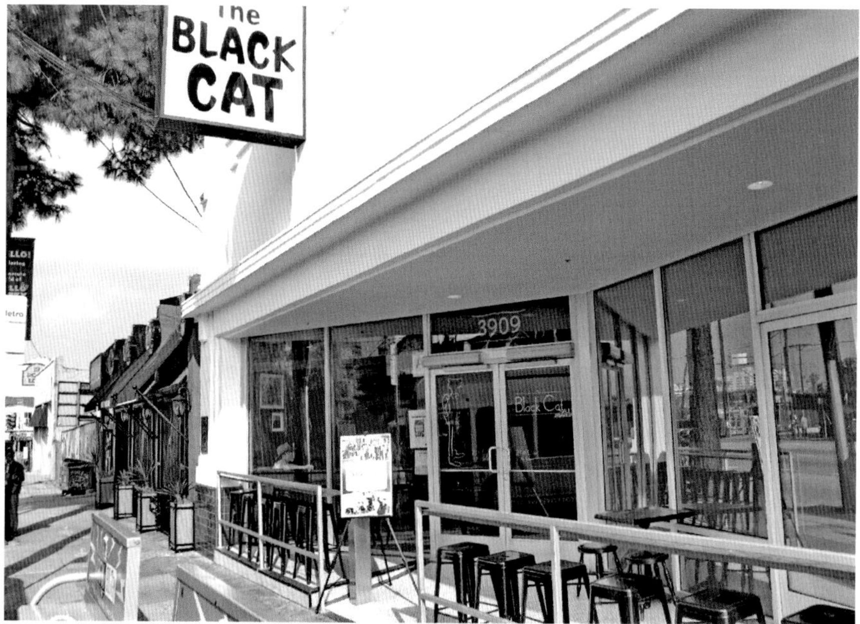

The Black Cat, June 2015.

October before, after an unsuccessful five-month fight over the post-raid suspension of its liquor license, was forced to close on May 21, 1967.

But all was not lost. The bar itself survived and initially even retained its gay identity through subsequent ownership and name changes, among them Basgo's Disco ("home of the notorious Club Fuck! in the 90s") and the gay Latino-oriented Le Barcito.[318] In 2008, thanks largely to the man who helped mount the Mattachine Steps sign campaign, Wes Joe, The Black Cat was officially designated Los Angeles Historic-Cultural Monument No. 939. In November 2011, restaurateurs and Silver Lake residents Charlie Conrad, Lindsay Kennedy and Dean Malouf purchased the property and, on December 2, 2012, reopened the elegantly renovated bar and restaurant under its original, and historic, name.

The reincarnated Black Cat, an instant hit with Silver Lake hipsters, is no longer a gay bar, per se. "Given the changing times, and demographics, we wanted it to be all-inclusive," Conrad says.[319] The new owners are hyper-aware of the site's historical significance, however, and have paid homage in the interior and exterior design. The bar counter's original base has been preserved; a panoply of black cat images, interspersed with actual photos of the

1967 protest, grace the inside walls; and the front entrance, with its iconic "The Black Cat" sign, has been restored as closely as possible to its former state.[320] The new Black Cat's pre-opening "LAPD-LGBT" cocktail party, meanwhile, demonstrated just how much the times have changed—immeasurably for the better.

Attendees included an array of top city and police officials, including the first lesbian head of the vice squad, an openly gay member of the Police Commission and representatives from various LGBT groups.[321] The crowning touch came on June 3, 2014, with the unveiling of a plaque beside the bar's main entrance, declaring: "The Black Cat—Site of the First Documented LGBT Civil Rights Demonstration in the Nation—Held on February 11, 1967." Featured speakers included Alexei Romanov, Mark Thompson and openly gay city councilmember Mitch O'Farrell.

The Cat's Meow

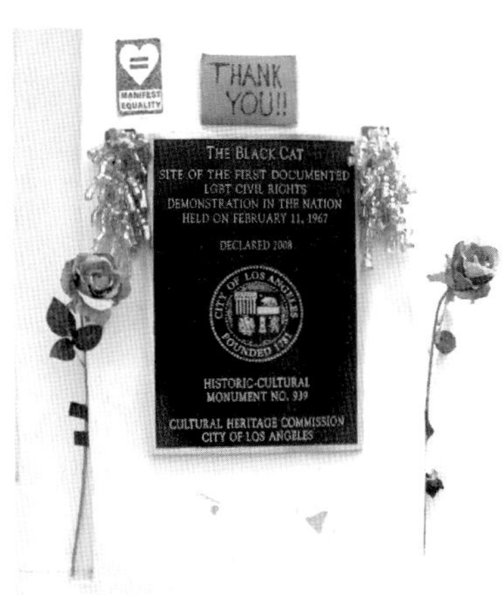

Celebrating the legalization of gay marriage at The Black Cat, June 2015.

Nothing speaks louder about the living legacy of "the crucial spark that ignited a whole movement" than the spontaneous Silver Lake street art inspired by the Supreme Court's decision, on June 26, 2015, declaring anti-gay marriage laws unconstitutional.[322] Shortly after the momentous ruling in *Obergefell v. Hodges*, The Black Cat's commemorative plaque was adorned with flowers, pink frills, a sticker with a heart design, a caption reading "Manifest Equality" and a note exclaiming "Thank You!!!"

More than just a touching display, the sign fortuitously acknowledged an actual legal through-line between the high court's 2015 decision and The Black Cat's "temerity of a kiss" trial of 1967. In a petition to the U.S. Supreme Court seeking consideration of The Black Cat case, the defendants' attorney "broke legal precedent by asserting for the first time that homosexuals are entitled to equal protection under the law."[323] "Before that," Romanov's husband, David Fahar, elaborates, "you would pay it off with a lesser charge, or say you were trapped, 'We didn't do it.' This was the first time that they actually defended—and lost—but defended, saying the Constitution of the United States applies to gay men equally as it does to straight men."[324]

A Different Light

Another Silver Lake business that played a key role in enhancing LGBT life in general is A Different Light bookstore. Three Canadians—Toronto bookstore employee Norman Laurilla and *Ottawa Citizen* journalist Richard Labonte, with funding from attorney and businessman George Leigh—opened A Different Light in October 1979 at 4014 Santa Monica Boulevard.[325] Located at the junction of Santa Monica and Sunset Boulevards, directly across from Circus of Books and kitty-corner from The Black Cat, the store struck a chord with the gay and lesbian community in the post-Stonewall era, eventually expanding to outlets in West Hollywood, San Francisco's Castro district and New York's Chelsea.[326] Like the original site, the store's name, taken from a sci-fi novel written by lesbian author Elizabeth A. Lynn, was well chosen. It was "there," lesbian author and rabbi Ruth Podolsky, who worked at A Different Light, recalls, "we reclaimed, for ourselves, the daylight."[327]

At its height in the 1980s and '90s, A Different Light "was one of the most influential LGBT booksellers in the United States, serving as a cultural hub and social center for LGBT people."[328] Malcolm Boyd and Mark Thompson launched all their new books at the Silver Lake store.[329] Other LGBT luminaries who gave readings or held book signings there included gays John Rechy, Allen Ginsberg, Christopher Isherwood, Larry Kramer, Armistead Maupin, Quentin Crisp and Ned Rorem and lesbians Judy Grahn, Katherine Forest, Eloise Klein Healy, Carolyn Weathers, Olga Broumas, Cherrie Moraga, Dorothy Allison and Pat Parker, among others.[330]

"A Different Light was a historic place," Boyd recalled in an interview, "not just for Silver Lake but for all Los Angeles."[331] "It was a center for community," Rabbi Podolsky adds; "our hang-out, our lifeline, our not-so-secret headquarters." Of special significance was the trailblazing "Lesbian Writers Series," inaugurated at A Different Light in February 1984, where lesbian authors "wrote ourselves out of the margins, into manifestation."[332] "For many years," former events coordinator Sophia Corleone noted in

2014, "the Lesbian Writers Series was absolutely the only place where lesbian-themed authors could safely share their work. In many ways, this is still true."[333]

Besides showcasing authors, the store featured reading groups, writing conferences, panel discussions and art openings and displayed work by local artists on a rotating basis. A victim of its own and the LGBT movement's remarkable success, along with the rise of big chains and the Internet, the flagship store sadly closed in 1992, with its three branches (since sold to new owners) following in 2001 (Chelsea), 2009 (West Hollywood) and 2011 (Castro).[334]

The closings couldn't dampen the stores' place in history. When A Different Light and the lesbian-owned and -oriented Sisterhood Bookstore opened their doors (the latter in 1972 on Crenshaw Boulevard in South L.A., later moving to Westwood), no "Gay & Lesbian" sections existed in mainstream bookstores, much less on Amazon. After the original Different Light's demise in 1992 (Sisterhood survived to 1999), people could still wax nostalgic when passing the quaint old row of storefronts whose rickety but charming Tudor-style façade seemed part of a Potemkin Village or B-movie set. A measure of poetic justice also derived from one of the last remaining store's selling computer-related products (the likes of which would, or already had, "creatively destroyed" the bricks-and-mortar chains). Then came the literal (in more ways than one) creative destruction.[335]

On September 24, 2011, *The Eastsider LA* reported, "Shoppers and visitors at Silver Lake's Sunset Junction on Saturday were met with the sight and sounds of a bulldozer that mowed down a row of storefronts and, along with them, a piece of gay neighborhood history." The *Patch* and *Queerty* blogs also covered the story, but the mainstream media, eerily reminiscent of their reticence on The Black Cat raid and protest, cast a blind eye to A Different Light's biting the dust.[336] The difference was that while atavistic local law enforcement was behind the brutality perpetrated at The Black Cat and New Faces, responsibility for A Different Light's demolition must be laid squarely at the feet of Big Capital.

Los Angeles mega-developer Frost Chaddock had recently purchased the storefront lot where A Different Light had once been located, along with two other Silver Lake lots: one right across the street on Santa Monica (site of another one-time gay bar, The Detour) and a second a few blocks west on Sunset (site of the long defunct, so-called Bates Hotel). All three properties were (and remain years later) slated for multi-story, multi-unit, mixed-use behemoths not only out of scale with surrounding residential and commercial buildings but also destined to aggravate already crisis-level traffic and parking. It was certain to meet stiff local resistance, even without the Different Light disaster. The disdain shown Silver Lake history—and the community, in events leading to the demolition—further chilled relations with Frost Chaddock.

As *Patch* reported at the time, Frost Chaddock had informed the Thirteenth District City Council office that oversaw the project, and the Design & Preservation Committee of the Silver Lake Neighborhood Council, that it "had no immediate plans to demolish the site." This assurance, given on August 24, a month before the demolition, was clearly a smokescreen, however, as design committee co-chair Elizabeth Bougart-Sharkov learned when she "discovered that a permit to demolish the site had been pulled that same day." Most egregiously, the council office, which had been working to facilitate another community meeting to discuss possible historic designation for the site, was assured by Frost Chadduck, "even as late as two days before the demolition," that "they would not take action without notice."[337] The developer's representatives, at several highly contentious post-demolition community meetings, apologized for the "mistake" and offered to compensate by including, in the building planned for the Different Light site, space for a small LGBT museum.

Better than nothing, but small recompense for the wanton destruction of a local landmark. Mark Thompson says he cried when he saw the ruins of the once beloved bookstore. Malcolm Boyd was still fulminating about it two years later: "Why isn't there more opposition to developers coming in and crushing everything? A Different Light was a historic place....Imagine having someone come in and wipe that out!"[338]

10

CONSCIENCE OF THE REVOLUTION

Ricardo Flores Magón

The Mexican Revolution of 1910–20 (with continued unrest through the 1920s) transfigured Mexican society and had significant impact on Los Angeles as well. The thousands of Mexican refugees driven to El Norte by the decades of social upheaval were attracted to L.A., specifically, by the city's phenomenal industrial spurt during the same period. The immigrant influx was so great that the city's population, whose Mexican proportion had dwindled from 90 percent at the outset of the American period in 1850 to 10 percent by 1900, by 1929 boasted the largest Mexican community in the United States.[339]

Mention the Mexican Revolution to the average Angeleno today, however, and you're lucky if the names Zapata and Pancho Villa—its legendary rebel leaders—spring to mind. The better informed might dredge up Madero, Huerta, Carranza and Obregon, who played musical chairs replacing dreaded dictator Porfirio Diaz as heads of state. Odds are only a rare individual has heard of Ricardo Flores Magón. Yet not only was he a key figure in the revolution; he alone among the figures listed above also lived, before and during the revolution, in Los Angeles and a good portion of that time in Silver Lake.

Ricardo had been a thorn in the side of the dictatorship since cofounding the opposition newspaper *Regeneración* in 1900. He also would have been among the first to mount the barricades in 1910 had he not been forced to flee with his younger brother Enrique in 1904, to escape almost certain execution by the Diaz regime. Nor did the brothers' agitation stop at the border. From

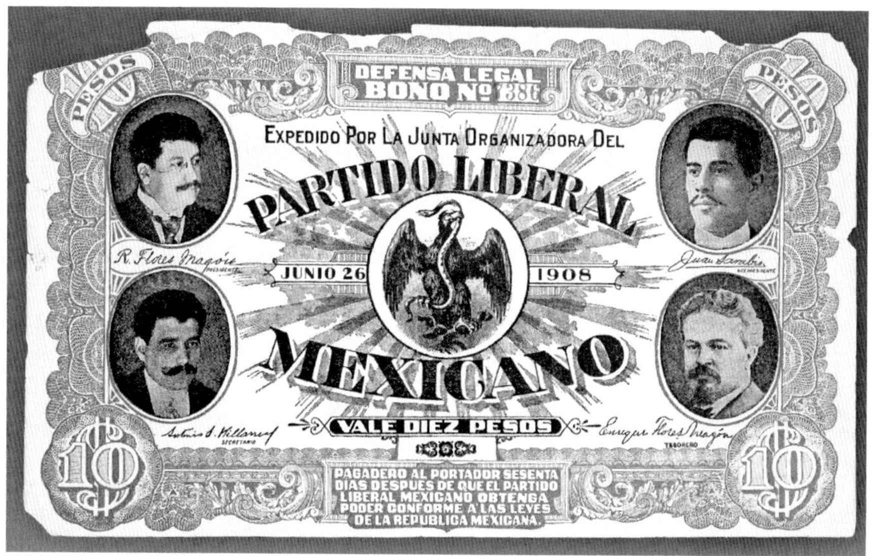

"Legal tender" issued by the PLM in 1908, redeemable after the revolution. *Portraits clockwise from upper left:* Ricardo Magón, Juan Sarabia, Enrique Magón and Antonio Villarreal.

exile in the United States, despite hounding by Diaz operatives and their American accomplices, Ricardo and Enrique, together with fellow exiled dissidents and supporters in Mexico, continued to publish and distribute *Regeneración* in their homeland. In 1905, they formed a new political party, Partido Liberal Mexicano (Mexican Liberal Party, or PLM), with Ricardo as president. In 1906, they formulated a Program and Manifesto (or Plan), which historians regard as "perhaps the most important, comprehensive, and far-reaching document of the Mexican Revolution…[inspiring] the relatively mild reforms of Francisco I. Madero as well as the revolutionary agrarian program of Emiliano Zapata. The framers of today's Mexican Constitution also borrowed heavily from it…[including] probably the most radical labor code at that time."[340]

NO OTHER CHOICE

Unlike Aline Barnsdall, Harry Hay and Malcolm Boyd, whose progressive politics defied their privileged origins, Ricardo was primed for his prominent role in the revolution. His birthdate, September 16,

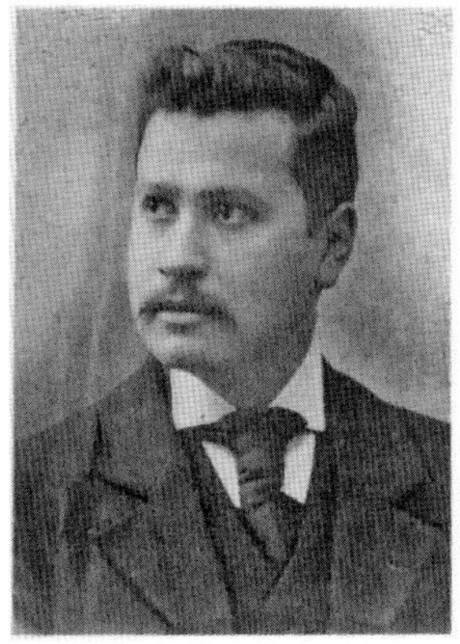
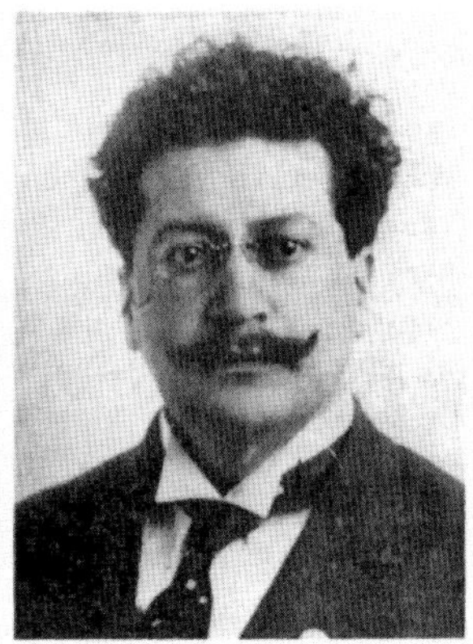
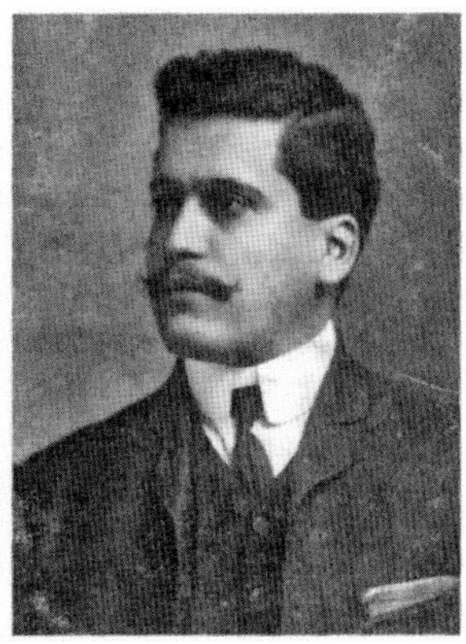

Left to right: Jesús, Ricardo and Enrique Magón. *Courtesy of Casa del Hijo del Ahuizote, Mexico City.*

1874, coincided with Mexican Independence Day. His birthplace, a *pueblo comunero* (communal village) in the Oaxacan town of San Antonio Eloxochitlan, was organized on an egalitarian basis stemming from the pre-Columbian period. His Zapotecan Indian father, Teodoro Flores, a respected elder in the community, reinforced egalitarian principles by constantly proclaiming, and having his three sons (Enrique, Ricardo and Jesús) repeat back to him: "All belongs to all!"[341] The boys' half-Indian/half-Spanish mother, Margarita Magón, who had drawn from revered Mexican liberator Benito Juarez the importance of education for politicizing the masses, moved the family to Mexico City for the access to better schools it provided.[342]

Ricardo would eventually go to law school and briefly practice, but what he mainly learned from his cosmopolitan surroundings were the strategies of political resistance. His first arrest came in 1891, when he was seventeen, at an anti-Diaz student protest. At eighteen he founded his first opposition newspaper, *El Demócrata*, which was suppressed, and he barely escaped a second arrest. After his father's death in 1893, he decided to exchange activism for lawyering to pay the rent, provide for his mother and, for a time, lead a "bohemian café life."[343]

Rejoining the revolutionary struggle with a vengeance in 1900, Ricardo cofounded, with older brother Jesús and fellow law school alumnus Antonio Horcasitas, the aforementioned *Regeneración*. He also began demonstrating a flair for fiery oratory in support of the newly formed Liberal Party and, during downtime from the paper's serial shutdowns and his own multiple imprisonments (one for as long as a year), honed his ideology, synthesizing his father's agrarian communalism with the industrial anarcho-syndicalism of Proudhon, Kropotkin and Bakunin.[344]

As Ricardo's threat to Diaz grew, so did the regime's countermeasures. In 1903, at a demonstration Ricardo and Enrique took all the way to the dictator's palace, "only the crowds around them saved them from execution." And when the courts declared any further publication of Ricardo's writings illegal, and one of his jailers told Ricardo point blank that if he wrote another word in Mexico "you are a dead man," exile became the only alternative.[345]

The Land of the Free would prove anything but for Ricardo, Enrique and a small group of supporters. Collusion between the Diaz and American governments, spearheaded in the United States by ex-Pinkerton detective Thomas Furlong, forced the revolutionaries, when they weren't behind bars, to be continually on the run—from Laredo and San Antonio to St. Louis and Toronto, to Quebec and back down to El Paso and, finally, in 1906, to Los Angeles.[346]

Neither nonstop harassment nor distance from Mexico curbed Ricardo's revolutionary activity. Besides founding the PLM and formulating the Plan, his writings in *Regeneración* helped foment strikes and uprisings in Mexico as early as 1906, carried out by a network of insurgents in forty secret clubs the PLM had organized in every Mexican state. The rebellions were quashed, but "the nation was shocked by the amount of innocent blood spilled by federal troops. People once again became aware of the need to overthrow the dictator, making them more responsive to the message of the PLM." Even as persecution of the PLM increased, leading to Ricardo and fellow party members' arrest in Los Angeles in 1907, they succeeded, this time from prison, in spurring another large, if again abortive, Mexican rebellion in 1908.[347]

Undeterred by unceasing surveillance, interception of the PLM's mail and even the murder of supporters in the United States and Mexico, Ricardo plodded, and plotted, on. How significant a force he, and the PLM, remained is evidenced in a March 13, 1909 issue of *Appeal to Reason* ("the most important socialist newspaper in the states" and "prior to WWI the largest-circulation periodical—of any sort—in the world"), which devoted the entire issue "to the PLM cause."[348]

Of All Places

The party's peak of popularity was celebrated in Los Angeles in August 1910. Upon their latest release from prison, Ricardo and other PLM members received a hero's welcome from the city's sizable progressive community. Riding high on expectations of socialist Job Harriman's election as mayor the following year, a cheering crowd at the train station threw flowers at the anarchists' feet, and a few days later they were feted by two thousand supporters at the recently constructed Temple of Labor on Maple Street.[349] As an orchestra played the Mexican national anthem, Ricardo and Enrique were carried on the shoulders of Job Harriman and muckraking journalist John Kenneth Turner, and Harriman read a letter of support from novelist Jack London:

> *We socialists, anarchists, hoboes, chicken thieves, outlaws, and undesirable citizens of the U.S. are with you heart and soul. You will notice that we are not respectable. Neither are you. No revolutionary can possibly be respectable in these days of the reign of property. All the names you have been called, we have been called.*[350]

Name-calling henceforth would be the least of Ricardo's concerns. Two explosive events—the *L.A. Times* building bombing in October 1910, which killed twenty-one people and Harriman's election chances, and the start of the Mexican Revolution in November—triggered a double-barreled assault on Ricardo personally. Arising from both the right and the left, in both the United States and Mexico, the attacks would muffle but not silence the "sacred rage," the "hatred and love," the "divine madness" of this "fierce, gentle saint."[351]

The first Los Angeles edition of *Regeneración* was published on September 3, 1910, and reached a circulation of over twelve thousand by November.[352] Beyond the geographical relocation, the L.A. edition signaled an ideological redirection for the paper and the PLM, which more accurately reflected Ricardo's political stance but would backfire on him and his party. Since the PLM's founding, Ricardo had strategically muted its radical polemics in favor of a more broadly palatable, Juarez-inspired slogan of "Reform, Liberty, and Justice." The new *Regeneración* "proclaimed a motto that had originated with the nineteenth-century Russian Narodnik movement and was employed by Spanish anarchists" but that also echoed Papa Teodoro's agrarian communalism—*Tierra y Libertad* (Land and Liberty).[353]

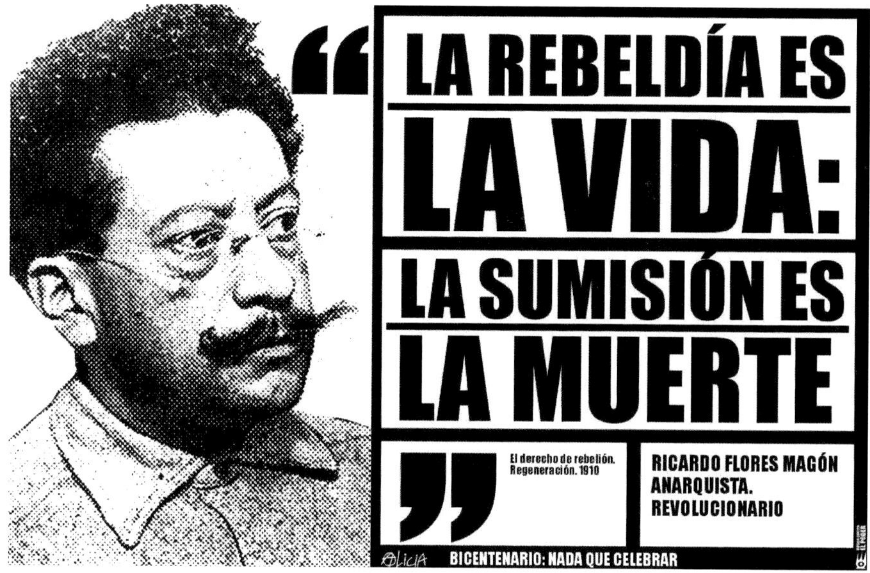

Asociación Los Promoventes "Ricardo Flores Magón" La Paz BCS. *Courtesy of Cuauhtemoc Morgan.*

The paradigm shift provided fresh fodder for right-wing forces, which in L.A. included newspaper tycoons Harrison Gray Otis, Harry Chandler and William Randolph Hearst and oil magnate Edward Doheny, whose vast land and oil interests in Mexico had long placed them at loggerheads with the PLM. But the party's radical turn also had political benefits for the city's power brokers. Following the *Times* bombing, Otis and Chandler, the paper's rabidly anti-union publishers, were able to paint the McNamara brothers, the laborites indicted for the crime (and eventually convicted of it), with the anarchist brush through alleged (but unproven) links to Ricardo and the PLM.[354]

Counterintuitively, Ricardo's new platform also put him on a collision course with leftists in the United States. The rousing reception he received in L.A. in 1910 was only the most public example of the American Left's support for the PLM. Indeed, without its sympathetic treatment in the leftist press and the legal aid it received, Chaz Bufe and Mitchell Cowen Verter assert, "Flores Magon's dream could not have survived…especially as his opportunities in Mexico collapsed and his legal troubles in the U.S. mushroomed."[355] Job Harriman, for example, who had represented Ricardo and his cohorts after his first arrest in Los Angeles in 1907, and had successfully argued against their deportation before the U.S. Supreme

Court, now disassociated himself from them. Other socialist and labor leaders followed suit.[356]

The flip-flop was a matter of ideology and survival. Teaming with fire-breathing radicals in the post–*Times* bombing era clearly carried political risks. The PLM's opposition to Francisco Madero after his ousting of Diaz and assumption of the Mexican presidency in 1911 also ran counter to the moderate U.S. Left's position. But the final blow came from the Madero camp itself.

A "bourgeois liberal" from a wealthy landowning family, Madero had supported Ricardo financially prior to the revolution. Ricardo, in the interests of a united anti-Diaz front, responded in kind during the PLM's reformist phase. Soon after the first shots of the revolution were fired in Puebla, however, Madero actively undermined Ricardo's independent military efforts in Baja, California, published a phony version of *Regeneración* in Mexico City and, when Ricardo refused to join forces with him, even threatened Ricardo's life. Ricardo's physical person survived, but his reputation never fully recovered from Madero's vicious disinformation campaign.[357] Ricardo didn't help his cause by calling Madero and his followers "a fresh set of jackals, moving in to take up where the old jackals left off." But the Maderistas crossed the line in branding Ricardo an opportunist and megalomaniac, a scoundrel and philanderer and, most slanderously, a pocketer of party funds.[358]

Besides Job Harriman, former U.S. allies who withdrew their support from Ricardo included Samuel Gompers' American Federation of Labor, union organizer Mother Jones and Socialist Party leader Eugene Debs. European leftists, such as Jean Grave, joined the attacks, charging that Ricardo was "not a true anarchist" and the Mexican social revolution a figment of his imagination. Anarchist patriarch Peter Kropotkin came to Ricardo's defense, but as he himself admitted, "the damage was done. I was a pariah."[359] Bloodied but unbowed, he published a new manifesto in September 1911, replacing the PLM's Plan of 1906 and laying out what was clearly an anarchist platform but avoiding any reference to the dreaded "A" word.[360]

"A" word or not, Ricardo, Enrique and other PLM loyalists, posing a graver threat than ever to the powers that be, were arrested again in 1912, on federal subversion charges. The trial in Los Angeles, a corrupt farce with the government resorting to manufactured evidence, bribery and kidnapping, ended in a twenty-three-month sentence for the defendants but also in a public protest of the miscarriage of justice, which, according to historian Juan Gómez-Quiñones, "sparked one of the wildest riots in Los Angeles history."[361]

Land and Liberty

Upon their release in 1914, Ricardo and company sought sustenance for the ongoing revolutionary fight in a new lifestyle and more sympathetic part of town. Ricardo, his wife, Maria Talevara, and her daughter Lucia Norman, brother Enrique and his companion Teresa Arteaga, trusted friend Librado Rivera and several other PLM members and their families rented a five-and-a-half-acre farm on Edendale Place in the hills above Glendale (then Alessandro) Boulevard between Loma Vista Place and Cove Avenue, just east of the Silver Lake Reservoir.[362]

Here, finally, the band of anarchists could put their principles into practice. Adhering to communalism and sexual equality, they balanced work and play, "enlivening their daily struggles with dances, public oratory, publishing, and selling their farm produce."[363] Holiday celebrations tilted leftward, honoring the Paris Commune on March 18, International Workers Day on May 1, the Day of Martyrdom (commemorating the 1886 Chicago Haymarket Square riots) on May 4 and a special double tribute on September 16 to Mexican Independence Day and Ricardo's birthday. Musical concerts and theatrical performances abounded, including a play by Ricardo performed outside the commune as well, aptly titled *Tierra y Libertad*.[364]

Whether the politicos had any time or desire to go to the movies, they surely must have sensed the irony of their communal farm sandwiched between two of the biggest and most popular movie studios in the world: Mack Sennett's Keystone Film Company, housed on Glendale Boulevard, a few blocks to the south, and Tom Mix's Mixville studio on Glendale, a few blocks to the north. That Keystone was noted for an anarchic style of comedy that literally threw pies in the face of bourgeois decorum, and Mixville doubled as a Wild West set replete with dusty town and Indian teepees, added more than a soupcon of surrealism to the situation.

The saga of Ricardo Flores Magón, alas, lacks a Hollywood ending. His utopian Silver Lake dream turned into an American nightmare when, like clockwork, he and Enrique were arrested in February 1916 for "defamation and sending indecent materials through the mails."[365] Fellow anarchist Emma Goldman, whom Ricardo had met in 1905 in St. Louis and who published his 1911 manifesto in *Mother Earth* in 1915, spoke in the brothers' defense at L.A.'s Central Plaza and nearby Italian Hall. Had Goldman's pal Aline Barnsdall already been ensconced on Olive Hill, one of her political billboards likely would have trumpeted Ricardo's cause as well. But Goldman's efforts, lacking moderate leftist support, were to no avail, and again like clockwork, Ricardo's one-year sentence, not justice, was served.[366]

Upon his latest—and last—release in 1917, Ricardo "gave what was perhaps his most compelling public speech at the Italian Hall to the International Workers Defense League." Addressing an estimated crowd of seven hundred people, he denounced the third Mexican president since the revolution, Venustiano Carranza, as a "lackey" of U.S. President Woodrow Wilson and a "bandit of Wall Street."[367]

As if Ricardo needed additional spurious grounds for prosecution, World War I supplied them. The intercepted Zimmerman telegram of January 1917, which offered to return to Mexico the American spoils of the Mexican War of 1846–48 (including California and much of the Southwest) in exchange for Mexico's wartime aid to Germany, instantly branded all Mexicans in the United States, immigrants and citizens alike, as potential traitors. This left radically inclined Mexicans especially vulnerable to the draconian Espionage Act of June 1917, under which Goldman (a Lithuanian immigrant) was deported and Ricardo and Librado Rivera sentenced to prison terms of twenty and fifteen years, respectively. As the "Conscience of the Revolution" rotted in prison, the curtain was lowered not only on his Silver Lake idyll. As William David Estrada eulogizes, "The presence of the PLM in Los Angeles and the colorful oratory it brought to the [central] Plaza had come to an end. By 1920, organized PLM activities…were gone, and *Regeneración* went out of circulation."[368]

Ricardo Flores Magón died in the high-security federal penitentiary in Leavenworth, Kansas, in 1922. He had been in failing health from the prison's harrowing conditions and lack of medical attention. The officially listed cause of death from cardiac arrest reeks of manslaughter, and a murder charge against prison guard A.H. Leonard, himself stabbed to death by a devoted Ricardo admirer, Jose Martinez, cannot be discounted. Ricardo's corpse's neck bruises and contorted facial features pointed to death by strangulation, a scenario strongly supported by Librado Rivera.[369]

Through the efforts of his supporters, Ricardo's body was returned to Los Angeles. Thousands paid their respects at Breese Brothers Mortuary on South Figueroa Street downtown. Initial plans to bury him in the new Calvary Cemetery in East L.A. were scotched in favor of returning him to Mexico City, where another enormous crowd greeted his coffin and the government gave him a "massive state funeral."[370] In 1945, the oxymoronic *Partido Revolucionario Institucional* (Institutional Revolutionary Party, or PRI), transferred Ricardo's coffin to the Rotunda of Illustrious Men—an act he would have been horrified by, because of the corrupt party that carried it out and, even more, because of its reinforcing the *personalismo* (cult of personality) he had spent his life reviling.[371]

Despite the PRI's sugar-coating, Ricardo's true legacy has lived on in Mexico and beyond. He influenced the Nicaraguan revolutionary Augusto "Cesar" Sandino, whose name in turn was passed on to the Sandinistas who deposed dreaded dictator Anastasio Somoza DeBayle in 1979. Ricardo's name and example were invoked in the student and labor protests in Mexico City in 1968. More recently, in his home state of Oaxaca, three indigenous groups fighting for their rights along the lines of the Zapatistas in neighboring Chiapas have attached his name to their organizations.[372] It seems high time that Angelenos as well did something to honor this extraordinary figure who once made Los Angeles, and Silver Lake, his home.

11

CIVIL RIGHTS CHAMPION

LOREN MILLER

Another underappreciated Silver Lakean, despite his supreme accomplishments, is journalist, civil rights lawyer and superior court judge Loren Miller. Born in 1903 in Pender, Nebraska, his father, John Byrd Miller, was a former slave and his mother, Nora Magdalena Herbaugh, a white midwesterner whose love of her husband—as Loren artfully describes in the dedication to his classic book on the Supreme Court, *The Petitioners* (1966)—"led her to cross the color line and to my birth."[373]

Less artful was his parents' need to cross the state line to Iowa to get married—biracial unions being illegal in Nebraska and several other, mostly southern states (as they would remain until the Supreme Court's *Loving v. Virginia* decision of 1967). The family of seven children eventually moved to Kansas, where Loren (the third eldest) graduated high school with honors, attended the University of Kansas and, after a stint at Howard University in Washington, D.C., earned a law degree in 1928 from Topeka's Washburn University and was admitted to the Kansas bar the same year.[374]

As the most academically promising of the siblings, Loren was "the chosen one" in the family. His brothers Cloyd and Cecil "worked to support the family and help finance Loren's education," and soon after their father died in 1920, everyone except Loren moved to Los Angeles in search of better jobs.[375] The relocation was doubly auspicious for Loren and the fate of people of color. It prompted his own move to L.A. in 1929 and, upon confronting widespread racial discrimination in the city hailed as the world's entertainment capital, fired his lifelong passion for civil rights.

KICKING AND SCREAMING

"He felt it in his bones," is how Robin Miller Sloan describes her grandfather's dedication to social justice, much of which stemmed from his ancestral legacy.[376] Loren's granduncle, Bird Gee, played a crucial, if also tragic, role in American civil rights history. Setting out to test the newly passed Civil Rights Act of 1875, which expanded the "equal rights" clause of the Fourteenth Amendment to include public accommodations, Gee requested, and was duly refused, dining service at a posh Kansas hotel. Unfazed, Gee took his case to the U.S. district attorney for Kansas, who indicted the hotel's owner. The trial judge, unable to decide the case, certified it to the Supreme Court, where it languished until 1883. Finally, in a landmark decision that would sanction eighty years of Jim Crow, the court, in an eight-to-one vote, annulled the Civil Rights Act by ruling that Congress had "no authority to enact public accommodations statutes."[377]

Loren's taking up the legal brief for Bird Gee was delayed, however, by his intense aversion to lawyering. "I had to be dragged kicking and screaming into the practice of law," he later admitted.[378] His first love was creative writing, but the obstacle there was the unlikelihood, especially for blacks, of making ends meet. Journalism offered a more reliable source of income and a compromise between his literary ambitions and concern for social justice. Putting his legal practice on hold in his first few years in L.A., Loren joined the staff, and soon rose from feature writer to city editor, at the *California Eagle*, the city's first (since 1879) and leading black newspaper.[379]

One of his early articles, on Los Angeles's sesquicentennial celebration in 1931, demonstrated the forthrightness and acid wit that would become his trademark, both in his columns and later oral arguments. In an op-ed titled "Failure of the Fiesta," which indicted the city's portrayal of the *pobladores* (founders) as white Europeans rather than as the African, Indian and mixed-race group they actually were, Loren lambasted the organizers for deigning "to change the color of the founders' skins one hundred and fifty years after their death."[380]

Like many of the socially minded during the Depression, Loren tilted increasingly to the left. In 1931, as spokesperson for the Labor Defense League, the legal arm of the American Communist Party (CP), he helped defend the Scottsboro Boys, the nine black teenagers falsely accused of raping two white women on a train in Alabama. He joined the Los Angeles branch of the Communist-oriented John Reed Club and literally became a "fellow traveler" by joining Langston Hughes and other African Americans

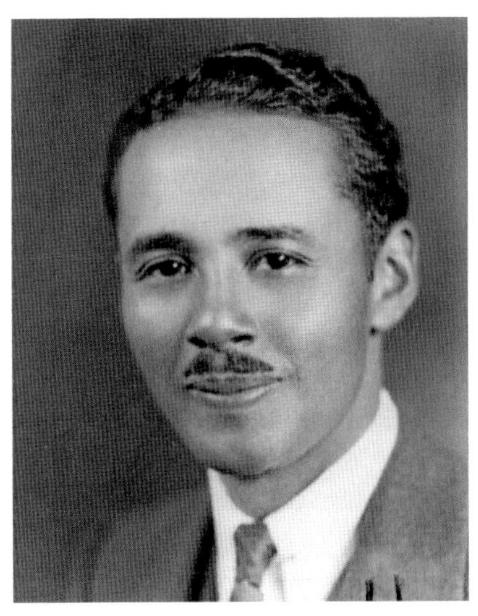

Loren Miller portrait. *Courtesy of Robin Miller Sloan.*

on a trip to the Soviet Union to make a film about black life in the United States. Though the film was shelved due to a backroom deal between the United States and Stalin, through which American businesses gained partial access to the USSR in exchange for formal recognition of the country, Loren remained, for the time being, a naïve apologist of all things Soviet.[381]

Upon his return to Los Angeles in 1933, Loren married Juanita Ellsworth, a graduate of both USC and UCLA and a member of the city's black elite, who, from entry-level county social worker, rose to become head of the California Housing Authority. At Juanita's urging, Loren passed the California state bar in 1934, but the journalistic, and Communist, strains retained their pull. After a stint at the *Sentinel*, a left-leaning black newspaper he helped found with his cousin Leon Washington, Loren moved to New York in 1935 to join the editorial staffs of two openly Communist papers, the *New Masses* and *Crusader News*. Ideologically frustrated and financially strapped despite the dual posts, Loren returned to Los Angeles in 1936 and resumed his legal, and conjugal, practice—the latter leading to the birth of the Millers' first son, Peter, in 1937.[382]

Whether Loren ever actually joined the CP is a matter of dispute. The FBI listed him as joining in 1936 and monitored him for the rest of his life, but a former party member turned informant claimed he was never a member. Robin Miller Sloan believes he was initially drawn to the CP because, as the main nonblack organization working actively for civil rights, "it offered the best chance of helping blacks attain their freedom."[383] Loren denied affiliation, adding that he became disillusioned with communism in general and CP methods in particular years before the Hitler-Stalin pact of 1939 led many members and sympathizers to distance themselves. Whatever his qualms may have been, his leftist principles remained strong enough to file an amicus brief in *Communist Party v. Peek* (1942), supporting party members' right to run in California primary elections.[384]

During the McCarthy era, even a faded Pinko was as suspect as a died-in-the-wool Red, and Loren would pay the price career-wise, delaying, until the anti-Communist hysteria abated and California had taken a more moderate turn, his rise in the profession. Not that he failed to do important legal work or gain recognition among his peers. According to friend and client Don Wheeldin, Loren's rhetorical flourish in the courtroom matched his literary flair. His trial presence was so commanding that other lawyers made every effort, even postponing their own cases, to catch his oral arguments.[385] And there was much to argue about, especially in the civil rights arena.

Even for middle-class African Americans, life in L.A., if a step up from the Deep South, had long been a mixed bag. W.E.B. Du Bois, on an NAACP-sponsored tour of the city in 1913, began his report on a hopeful note: "Nowhere in the United States is the Negro so well and beautifully housed.…Out here in this matchless Southern California there would seem to be no limit to your opportunities, your possibilities." Then came the boomerang: "Los Angeles is no paradise. The color line is there and simply drawn.…The hotels do not welcome colored people, the restaurants are not for all who hunger."[386] Nor, he might have added, were neighborhoods for all who wished to reside there, given restrictive racial covenants in home sales and apartment rentals that barred people of color (and often Jews as well) from moving into white areas.

Loren himself managed to circumvent such restrictions in the Silver Lake section south of Sunset Boulevard he moved to in 1941. Although the "Temple area" or "the Flats," as this section was known at the time, may have been "more open to the Other" than the rest of the city, the bohemian capital was no utopia for people of color (see Chapter 14).[387] The original 1929 lease of my own (Vincent Brook's) Silver Lake home, legally valid until the late 1940s, stipulates the property not be sold to people of African or Asian descent. Loren's home at 642 Micheltorena Street was just three blocks from mine. And his neighbor at 657 Micheltorena was James Garrott, Gregory Ain's architectural partner and the second African American (after Paul R. Williams) admitted to the AIA, who had designed both Loren's and his own split-level house.

Apparent exceptions notwithstanding, housing problems for blacks in general took on new urgency in the 1940s. The increased employment opportunities afforded by World War II, crucially enhanced for blacks by FDR's Executive Order 8802 desegregating the defense industries, caused the city's African American population to soar. The Depression years had already seen a surge, with the number of blacks nearly doubling to 69,000 and their proportion of the population rising from 3 to 4 percent. From 1942 to 1945 alone, however, over 100,000 blacks migrated to Los Angeles; by 1950, their proportion had more than doubled to 8.7 percent.[388]

FDR's other, more infamous wartime Executive Order (9066), mandating the internment of Japanese immigrants and American citizens, unintentionally benefited L.A.'s blacks by helping ease the housing crunch. Their flocking to a Little Tokyo forcibly evacuated of its former residents briefly turned the enclave's nickname (until the residents' postwar return) into "Bronzeville." True to his principles, Loren's loyalties in this instance lay with the Japanese, whom he represented as a lawyer for the American Civil Liberties Union (ACLU), challenging the constitutionality of the internment, which, to its undying shame, the U.S. Supreme Court upheld.[389]

Bronzeville did not solve blacks' overall housing problems, and when discrimination began extending into areas not covered by racial covenants, or where ad hoc covenants were hastily concocted, the situation became dire. Approximately two hundred suits were filed on discriminatory housing practices in L.A. County over a four-year period in the early to mid-1940s, many of which, including two of the most significant, were taken up, and won, by Loren Miller.[390]

In the first case, *Fairchild v. Raines* (1944), a black family had been sued by whites attempting to block the family's buying a nonrestrictive lot in Pasadena. In the second, more high-profile case, *Anderson v. Auseth* (1945), Loren represented some of Hollywood's top black actors, Hattie McDaniel, Louise Beavers and Ethel Waters. Though the women were relegated to playing maids on screen, their movie-star salaries enabled purchase of elegant homes in the tony West Adams Heights section of Los Angeles popularly known as "Sugar Hill." After a lengthy court battle, Superior Court judge Thurmond Clark summarily threw out the case and added a statement that should have signaled the death knell for restrictive covenants altogether: "It is time that members of the Negro race are accorded, without reservations or evasions, the full rights guaranteed them under the 14th Amendment to the Federal Constitution. Judges have been avoiding the real issue for too long a time."[391]

And they continued avoiding it. By 1947, Loren had represented over one hundred housing discrimination cases and had become the ACLU's chief spokesperson on unequal treatment of people of color in both housing and education. Buoyed by the California Supreme Court's decision in *Mendez v. Westminster* (1946), which, eight years before *Brown v. Board of Education*, outlawed racial discrimination in the state's public schools, Loren set his sights on a similar decision in housing.

His strategy was double-pronged: appealing to the principle of equal rights and to the fear of racial violence. On the rights front, Loren, in a *Nation* article in 1948, accused the Federal Housing Authority (FHA) of fostering, in collusion with banks and developers, Jim Crow policies by refusing "to guarantee home construction loans unless race restrictions were inserted in subdivision deeds."[392] On segregation's social consequences, Loren argued that rather than easing racial tension and ensuring public order, as covenant proponents alleged, creating and maintaining minority ghettos generated "nothing but bitterness and strife."[393] Tension was mounting in the segregated areas, he presciently cautioned, because of the confinement and substandard housing conditions blacks were forced to endure.[394]

BREAKTHROUGH

In the landmark national housing case *Shelley v. Kraemer*, which Loren argued together with future Supreme Court justice Thurgood Marshall, the high court declared racial covenants in real estate unenforceable by the courts.[395] The decision was a major victory for fair housing, but failure to ground the ruling unequivocally, as Judge Clarke had done, in the equal protection clause of the Fourteenth Amendment would hamper enforcement. A violent racist backlash created further obstacles in Los Angeles, where blacks attempting to move into previously restricted areas were met by "a wave of cross burnings, shootings, and bombings."[396]

Loren pressed ahead, on both the housing and education fronts. As cochair of the West Coast legal committee of the NAACP, this time working with Franklin H. Williams, Loren won another housing case, *Barrows v. Jackson* (1953). In disallowing damage awards when racial covenants were allegedly violated, the case was "equally as important as *Shelley v. Kraemer*."[397] And in 1954, working for the NAACP with Marshall, Loren wrote the majority of appellate briefs in the historic *Brown v. Board of Education* case that declared segregation in all public schools unconstitutional.[398]

Loren's journalistic bully pulpit also expanded. In addition to writing numerous article on civil rights for prestigious journals such as *The Crisis*, *The Nation* and *Law in Transition*, the city editor of the *California Eagle* became, in 1951, its owner as well. An indefatigable advocate for

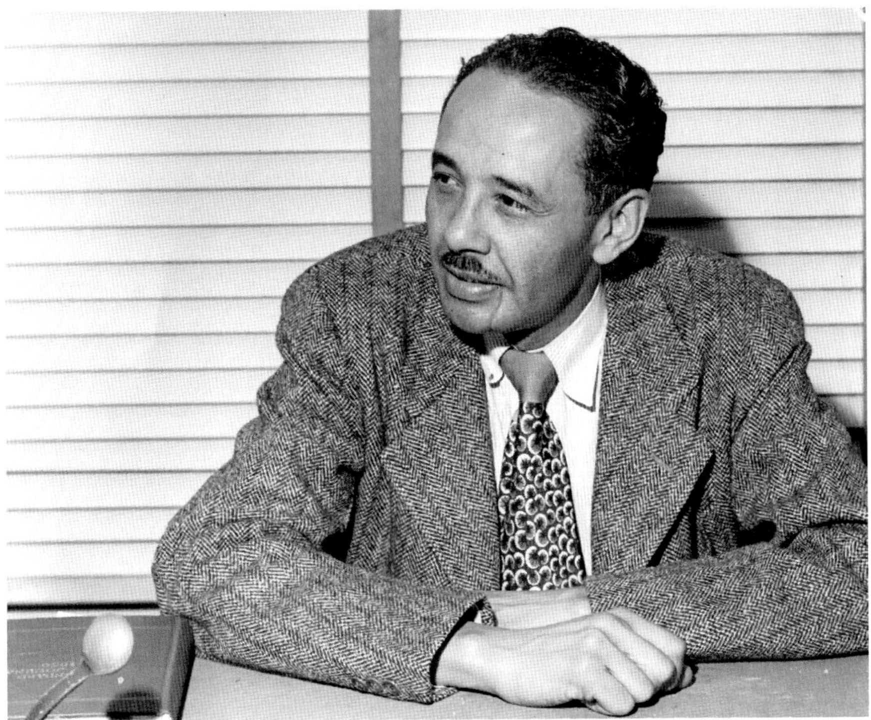

California Superior Court judge Loren Miller. *Courtesy of Robin Sloan Miller.*

oppressed minorities since its founding by Charlotta Bass, the *Eagle* under Loren cranked up demands for minorities' full protection under the law and an end to police brutality.

Stubbornly racist Los Angeles's inability to heed Loren's clarion call would have dire consequences for all concerned. Although the Watts Riots of 1965 were more than a decade away, the 1952 bombing of the home of a black schoolteacher and World War II veteran, William Bailey, and the failure of adequate police and judicial action showed how close to the tipping point the city had come. The imminence and extremity of the danger was certainly clear to Loren, as is evident from a statement he drafted for the local chapter of the NAACP: "The indifference of official Los Angeles to the serious lack of police protection for Negroes moving into the 'new' areas in the city is a problem that will explode into a race riot the next time an act of violence is visited upon a Negro family."[399]

The explosion's thirteen-year postponement was by no means due to improvement in the lives and circumstances of black people. "White supremacy may be scientifically dead," John Somerville, founder of the elegant Dunbar Hotel in South Central as a haven for blacks barred from the city's other fine hotels, stated. "But its ghost still walks the streets of Los Angeles."[400] Throughout the 1950s and into the 1960s, ghetto unemployment levels doubled and even tripled those in the rest of the city, and crime rates and police brutality rose to unprecedented heights.[401] As clear as the disastrous omens were to Loren and the NAACP, they somehow escaped, or were willfully ignored, by another prominent black organization. In 1964, one year before the deadliest and most destructive urban uprising in the country's history to that time, the Urban League deemed Los Angeles "the most desirable city in the United States for black people."[402]

That year did bring some belated personal satisfaction to Loren, when Governor Edmund G. "Pat" Brown, less prone than his predecessors to toe the anti-Communist line, appointed him to the California Superior Court, County of Los Angeles. Two years later, drawing on years of research and his wealth of firsthand experience, Judge Miller capped his illustrious legal and literary career with the aforementioned *The Petitioners: The Story of the Supreme Court of the United States and the Negro*. Both an encyclopedic survey and

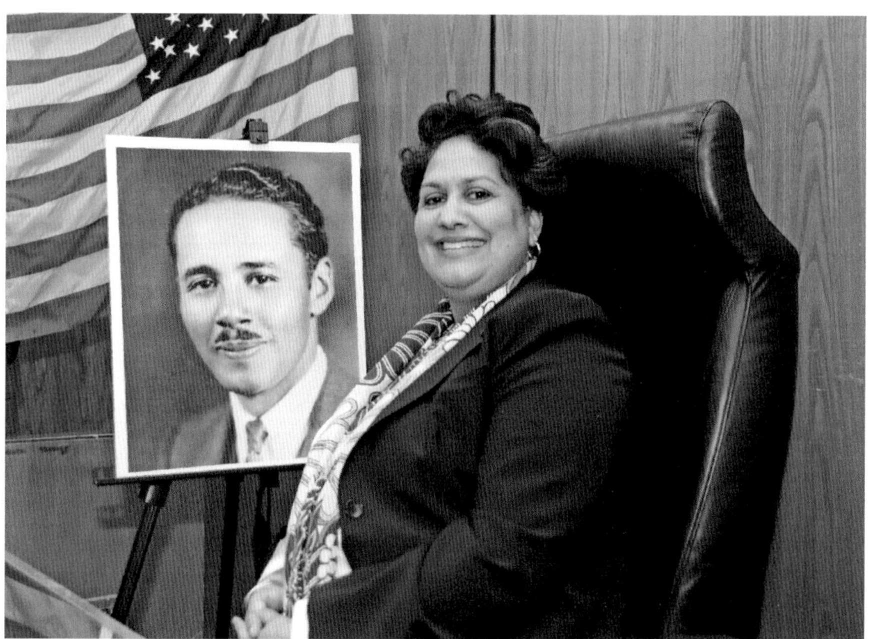

Judge Robin Miller Sloan with a portrait of her grandfather Loren Miller.

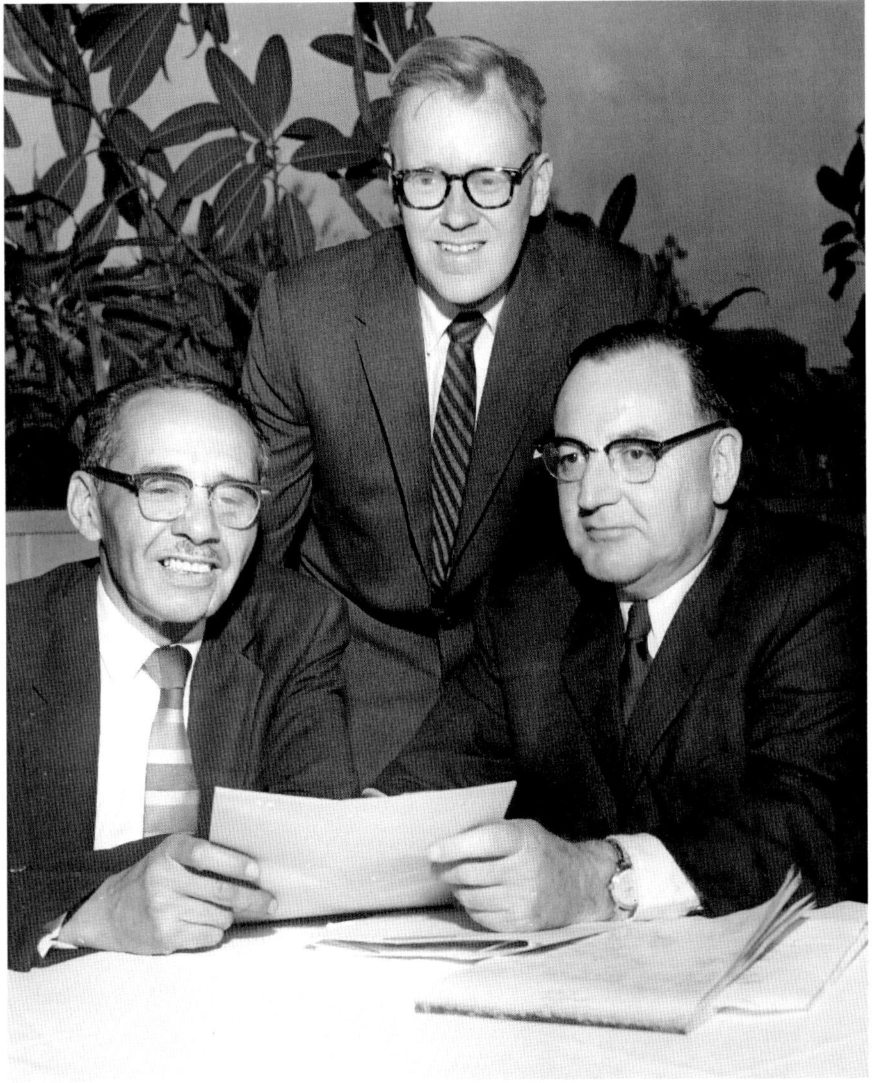

Loren Miller (left) with Governor Edmund G. "Pat" Brown (right). *Courtesy of Robin Miller Sloan.*

a critical analysis, the book deconstructs the crucial role of the U.S. Supreme Court in shaping the lives of African Americans, "who were systematically excluded from [American society], and who had to become petitioners to change its course."[403]

In July 1967, one year before the national Fair Housing Act hammered the final legal nail in the coffin of housing discrimination, Loren Miller died at Temple Hospital, a few blocks from his Silver Lake home. He was survived by his wife, Juanita, and two sons, Loren Miller Jr. and Edward Miller. Loren Jr. went on to serve on the bench in Los Angeles County Superior Court from 1975 to 1997, and his daughter, Robin Miller Sloan, "became the first linear third-generation judge in the history of the California court system."[404] Judge Sloan, unaware as a child of the towering historical legacy he bestowed, recalls Loren as a doting grandfather who "would pick me and my brother up every Saturday, take us to his Silver Lake home, and delight us with a supply of Van de Kamp's pastries."[405]

Juanita Miller, a driving force in her husband's life, carried the torch posthumously as well.[406] In 1968, thanks to her efforts, a new elementary school in South Central was named for Loren Miller. The Loren Miller Bar Association, a civil rights organization, was formed the same year in Seattle, Washington. And in 1977, to commemorate the fiftieth anniversary of the California State Bar, the Loren Miller Legal Services Award was inaugurated. It has been given every year since to a lawyer "who has demonstrated long-term commitment to legal services and who has personally done significant work in extending legal services to the poor."[407]

12

PIONEER IN PROGRESSIVE EDUCATION

ROSE SCHARLIN SCHOOL

Whether Rose Scharlin Cooperative Nursery School was the "very first" cooperative nursery school in Los Angeles, as the school's website claims, it was unquestionably a pioneer in progressive childhood education and a model for other such schools in Silver Lake and the rest of the city.[408] Called Echo Park Cooperative Nursery School upon its founding at Echo Park Playground in the late 1930s (or early 1940s), the school split into two groups in 1946, apparently over a political dispute.[409] One of the groups started a new school at 2414 Lake View Avenue in Silver Lake, on an abandoned tennis court over the hill from the old Mixville studio lot (now a shopping center housing CVS Pharmacy and Whole Foods Market). Called Lakeview Cooperative Nursery School for its first few years, the name was changed to Rose Scharlin Cooperative Nursery School, in honor of its first director, after her death in 1949.[410] In 1955, the Echo Park school dissolved, and some of its former rival members merged with Rose Scharlin. Adding another twist to the fractious affair, one of the groups involved in the 1946 rift included none other than Harry Hay and his wife, Anita. Here, however, the historical record gets a bit muddled and forces us, as with much of the Rose Scharlin story (her own and the school's), to rely on informed speculation.

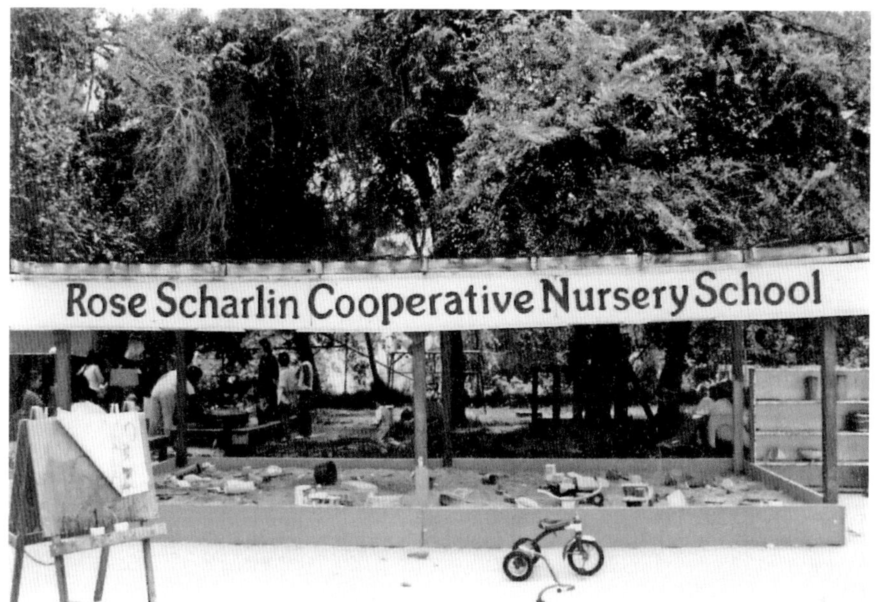

Rose Scharlin School vintage photo. *Courtesy of Rose Scharlin Cooperative Nursery School.*

CONFLICTING TIMELINES

Daniel Hurewitz, in *Bohemian Los Angeles and the Making of Modern Politics* (2007), offers a brief account of the Echo Park and Rose Scharlin schools' early history. Based on interviews with Hay and fellow leftist Max Hillerman, this account contradicts information on the school's website and contains its own discrepancies. Hurewitz relates that Hay, Hillerman, their wives "and a few other families set up a cooperative nursery school—the first in the city—at Echo Park Playground. They began the school during the war as a way to help people working in the defense industries care for their children."[411] The phrase "during the war," however, would place the school's founding date no earlier than 1942, or at least three years later than the website's listed date of 1939. The website's date is also compromised by a newspaper clipping in 1941 applauding the Echo Park community's "at last" getting a Pre-School Play Group.[412] Further complicating the timeline, and especially the Hays' part in starting the school, is the fact that Harry and Anita were in New York from 1940 to 1942 and only adopted their first daughter in 1943—who at five weeks old would have been too young to attend a nursery school at *any time* during the war.[413]

A more likely scenario for Hay's involvement with the school is the following. By 1946, his three-year-old daughter would have been old enough for nursery school. That also happens to be the year the rift at the Echo Park school took place. Hay and Anita, and likely most other parents in their group, were Communists, providing ample cause, especially in the early Cold War period, for dissension among the school's members. Add to the mix Hay's compelling (some would say overbearing) personality and a tendency to push radical causes, and a recipe for the school's breakup seems readily at hand.

Hay's group also, from Hurewitz's account, appears to be the one that hired Rose Scharlin, "also a leftist émigré to Edendale," to direct the Echo Park school. She then likely "joined with several parents," including Hay and company, to form the Silver Lake school. Besides her leftist connection with Hay and his cohort, Scharlin shared a special camaraderie with Max Hillerman—not only did he hail "from the same area in Cleveland" as Scharlin, but their families also "came from the same shtetl in Europe."[414]

RUSSIAN ROOTS

Census records indeed show Rose Scharlin's birth taking place in Gomel, Belarus, in 1902, to Nachman and Rachael Rivkin.[415] The family immigrated to the United States in 1906, possibly fleeing, along with many other Russian and Eastern European Jews, the latest in a series of pogroms that began in 1903 and intensified following the publishing of the infamous Protocols of the Elders of Zion in 1905.[416] This bogus document of a secret meeting among the Jewish elite, fabricated by Czarist agents to stir the anti-Semitic pot after Russia's defeat in the Russo-Japanese War, reinforced longstanding charges of a Jewish conspiracy to rule the world. Auto magnate Henry Ford notoriously republished the thoroughly discredited Protocols as factual in the early 1920s in his *Dearborn Independent* newspaper, providing other anti-Semites, including Adolf Hitler, fodder for their hateful propaganda and eventual genocidal crimes.

Scharlin was raised in Cleveland and, as a young adult, moved to Los Angeles, where in 1924 she and her sister Bessie were living at 912 South Figueroa Street downtown and working as teachers.[417] One can presume the young women brought with them the leftist bent Hurewitz attributes to Scharlin. For while anti-Semites have falsely imputed conspiratorial intent to the Jewish Left, as well as to Jews in finance and the media, Jews indeed were, and women prominently among them (e.g., Emma Goldman), at the forefront of the various socialist, communist and anarchist movements roiling major American cities, including Los Angeles, in the early 1900s.[418]

Politics didn't preclude romance, and in 1926, Rose married the American-born Abraham Scharlin and bore two children, Rachel and David. Although Abraham's occupation is listed in census records simply as "accountant/credit manager," he likely came from money or had a thriving business.[419] After living in patrician Pasadena through the 1930s, the Scharlins moved in 1940 to a spectacular new, Gregory Ain–designed home at 2932 Silver Ridge Avenue, a stone's throw from Rose's school-to-be. That the architect of the celebrated Avenal Cooperative Housing Project would build a Silver Lake home for the director of the area's pioneering cooperative nursery school adds another interpersonal link to this book's ever-expanding chain.

The school's naming after Rose Scharlin was, by all accounts, richly deserved. She was the school's "moving force," the Rose Scharlin website extolls, "fostering the idea of parents and children growing and learning together within the group." Her spirit and philosophy infuse the school's

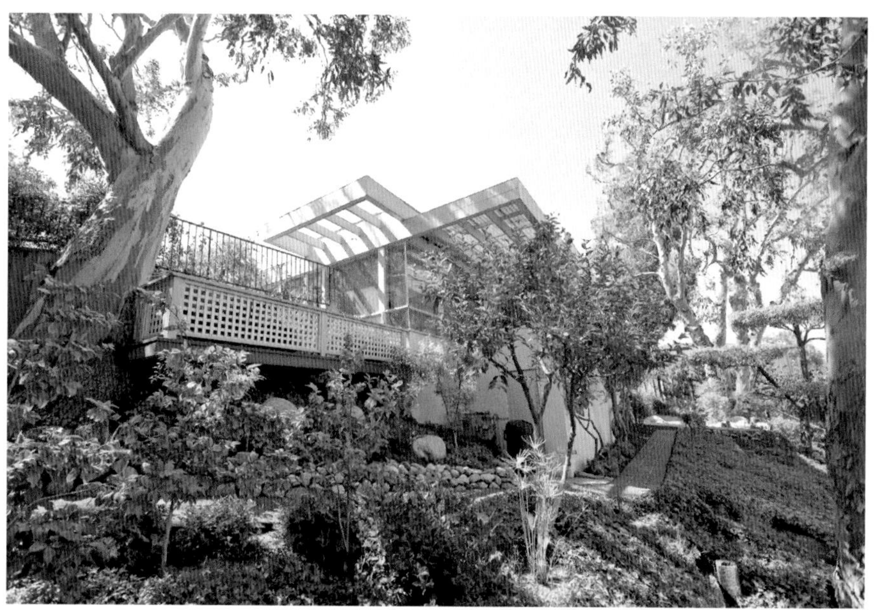

Abraham and Rose Scharlin Residence, 2363 Silver Ridge Avenue, Gregory Ain, 1939.

"communal and non-authoritarian" structure, current school director Gilbert Brebes elaborates. "As it's always been, families essentially run the school, in cooperation with each other and with the school's teachers." Parents serve as teaching assistants and make up an executive board, overseeing operations and handling administrative duties. "The educational approach is personal and progressive, focusing more on social learning and interaction than academics."[420]

The school's location and surroundings support the loose-structured approach. Nestled below street level on a tree-circled plateau above the Coralitas Red Car trail, with snippets of northeastern Los Angeles and the San Gabriel Mountains visible in the distance, the modest facility has the feel of a summer camp. In the center of the yard, among a smattering of clapboard sheds, playground equipment and lean-tos, stands a structure resembling a merry-go-round with a sign reading "Gathering Place"—a fitting motto for the Winnie the Pooh–like world the school creates.

Cooperative Branches

As uniquely charming and historically rich as Rose Scharlin Cooperative School certainly is, the cooperative school movement originated centuries before. The idea of "learning through play" is credited to Moravian minister Jan Amos Comenius (1592–1670) and the notion of cooperation between parents and teachers to Swiss schoolmaster Johann Heinrich Pestalozzi (1746–1827).[421] But it was mainly through the work and writings of German kindergarten pioneer Friedrich Froebel (1782–1852) and his adherents that these ideals and practices became more widespread in twentieth-century America. Froebel's notion of self-realization, and his espousing a "communal…noncompetitive approach to child-rearing," has particular resonance with that of Rose Scharlin School.[422]

Ironically, the American progressive school movement stalled in the early 1900s due to the wave of southern and eastern European immigration that brought Rose Scharlin to America's shores but also produced school overcrowding and a drain on resources. As a progressive educator recounted her experience in Pasadena in 1905: "I had forty children in one room and the toilets were out behind the grocery store next door. All I could do was *herd* them. Who had time for philosophy?"[423] Another deterrent came from a competing "scientific" child study movement promulgated by Edward

Thorndike and other social scientists, who tended to dismiss the humanistic methods of "'sentimental women' who were mere classroom teachers."[424]

It took two British women, Rachel and Margaret McMillan, and one Italian, Maria Montessori, to keep the cooperative movement alive, with Montessori's system becoming integrated into some U.S. nursery schools by the 1920s as economic conditions improved.[425] Worsening conditions in the 1930s led the federal government, under the Roosevelt administration, to become involved in preschool education, but Los Angeles was ahead of the curve. "Already in 1926," Dorothy Hewes reports, "the Los Angeles Board of Education established Normandie Nursery School to demonstrate scientific child care for the benefit of secondary school students, parents, nurses and teachers." The Normandie school closed in 1931 "due to increased population and decreased funds," but the Parents Cooperative Nursery School, formed by some of Normandie's families, continued the co-op tradition.[426]

As would Rose Scharlin School, initially under the Echo Park banner, by the late 1930s (or early 1940s). A decade or so later, under more favorable economic conditions, two other Silver Lake–based cooperatives would follow: Hilltop Nursery School in Bellevue Park, founded in 1951, and Neighborhood Nursery School at Ivanhoe Reservoir, founded in 1952.[427] The more recent schools follow the same principles as Rose Scharlin's, whose mission statement echoes the aims, adapted to the times, of its European and American precursors:

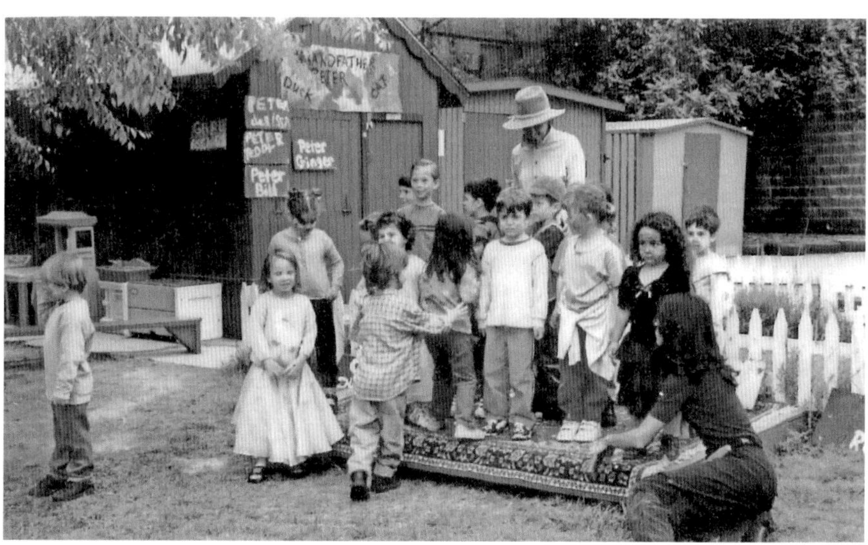

Rose Scharlin School vintage photo. *Courtesy of Rose Scharlin Cooperative Nursery School.*

Our purpose is to provide a safe, secure and challenging environment for our children; to offer them a range of developmentally appropriate activities; and to reflect the diversity of our backgrounds, our community and our world. We emphasize the process of parents and children learning and working together for the social, emotional, physical, intellectual and spiritual growth of all. We cherish each child's need to play. We acknowledge and value our differences, and respect our children as unique individuals with their own abilities and needs. We actively seek to challenge the impact of bias on our children in our interactions with them and each other and in our choice of educational materials and activities. We work to encourage the growth and empowerment of children and adults in building the cooperative community of Rose Scharlin, *respecting all individuals as we work toward our shared goals.*[428]

13

HARBINGER OF THE FUTURE

John Lautner and Silvertop

John Lautner was ahead of his time. Had his debut as an architect occurred thirty or even twenty years later, he might not have been denied the large commercial projects awarded to those who worked in the more conventional styles favored by planning departments. Still, he left us some of the boldest residential designs of the modern era, and current L.A.-based avant-gardists such as Frank Gehry, Thom Mayne, Michael Rotondi and Eric Owen Moss have built on the "remarkably complex, thoughtful and inventive" sculptural qualities Lautner pioneered a half-century before.[429]

Lautner shares with Schindler and Neutra, Flores Magón and Ain an upbringing and early environment that encouraged his creativity and unconventional outlook. His free spirit was nurtured by his artistic, progressive-minded parents and the small town of Marquette on the shores of Lake Superior in Michigan's Upper Peninsula, where he was born in 1911. Both the town's surrounding landscape of "deep, green forests and fish-filled lakes" and the region's rich history affected him deeply.[430] The Nordic lumbermen and German mining engineers who had settled the area in the mid-1800s, Lautner biographer Nicholas Olsberg floridly describes, brought "their myths of the forest and a culture that had, for a hundred years, brooded on the consonance between nature and knowledge, imagination and space, and upon a Romantic vision of societies constructed to aid the individual quest to grasp great truths."[431]

His father, John Ernest Lautner, had emigrated from Germany as a child. Largely self-educated, he went on to the University of Michigan

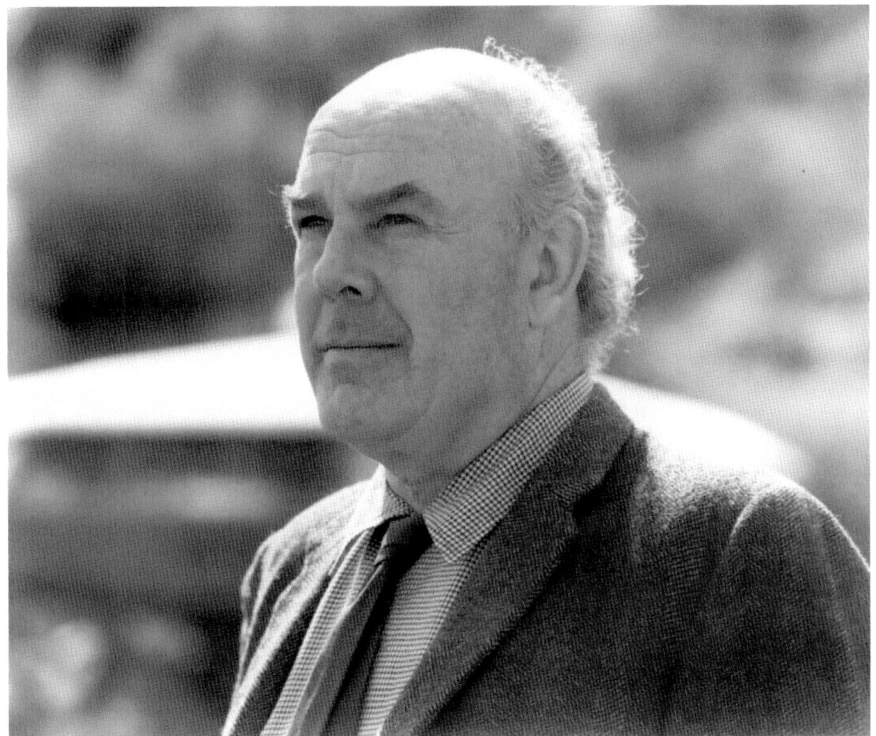

Portrait of architect John Lautner. *Courtesy of Getty Archives.*

and later studied philosophy in Paris, Geneva and Göttingen. In 1901, he was appointed head of the French and German language departments at Northern State Normal School (now Northern Michigan University), where he met Cathleen Gallagher, Lautner's mother, an art student at the school. The two were married in 1907. As nonconforming as her husband, Cathleen adopted the name "Vida," took as her personal motto the ancient Egyptian symbol "ankh" (signifying religious pluralism) and had cultural and spiritual interests ranging from the art of Gaugin and the Fauves to Goethe's color theories, Nordic myths, Sufism and Sanskrit poetry. By the time Lautner's sister Katherine arrived in 1915, Olsberg relates, their parents had merged their mutual "philosophical, metaphysical, and artistic enthusiasms into an entire program…in which their two planned children would be raised."[432]

Midgaard

The family's environmental centerpiece was a self-consciously designed summer home, "reminiscent of the sturdy austerity of the pioneers." A "great lodge of logs," it was built by hand by the family between 1921 and 1928, based on designs Vida discovered while doing research on Norwegian folk architecture. The experience taught young Lautner the fundamental lessons of architecture and a "near-mystical passion for the cabin on the lake—a single open space with a high, surrounding mezzanine for sleeping." They named the home Midgaard, meaning "midway between heaven and earth" and referring, according to Nordic legend, to the "bridge between the describable phenomena of earthly knowledge and the indefinable knowledge of the heavens." Lautner literalized the concept when he returned to Midgaard in 1932, rebuilding the roof on a heroic scale and having his mother paint a sky on its timbers, thereby expressing what he came to see as the first function of architecture: "to build the space between."[433]

Lautner's Midgaard redesign also bore the fruit of his education, which began in 1929 at his father's (since renamed) Northern State Teachers College, where he studied art, architectural history, drafting, ethics, literature and physics. He also learned to play woodwinds and piano, listened to jazz and traveled with his father to Boston and New York, "where he experienced the urban riches of museums and concerts not available in Marquette."[434] After college, he became engaged to one of the family's neighbors, Mary "Marybud" Roberts. Thanks to Marybud's mother, Abby Beecher Roberts, who had helped fund Frank Lloyd Wright's Taliesin Fellowship in Spring Green, Wisconsin, he and Marybud entered a joint apprenticeship program there in 1932.[435]

Digging In, Branching Out

Just as Wright found in Lautner his ideal apprentice, Lautner found in Wright his ideal architect. "Individualism" drove both men's work, with the goal of producing "singular works of architecture—perfectly positioned, variously formed, and ignoring rhetorical distinctions between public and private so that every space inhabited becomes one of its own."[436] The Lautner-Wright association would continue, off and on, for eleven years, gradually moving from apprenticeship to collaboration.[437]

After wife Marybud became pregnant in 1938, Lautner decided to cut the cord with Wright—at least partially. In moving to Los Angeles, he chose a city whose promising architectural environment had been catalyzed by Wright, and his first L.A. assignment was the supervision of the construction of the Wright-designed Sturges House in Brentwood. But he also purchased a hillside lot in Silver Lake and developed plans to design his first solo project: a house for himself and his growing family. And in contrast to the Sturges House, the Silver Lake house would "be something *of* the hill rather than in spite of the hill…simple in plan and economical in execution."[438] The house, at 2007 Micheltorena Street in the Moreno Highlands section, was an instant triumph, with a feature article in *House Beautiful* magazine complete with accompanying handbook on plans and specifications for do-it-yourself model homes.[439]

The splashy publicity did not immediately lead to new residential commissions or commercial projects, and all work came to a standstill during World War II. Still in need of reliable income after the war, Lautner entered into a partnership with Douglas Honnold, an established architect with a string of lucrative, large-scale projects including "commercial buildings, society restaurants, and the homes of movie stars and moguls in Beverly

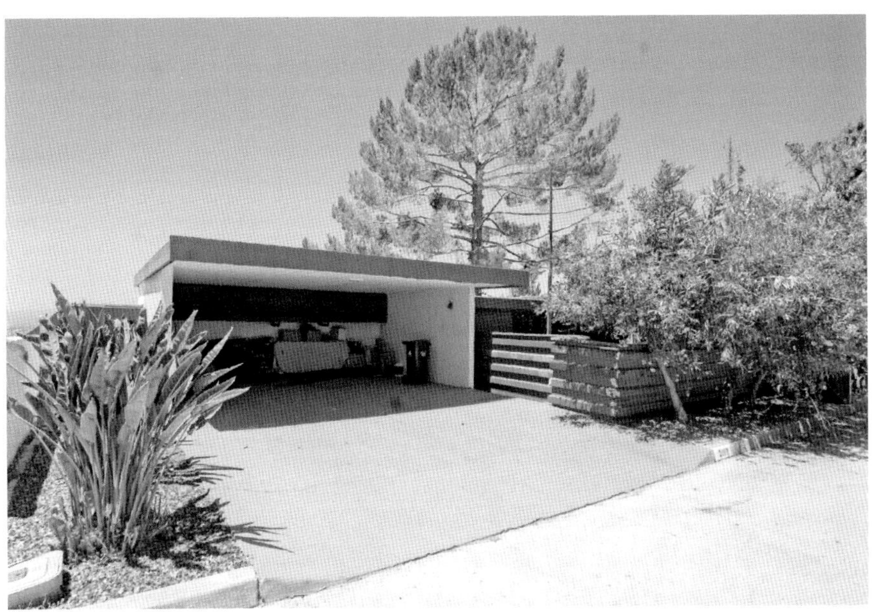

John Lautner House, 2007 Micheltorena Street, John Lautner, 1940.

Hills and Malibu." Recognizing Lautner's talent, Honnold allowed him to pursue his interest "in the spatial exploration of organic modernism," as opposed to "the shiny minimalist structures of Los Angeles' [then] leading high-art architect Richard Neutra."[440]

Lautner also gained from the partnership closer contact to the often maligned but distinctive "Googie" style of coffee shops, motels, car washes and gas stations that began dotting the Southern California landscape in the late 1940s. Following in the Schindler tradition on a personal level, Lautner made quite an impression on the women in the Honnold household. Honnold's daughter Elizabeth Harris told historian Alan Hess that Lautner was "the most exotic creature imaginable," arriving to work in "red shirt, brilliant tweedy tie, and a giant turquoise ring on his giant fist. He also had a gorgeous guffaw and in every respect was a gorgeous giant of a man. He electrified the drafting room."[441] Honnold's wife, Elizabeth, was similarly impressed, openly admitting to her husband that she had fallen in love with Lautner.[442]

Whether the "Schindler effect" contributed to the eventual dissolution of the Lautner-Honnold partnership in 1947, Honnold continued to hold Lautner, the artist and architect, in high esteem during the construction of Lautner's second Silver Lake commission, the Hancock Residence, built in 1949. Marybud was not as forgiving; she moved with the children back to Marquette, ending a twelve-year marriage.[443]

SILVERTOP

Lautner's final contribution to the architecture of Silver Lake was the first that allowed him to "turn the corner from small innovative houses bursting with ideas" to "sprawling houses" that could demonstrate his "creative dexterity."[444] His client, Kenneth Reiner, was a forty-year-old millionaire and inventor who made his fortune designing and manufacturing specialized parts for the aerospace industry. Reiner would typify a handful of wealthy clients who were open to imposing designs of heroic proportions and had the bank accounts to support them. Reiner named the house Silvertop, in reference to its sitting atop the Moreno Highlands hillside overlooking Silver Lake Reservoir and the hills and mountains beyond. The house would become a virtual laboratory, as architect and inventor-client together explored and implemented new technologies in design. Building for the future, they planned for the future as well, incorporating a system of tunnels under the house so that "any room could be reached from below, and new wiring, plumbing or other changes could be added for the future."[445]

Silvertop's original budget in 1956 was in the range of $55,000 to $75,000, but by 1960, nearly $700,000 had been spent and the house was still unfinished. In the end, the lack of restraint was Reiner's undoing. His financial and personal fortunes took a turn for the worse in 1964 when his business partner sued him and his marriage ended in divorce. Perhaps most tragically, Reiner never got to live in his and Lautner's masterpiece. The house sat empty, neglected and still unfinished for another decade and was finally sold in bankruptcy court in 1974 to Phillip and Jacklyn Burchill for $150,000. The new owners considered it a bargain. Phillip Burchill recalled asking his wife, "What did we ever do to deserve this?"[446] The Burchills lived in and lovingly maintained Silvertop for the next forty years and are remembered for their joy in sharing the house with others, particularly local charities and nonprofits interested in architecture and preservation issues. The house was last sold in October 2014 for $8.55 million—a Silver Lake record and well above the asking price of $7.5 million.[447]

Silvertop remains, literally and figuratively, Silver Lake Modernism's crowning achievement. Looming like a flying saucer or futurist castle, its

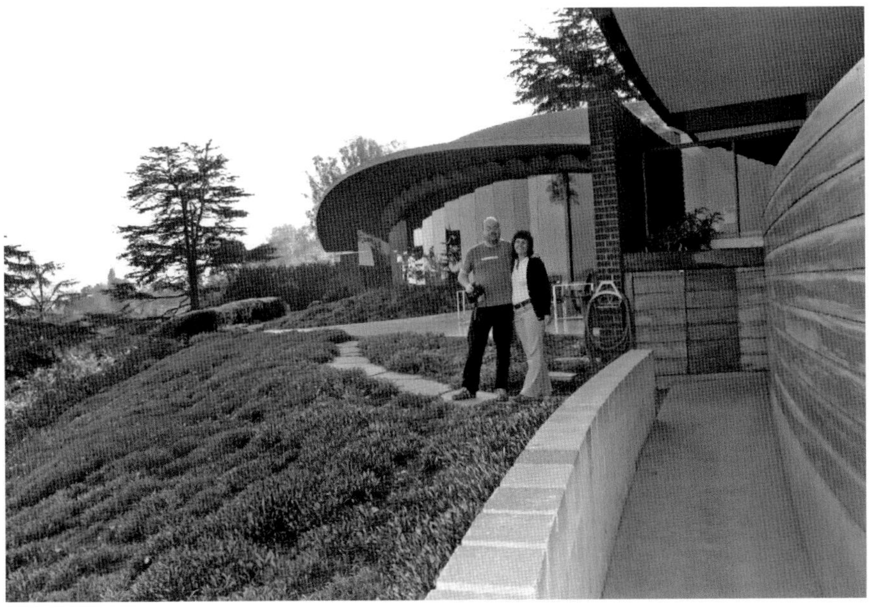

Martin Shall (you-are-here.com) with friend Rita Wirth on a visit to Silvertop, November 2006.

curved roof mirroring the arc of the hillside above and its infinity pool seeming to spill into the reservoir below, the house both stands regally apart and merges seamlessly with the surroundings. History and geography also come together in Silvertop's placement across the reservoir from Neutra's VDL House, as if the two modernist icons were in conversation, if not full agreement, about their architectural approaches and reputations.

Lautner went on to design approximately two hundred projects in his fifty-year career. Several have been featured in movies and other media, most famously, the Space Needle–like Chemosphere house in the Hollywood Hills; collectively they have helped define Southern California.

Shortly before his death in Los Angeles in 1994, Lautner returned to Midgaard, the mystical home his family built, and he redesigned, more than a half century prior. Olsberg imaginatively describes the experience:

> *As Lautner sat on the terrace, perched on his billion-year-old rock, looking at the evanescent horizon, he gave his nephew some parting advice. Be faithful, he said, to first beliefs. For in spite of the things he could not change, he felt he had opened up as much of the world as he could to its inherent truths and beauty.*[448]

14

JOINING CULTURES EAST AND WEST I

David Hyun, Eugene Kinn Choy, Gilbert L. Leong and Delbert Wong

David Hyun's name doesn't generally pop up in discussion about Silver Lake architecture. His name isn't even mentioned in Thomas S. Hines's comprehensive study of Los Angeles Modernism, *Architecture of the Sun*. His signature achievement, the Japanese Village Plaza in Little Tokyo, gets brief notice in David Gebhard and Robert Winter's "bible" of Los Angeles architecture, *An Architectural Guidebook to Los Angeles.* Googling his name uncovers bits and pieces about his life and work, but nowhere will you find a comprehensive examination of this extraordinary man and his exceptional accomplishments.

I (Michael Locke) first met David Hyun while campaigning for a seat on the Silver Lake Neighborhood Council (SLNC) in 2003. I had always been curious about the house at 1954 Redesdale, with the seven-gabled roof of blue ceramic tiles, which he designed and lived in with his wife, Mary. I was delightfully surprised when he opened his home to me on more than one occasion, first to share his story as the first Korean American to obtain an architect's license and, again, to host one of the first meetings of SLNC's Beautification Committee.[449]

Born in Korea in 1917, David Hyun was the youngest son of Reverend Soon and Maria Lee Hyun. David was profoundly influenced by his father, who as a college student during the Japanese occupation of Korea found inspiration in Western history and culture, specifically the American struggle for independence from Great Britain, Abraham Lincoln's Emancipation Proclamation and Moses's biblical admonition to Pharaoh, "Let my people go!"

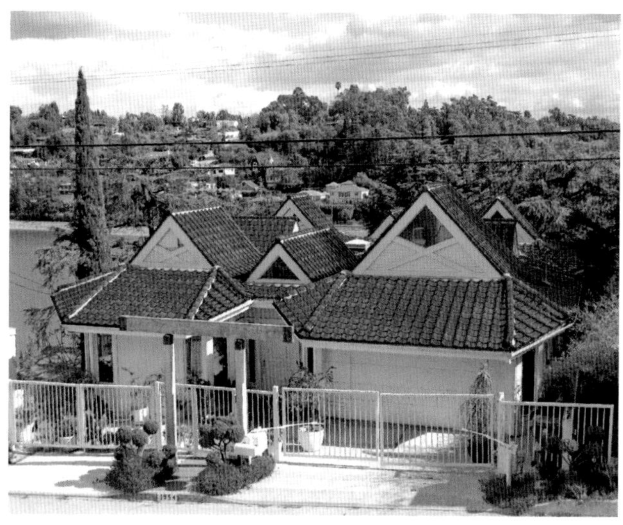

David Hyun residence, 1954, Redesdale Avenue, David Hyun, 1993.

His father converted to Christianity and joined the Mansei Movement of 1919, in which two million Korean youth rose in protest against their Japanese overlords. He became spiritual leader of the largest Protestant church in Korea, traveling across the country to advocate for the revolutionary principles he found in political struggles throughout the ages and in the teachings of Jesus. During the brutal suppression of the Mansei demonstrations that ensued, Reverend Hyun and his family fled to Shanghai, where he served as Minister Plenipotentiary and envoy to the United States of the free Korean government-in-exile. He declined an invitation to be nominated as president and instead supported Syngman Rhee, a decision he would come to regret.

In 1921, Reverend Hyun, representing the provisional government, petitioned the U.S. Congress for American recognition of Korean independence. While the petition was undergoing Congressional review, conflicts arose within the provisional government, and the request was withdrawn. In a power play by Rhee, Reverend Hyun was accused of using false credentials and labeled a Communist. Denied reentry into Korea, the Hyun family moved to Hawaii, where Reverend Hyun continued to fight for Korean independence in exile.[450]

David Hyun revered his father and felt imbued with his sense of patriotism and idealism. Growing up as a political refugee in Hawaii, David excelled in school and graduated from the University of Hawaii in math and physics but soon discovered that his real love was architecture. He made his way to Southern California determined to become an architect. Taking night classes

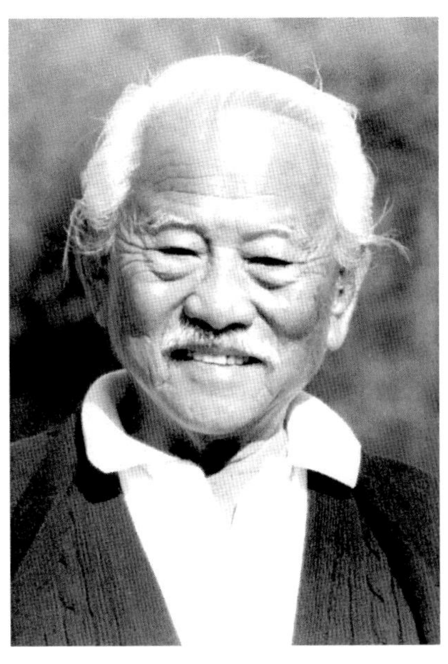
David Hyun portrait. *Courtesy of David Hyun.*

at the USC School of Architecture, working janitorial jobs during the day and studying on his lunch breaks, he managed to pass the state licensing exam on his first try. Given his quick mind and engaging personality, he readily found work at some of the leading architectural firms in Los Angeles, among them A. Quincy Jones Jr., Arnet & David and (guess who?) Neutra and Alexander.

In the hysteria of the McCarthy era, David was accused of being a Communist and underwent deportation hearings. His alleged affiliation resulted from the union meetings he had attended while working in the sugar cane fields of Hawaii during his undergraduate days. Despite the dearth of evidence, the hearings dragged on for many years. His wife, Mary, campaigned and raised funds for his release, and the case was eventually dropped. This was a fortunate turn of events for the whole family; had they been sent back to South Korea, their lives certainly would have been in peril due to the bad blood between Hyun and strongman Syngman Rhee.[451]

With a new lease on life, David opened his own Los Angeles architectural firm, David Hyun and Associates, Inc., in 1953. His designs expressed a philosophy based on his father's teachings: an "architecture of the present that best expresses the hope of the future by uniting not only with the past, but by joining cultures both East and West."[452]

In the 1970s, David contemplated his first ambitious enterprise, called "Korea City" and envisioned as a showcase of the Korean American experience. "Without a showcase, our heroic efforts to participate fully in American life are disadvantaged," he told the *Koreatown Weekly* in 1979. "Many Americans see Koreans as second-class Japanese and are completely unaware of the great history and ancient culture of Korea." The undertaking would have transformed embryonic Koreatown into the likeness of a traditional Korean village. K.W. Lee, founder and editor of the *Koreatown Weekly*, supported the endeavor, calling it "the cutting edge for real growth of Korean Life in our adopted country."[453] Though the project was never realized, David's vision for a revitalized Koreatown has since been achieved, many times over.

His most notable accomplishment—ironic, given his family's traumatic past but fully in keeping with his unifying principles—was Japanese Village Plaza in Little Tokyo in the early 1980s. The centerpiece of Little Tokyo's revitalization, the project heralded the area's transformation from a place that had seen better days into a thriving community. David's architectural and engineering skill, his experience gained in the preceding four decades in all facets of real estate development, coupled with his passion for bringing people together, uniquely prepared him for the Japanese Plaza undertaking. In a climate of "it can't be done," David, armed with vision and determination, managed to merge private, institutional, community and government resources to revitalize a neighborhood against seemingly impossible odds. As author and documentary filmmaker Helie Lee observed, David Hyun believed that "any neighborhood could be revitalized if you bring in commerce and good will."[454]

Japanese Village Plaza, while not completely compensating for the aborted Korea City project, remains a lasting testament to David's core belief that,

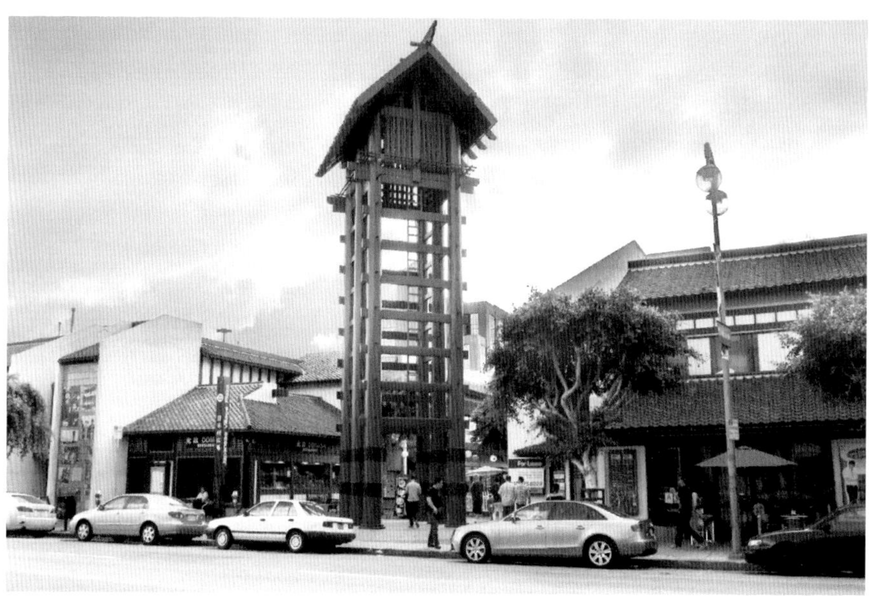

Yagura Fire Tower, Japanese Village Plaza, David Hyun, 1978.

in spite of Koreans' historical rift with the Japanese over their occupation of Korea from 1910 to 1945, rising above the wounds of the past could be achieved by answering the age-old question "Who is my neighbor?" David answered with a resounding "Everyone!"[455] Besides expressing his principles through his architecture, David was socially engaged as well, serving as first chair of the Korean American Coalition (KAC) and as a founding board member of Leadership Education for Asian Pacifics (LEAP).

In 1993, David designed the seven-gabled Silver Lake home for himself and his family. The distinctive roof of ceramic blue tiles that first caught my eye, reminiscent of those used in his Japanese Village Plaza design, are not only strikingly beautiful but purportedly have a lifespan of four hundred years. Another nearby house, designed in Los Feliz in 1970 for civil rights attorney John T. McTernan, was recently granted historic designation status (LAHCM No. 1065). The house held personal historical significance for David as well, as McTernan had defended Harry Hay and several other accused Communists and labor leaders during the McCarthy era, including David Hyun.[456]

Eugene Kinn Choy, Gilbert L. Leong and Delbert Wong

Eugene Kinn Choy was the first Chinese American architect in California to join the AIA, second nationally to New York–based I.M. Pei. Born in Guangdong, China, in 1912, Choy immigrated to the United States at age eleven, settling in Bakersfield, where his parents made their living selling blue jeans to farm workers. After graduating from the USC School of Architecture in 1939, Choy founded his own firm, designing commercial, industrial, educational and government buildings in Los Angeles and other cities. He built a number of residences and apartment buildings in and around Silver Lake, several in collaboration with his brother Allan Kinn Choy, and son, Barton Choy, and built his own home at 3027 Castle Street in 1949.[457]

Gilbert L. Leong, the first Chinese American to graduate from the USC School of Architecture, in 1936, was a highly successful architect whose work in Echo Park and Silver Lake reflected a "concern for affordable, practical and accessible housing."[458] Among Leong's more notable achievements was a modest home at 2416 West Silver Lake Drive built in 1954 for Judge Delbert Wong, notable himself as the first Chinese American appointed

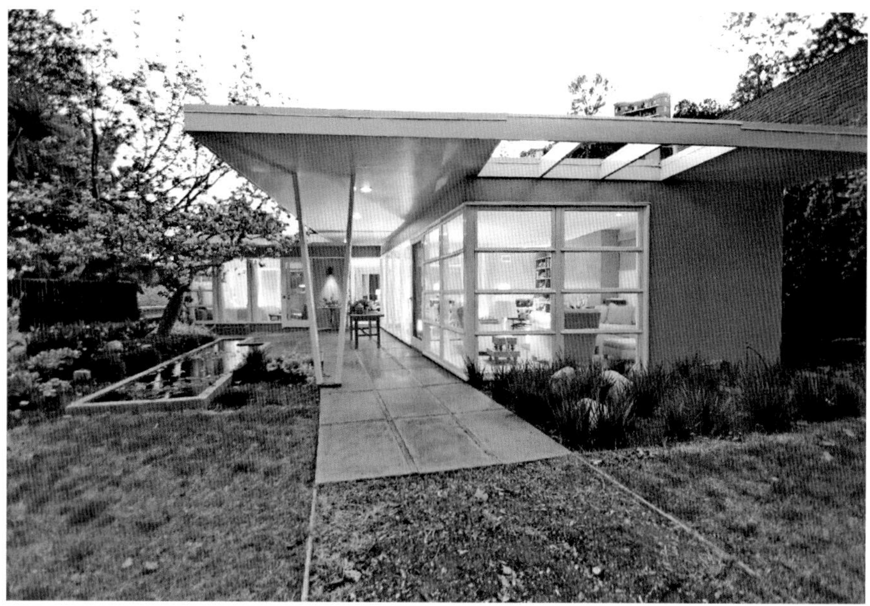

Eugene Kinn Choy residence, 3027 Castle Street, Eugene Kinn Choy, 1949.

to the bench on the U.S. mainland (by Governor Edmund G. "Pat" Brown in 1961).

Judge Wong played a significant role in Silver Lake history on at least two fronts. Although his judicial appointment marked significant progress for Asian Americans, his move to Silver Lake showed that even this leftist section of Los Angeles wasn't immune from the bigotry that still gripped much of the city. Although racially based deed restrictions had recently been lifted (largely through the efforts of Loren Miller), this did not prevent some of Judge Wong's Anglo neighbors from mounting a drive to block the sale. The ultimate defeat of this racist ploy is widely credited with helping break the color barrier for Asians in Los Angeles.[459] Judge Wong also contributed to Silver Lake's cultural life through his involvement with East West Players theater, as we'll see in the next chapter.

15

JOINING CULTURES EAST AND WEST II

EAST WEST PLAYERS

Founded in Silver Lake in 1965 and with its main stage in the area for more than three decades, East West Players (EWP), the nation's first Asian American theater organization, represents a remarkable confluence of talent, history and need. Need relates to the longstanding lack in U.S. culture of Asian American themes and meaningful roles for Asian American actors, which EWP, fired by the ethnic pride and identity politics zeitgeist of the 1960s, sought to redress. Talent and history come together in, and radiate out from, Japanese actor Mako, the prime catalyst for EWP's creation.[460]

Having begun to find work in film and television but frustrated by the continuing dearth of meaty, non-stereotypical stage and screen roles for Asian Americans, Mako (full name Makoto Iwamatsu) teamed with fellow actors Beulah Quo, Soon-Tek Oh, Pat Li, June Kim and Yet Lock to form EWP. When Mako was nominated for an Academy Award for Best Supporting Actor in *The Sand Pebbles* (1966)—only the third such honor for an Asian actor, after Miyoshi Umeki's Oscar and Sessue Hayakawa's nomination in 1958—he instantly became a magnet for additional talent to join EWP and for audiences to attend its plays.[461]

For its first seven years, the troupe trained and staged in the Bethany Presbyterian Church (founded in 1931), just off Silver Lake's main drag at the corner of Griffith Park Boulevard and Edgecliffe Drive. Why this particular venue was chosen brings us back to Judge Delbert Wong. Judge Wong was a member of the church and was as interested as EWP's founders in fostering an Asian-oriented theater. He also happened to be

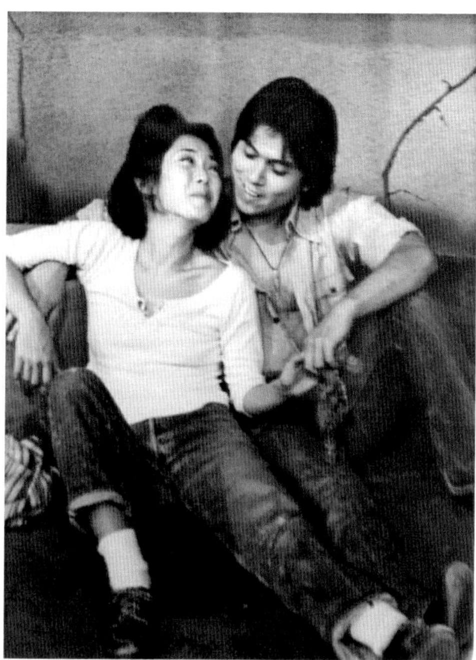

Right: Momo Yashima and Ralph Brannen portrait, circa 1975. *Courtesy of Momo Yashima and Ralph Brannen.*

Below: Mako Iwamatsu portrait.

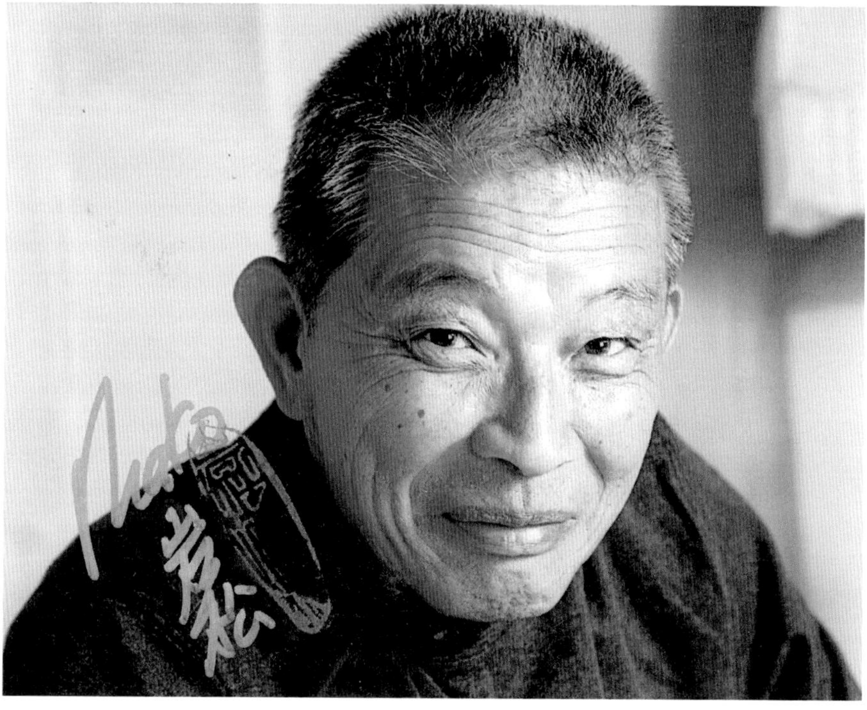

a former Stanford University classmate of EWP cofounder Beulah Quo, who lived in Silver Lake. Through the Quo connection, Judge Wong cleared the way for EWP to use the church basement for rehearsal and productions and helped fund the theater's operations as well.[462]

Building on its success and seeking a more autonomous space, EWP, in 1972, after a brief residence at a storefront at the corner of Santa Monica Boulevard and Virgil Avenue, moved to a cozier home at nearby 4424 Santa Monica Boulevard, where it remained until 1998. But EWP's ties to Silver Lake and Mako go deeper. Mako's younger sister, Momo Yashima, joined EWP soon after its founding, and her husband, Ralph Brannen, came aboard in 1973. Married in 1975, in Barnsdall Park of all places, Momo and Ralph rented a Silver Lake house at 1375 Angelus Avenue, where they lived for five years.[463]

The young couple's honeymoon phase with EWP would not last nearly as long. But to better understand why the countercultural spirit they brought to the company did not sit well with the older and more traditionally minded Mako, some knowledge of the traumatic but ultimately redemptive backstory of the Iwamatsu-Yashima family is required.

Taro and Mitsu

Mako and Momo's parents, Japanese-born Taro and Mitsu Yashima (born Atsushi Iwamatsu and Tomoe Sasoko), were leftist activists who bitterly opposed Japan's domestically repressive, militarily expansionist policies in the years leading up to World War II. Both were jailed several times in the 1930s for their resistance and were subjected to torture. Mitsu lost two children to miscarriage while incarcerated. Mako, born in 1933, she called a "ten-month baby" for having extended his delivery until after her release, so he would not be born in prison.[464]

Taro, a gifted artist, aided by fellow inmates who smuggled in art materials, documented their brutal mistreatment in drawings he would later incorporate into an illustrated, autobiographical account of life in prewar Japan, *The New Sun* (1943).[465] Neither the book, nor he and his family, would have seen the light of day had it not been for Mitsu's wealthy shipbuilder father (shades of socialist Aline Barnsdall's oil baron patriarch). With Taro and Mitsu's lives on the line with the onset of World War II, Mr. Sasoko arranged for their escape from Japan by sea in 1939. Unsure of their chances of survival abroad, they left six-year-old Mako with his aunt and grandmother in Kobe, an "abandonment," no matter how well-intentioned, that would mark Mako for life.[466]

Feeling the odds were better for Japanese on the East Coast rather than the West Coast of the United States, Taro and Mitsu took the Suez Canal route to New York City. Not only did they escape internment, unlike most of their compatriots following the bombing of Pearl Harbor; they were hired by the Office of Strategic Services (OSS) to aid in the U.S. war effort. Their intimate knowledge of Japan and their artistic skills were utilized in producing propaganda leaflets to be dispersed on the Pacific front. Fearing repercussions for Mako and other family members should the Japanese government learn of their service to the "enemy," the couple changed their names to Taro and Mitsu Yashima.[467]

After the war, the Yashimas were rewarded for their contribution to the Allied cause by a special act of Congress in 1949 granting them U.S. citizenship—a privilege still denied most Japanese (and other Asian) immigrants but a prerequisite for enabling Mako to rejoin his parents in New York.[468] Overjoyed at Mako's return but minus their OSS benefactors, the growing family (Momo was born in 1948) struggled financially into the early 1950s. Upon their move to the Boyle Heights section of Los Angeles in 1953, their fortunes began to improve, especially with the publication of Taro's Caldecott Honored children's book *Crow Boy* (1956) and a string of other successful, now classic texts, several created together with Mitsu and featuring a character named, and literally modeled after, young Momo.[469]

MAKO, MOMO AND RALPH

Mako, who studied architecture upon his arrival in the United States and realized his theatrical talent during military service, landed his first role in a major motion picture in 1959's *Never So Few*.[470] Soon after helping form East West Players in 1965, he brought on Momo, a dance major at Cal-State Los Angeles and USC, to instruct the troupe in dance, and Taro to design sets. The first play mounted by EWP was *Rashomon*, the classic tale told from multiple perspectives, made famous by acclaimed Japanese director Akira Kurosawa's 1951 awarding-winning film.[471] Chiefly concerned with fostering fresh Asian material and talent, EWP, in its first few years under Mako, also emphasized Western classical training and produced one play a season from the likes of Shakespeare, Ibsen, Chekov and Brecht.

Momo left the company for two years in the mid-1970s, studying acting in New York and doing dinner theater in North Carolina. Her work in the East with Sanford Meisner and introduction to the Grotowski technique, plus her romantic liaison with newcomer Ralph Brannen upon her return, would send the young couple and Mako on a collision course. Meisner's nontraditional, anti-Method approach stressed an actor's attunement to the immediate environment; Grotowski's aimed at a dynamic interrelation between actors and spectators. Both orientations meshed with Brannen's, who, as founder and lead singer of the multicultural rock band Heavy Nation, came to EWP with a similarly progressive sensibility.[472]

Initially, EWP benefited from the infusion of new ideas and personnel, as well as from Momo's joining the ensemble, often in lead roles. Besides its main-stage productions, the group held children's matinees and traveled to schools, colleges, community centers and prisons. With a grant from the California Arts Foundation, EWP expanded its outreach beyond Los Angeles, touring along the coast from San Diego to Ukiah. When a 1976 EWP play, *Asian American Hearings* (about seeking redress for the wartime Japanese internment), written and with music by Ralph and choreographed and starring Momo, became the company's biggest popular and critical hit to that time, a power struggle between Mako and his sister and brother-in-law ensued.[473] The issue was partly a matter of ego and control, but also one of differing artistic and political perspective. As Ralph explained in our interview:

> *When I came in, and through Momo, we took a very political stance, because we felt the roles being made available to Asian Americans at the theater were stereotypical and demeaning. So the plays we started doing were meant to be politically awakening. We would take a very strong stance against any kind of discrimination or stereotyping, and this became our theme. So we searched for plays and productions that had that sort of a theme, and we asked for writers to come in and to present their works in that direction....* Asian American Hearings *was the beginning of the second wave or youth wave at East West Players.*[474]

"And the patrons loved us," Momo added. "Because they had seen us developing from doing small roles and then to see us controlling a completely different style of theater was so exciting!"

But Mako was still in charge. As retribution, he stripped Momo of her roles by hiring directors who would do his bidding. He sent her and Ralph off as "emissaries," doing touring productions "so he could maintain control of the main stage." Most humiliatingly, he sent them to New York so they "could see what real actors are." The exile plan backfired, however, as the younger players' popularity with patrons at home forced Mako to bring them back by popular demand. In addition, Momo and Ralph's talents were starting to be noticed outside of independent theater. Through agent Guy Lee, a longtime EWP supporter, Ralph landed a television series, Momo scored five commercials in quick succession and other TV and film roles soon followed (including as fellow crew members in the first *Star Trek* movie).[475]

While the move to the large and small screens may not have been a step up artistically, the financial windfall allowed the couple in 1979 to purchase the charming Mid-City Spanish-style house they live in to this day. Nor did they turn their backs completely on EWP. Despite their problems with Mako, who had begun to alienate others in the company as well, they remained protective of him in the face of charges of financial improprieties and—ironic, given his past treatment of them—nepotism, particularly in the casting of his wife, actress Shizuko Hoshi.[476]

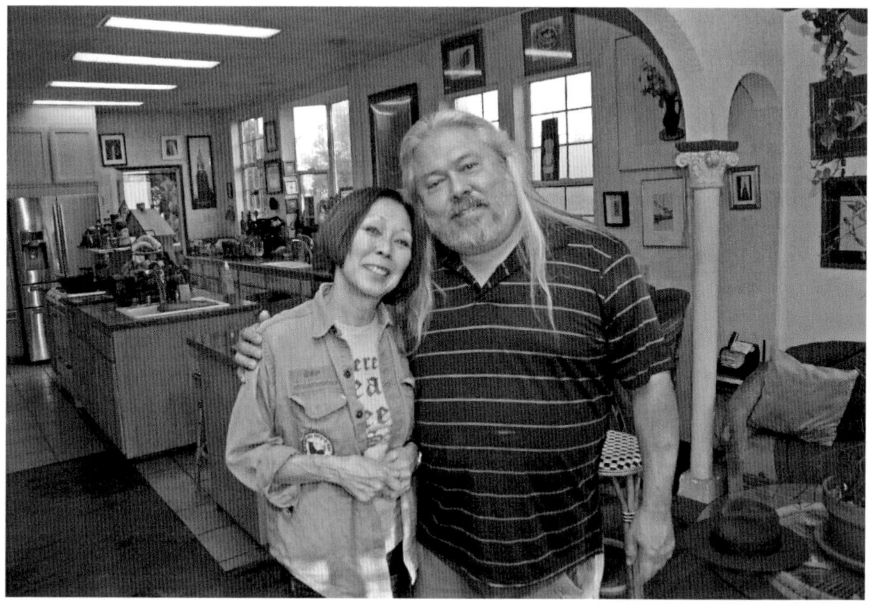

Momo Yashima and Ralph Brannen portrait, April 2016.

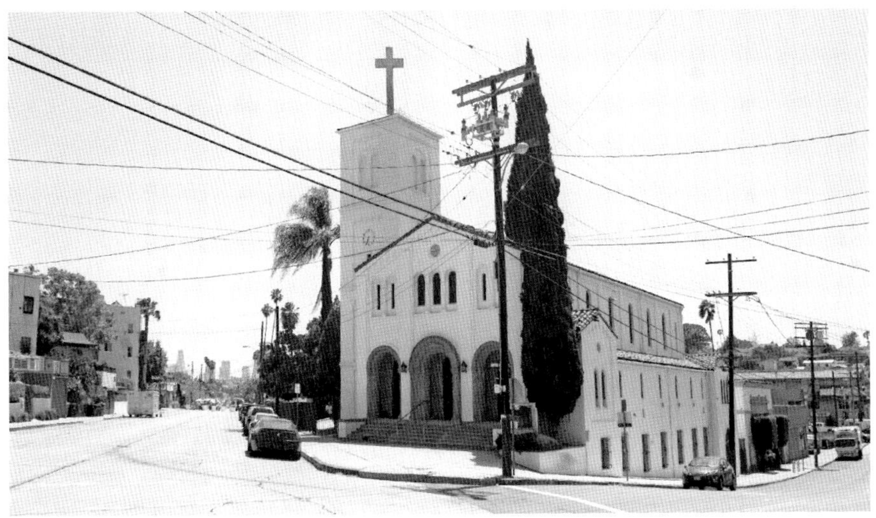

Bethany Presbyterian Church, 1629 Griffith Park Boulevard.

By the time Momo and Ralph left EWP for good in the early 1990s, Mako's influence had waned considerably. He finally left in 1998, when, under new director Tim Dang (taking over from Nobu McCarthy), the company moved from Silver Lake to Little Tokyo and from a 99-seat, equity-waiver theater to a new, 240-seat main stage within the historic Union Center for the Arts, where EWP remains today.

Mako, who has a star on the Hollywood Walk of Fame, died in 2006.[477] The Bethany Church building, where EWP got its start, is no longer a functioning church. It has been leased for several years by local developer Dana Hollister, who has rented it out for film productions and has dreams of turning it into a boutique hotel.

16

TRIUMPH AND TRAGEDY

William Kesling and His "Scintillating Structures"

Readers of the classic French historical novel *Les Misérables* might find it in their hearts to have a little empathy for William Kesling, a promising Los Angeles builder who made some comparatively minor mistakes for which he suffered grave consequences. Like the hero in the novel, Jean Valjean, sentenced to prison for stealing a loaf of bread, Kesling was indicted for embezzling $315 and sentenced to San Quentin Prison.

Kesling's life is the sort that plays out like a modern-day Shakespearean tragedy. His father, Adolph Kessling (William later dropped one of the *s*'s because it "sounded better"), was born in Germany in 1856. After moving to Russia at age twenty and learning the butcher's trade, he immigrated to America in 1881. Here he worked the coal mines, did some mining and prospecting around the country and finally settled, more or less, in Kansas City, where he married another German immigrant, Paulina Heisser, and started a family.[478]

On and off for the next forty years, Paulina shared in her husband's "many financial successes and failures and endured his personal failings."[479] The most galling of these occurred in 1911, when Adolph, without forewarning, took their eldest son and deserted his wife and four remaining children, including eleven-year-old William. Five years later, the peripatetic Adolph resurfaced, seeking reconciliation and asking Paulina to join him in Calexico, where he had managed to establish a thriving meat market and become one of the town's leading businessmen. Paulina joined him with the four children, but on her terms: she purchased a home of her own, and the couple never lived again in the same house.[480]

Not Far from the Tree

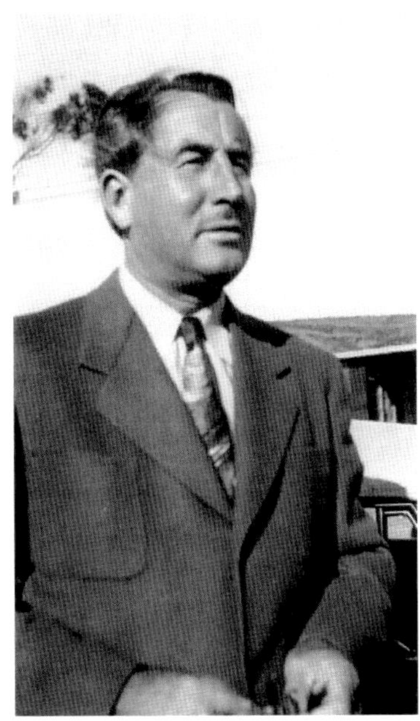

William Kesling, La Jolla, 1950. *Kesling Family Archive, courtesy of Patrick Pascal.*

William Kesling was sixteen when he arrived with his mother in Calexico. He worked at various jobs for Adolph but was inclined toward the building trades and, given an enterprising nature like his father's, easily found employment. Rising rapidly through the ranks, he soon landed a position as construction superintendent on a large Mexican ranch. Sharing his father's restless energy as well, he moved to Los Angeles in 1920, lured, as were so many, by the big city's seemingly boundless opportunity. Here, too, Kesling quickly moved up the ladder, climbing from apprentice to foreman to building superintendent in three years, eventually, by his claim, even working as a draftsman for R.M. Schindler.[481]

By 1935, without an architect's license, Kesling felt ready to open his own office, located at 1639 Silver Lake Boulevard. He called the place "Kesling's Modern Structures" and by 1936, license or no, boasted of having built "over 450 homes, stores and apartments in the Los Angeles area," adding more modestly, "While I have never made a fortune, I have made a fair living."[482]

Not in the same league as a designer with the premier modernists, Kesling's mark on Silver Lake and Los Angeles as a whole stems from one of modernism's more derivative but popular offshoots, Streamline Moderne. In 1935, during the period of Streamline Moderne's greatest popularity, Kesling was "far and away Los Angeles' most prolific and successful practitioner of the style, breaking ground on more than twenty projects."[483] Of the ten of his "scintillating structures" still standing, most are clustered around and above Silver Lake Boulevard, with five dominating Easterly Terrace's short dead-end street.[484]

Perhaps Kesling's greatest contribution was building sophisticated architecture that the average homeowner could afford. His first project, the "Model Home," established him as a player in Los Angeles's modernist

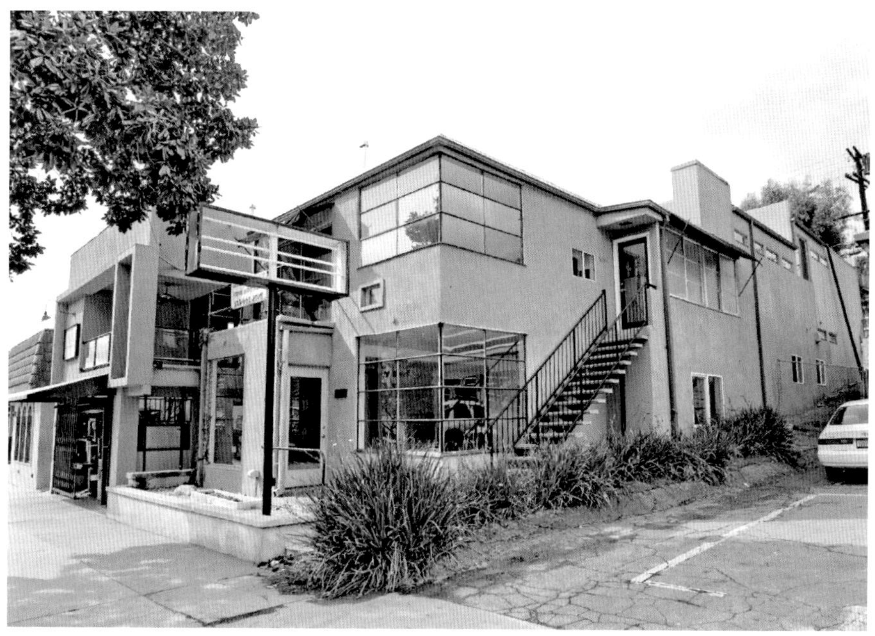

Kesling Modern Structures Office, William Kesling, 1935.

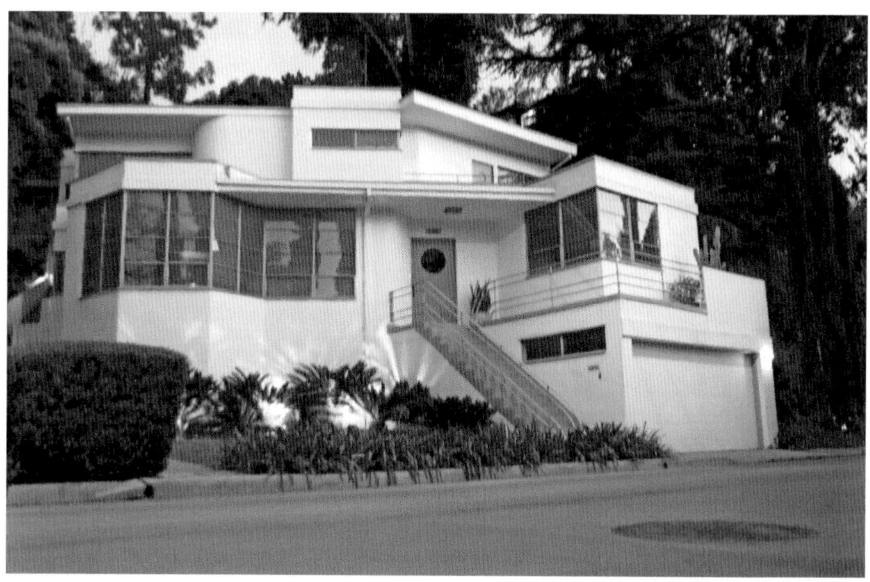

Skinner House, 1530 Easterly Terrace, William Kesling, 1936.

movement. The budget for the Model Home was only $3,600 (or $2.55 per square foot, compared to over $10 per square foot for Neutra's Lovell House). During the Great Depression, when most of L.A.'s prominent architects gained few commissions, Kesling thrived, bragging at one point that he had "signed 35 contracts without much effort."[485]

Rising labor and material costs, combined with low profit margins and simply taking on more projects than he was prepared to handle, proved Kesling's Achilles' heel. Promising more than he could deliver, he was sued by a handful of disgruntled clients for breach of contract after seeking additional funds for the completion of work at more than the agreed-upon price. Though he initially prevailed, two of the litigants (a Mr. and Mrs. Greene), abetted by LAPD detective Gerald Moore, threatened to file another complaint.[486]

Kesling was in fact guilty of overcharging, but the tactic of undercharging and compensating when sufficient funds were secured was a commonplace practice and rarely questioned. In the "desperate, suspicious atmosphere" of the Depression, Kesling biographer Patrick Pascal recounts, society was "disposed to react strongly against financial misdeeds and readily believe the worst about others, particularly those espousing new ideas."[487] The overreaction in Kesling's case seems one of the period's more egregious offenses.

In March 1937, Kesling pled guilty to one count of embezzlement. The monetary penalty was reduced from the original $315 to an even more ludicrous $24 and, spared Jean Valjean's fate, his sentencing to San Quentin was suspended. Instead, he was placed on two-year probation, during which time he was barred from conducting any business. In his report to the presiding judge, Deputy Probation Officer George Grist remarked, "The defendant apparently used some shady means in trying to get his client to pay additional for extras in order to make up for some shortage in another place. This however appears to be the method in meeting competition in many lines of business…[and I] cannot find where the defendant has profited by any of his activities." Mr. Greene, on the other hand, Grist noted, was "satisfied with living in a modern house which the defendant built [and] after doing everything he could to impede Kesling's progress by inciting others, contributing to his insolvency, extorting threats from others, and then filing a formal complaint with the district attorney… completed his vengeful streak of actions by selling Kesling's office and keeping the proceeds."[488] Kesling fared no better with the architectural power structure, Pascal explains, which "thumbed its collective nose at the brash interloper," holding Kesling up as an example of the "dangers of not hiring professional architects with proper credentials."[489]

With Kesling's finances and reputation in ruins and his Modern Structures office taken from him, the once proud builder, at age thirty-six, was destitute and broken. His architecturally significant homes were shunned and neglected as favor in the Streamline Moderne style faded. Barred from doing his own building under the terms of his probation, Kesling from 1937 to 1939 resorted to working in Salinas and San Francisco as a carpenter's assistant. Mirroring his father in the ability to bounce back from adversity, he resettled after his probation in the upscale seaside community of La Jolla and enjoyed a second successful architectural career. Yet, as before, he overcommitted himself and ended up in court.[490]

By 1962, at age sixty-three, like the Thackeray protagonist whose downfall is bound to the very traits that propelled his success, Kesling had lost it all again. Although he remained active until his mid-seventies, he never regained his earlier stature. He died of the complications of diabetes and Alzheimer's in 1983.

17

THE HOBO MILLIONAIRE

JAMES EADS HOW

With links to Aline Barnsdall, Rudolph Schindler, James Leo Herlihy and a unique brand of bohemianism, James Eads How, born in 1874, offers a colorful addition to the offbeat annals of Silver Lake.

Likened in his lifetime to St. Francis of Assisi, How was heir to a prominent St. Louis family's fortune but chose to live as a homeless wanderer and devote his life to the poor. His wealth derived from his grandfather James Buchanan Eads, a civil engineer and inventor who made millions retrieving salvage from riverboat disasters on the Mississippi River. Owing to his status and knowledge of the river, Eads was summoned to Washington to assist in the Union's defense of the river in the Civil War. After the war, he became world famous for designing the longest arch bridge in the world, the Eads Bridge, completed in St. Louis in 1874. An engineering marvel still in use today, the bridge was the iconic symbol of the city until the building of the Gateway Arch in 1965.[491]

The family fortune passed down to Eads's grandsons, Louis and James Eads How. Elder brother Louis "took to the gay bohemian life," becoming a prolific poet and biographer of his grandfather; James cast his lot with the "hobohemians."[492] From the beginning, he was a "stubborn idealist," eschewing the attention of servants and preferring to wait on himself. As *Time* magazine elaborated, "He was never able to understand how some people could be content with a string of porters or servants, while others had to make a desperate struggle to live at all." One day, in his early teens, he picked up a purse containing some money. He made an effort to find the owner and, not being successful, was told he could keep the contents. The experience proved revelatory. "Whose money is this?" he reasoned. "Why am I entitled to it? I didn't do anything for this; I didn't even have to thank anyone for it. And then I thought of all the other money that had come to me without any effort on my part."[493]

Furthering the analogy with St. Francis, How attended Meadville Theological School, a Unitarian seminary in Meadville, Pennsylvania, and lived like a hermit, "giving the poor his allowance, his possessions, everything but meager necessities; he wanted to live the life of Christ."[494] After seminary, he was admitted to Harvard, where, on the one hand, he excelled at football and baseball and, on the other, tried, unsuccessfully, to establish a monastic order, the Brotherhood of the Daily Life. Continuing on his altruistic path, he studied medicine at the New York College of Physicians and Surgeons and, while a postgraduate at Oxford University, joined the Fabian Society, a nascent British socialist organization.[495]

Taking literally Christ's message—"Whatever you do for the least of these my brothers, you have done it unto me"—How spent the rest of his life ministering to the needs of the wandering jobless, determined that every drifter could be coaxed into meaningful employment. He had less luck with the media, which mocked his utopian efforts and derided him as the "Hobo Millionaire."[496]

I Was an Hungred and Ye Gave Me Meat

Despite the embarrassment his notoriety caused his blueblood family, in the end How's mother, Eliza Eads How, supported him. Upon her death in 1915, her will bequeathed him $500,000, half in trust and half to be spent in furtherance of his efforts. The added income allowed How for the next fifteen years to travel around the country and abroad, offering aid to migrant farm workers, seasonal laborers or simple tramps forced to move from place to place in search of shelter and sustenance and without the means to extricate themselves from a life of hardship and degradation. No other endeavor held How's interest, "not even matrimony."[497]

In 1905–6, How organized the International Brotherhood Welfare Association (IBWA), a mutual aid society for hobos. Headquartered in Cincinnati, Ohio, the IBWA set up branches in more than twenty metropolitan areas around the country, including Baltimore, Philadelphia

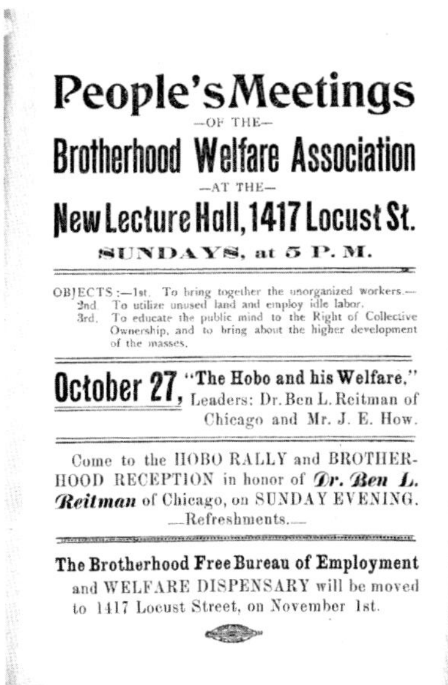

People's Meetings

—OF THE—

Brotherhood Welfare Association

—AT THE—

New Lecture Hall, 1417 Locust St.

SUNDAYS, at 5 P. M.

OBJECTS:—1st. To bring together the unorganized workers.—
2nd. To utilize unused land and employ idle labor.
3rd. To educate the public mind to the Right of Collective Ownership, and to bring about the higher development of the masses.

October 27, "The Hobo and his Welfare," Leaders: Dr. Ben L. Reitman of Chicago and Mr. J. E. How.

Come to the HOBO RALLY and BROTHERHOOD RECEPTION in honor of Dr. Ben L. Reitman of Chicago, on SUNDAY EVENING.
—Refreshments.—

The Brotherhood Free Bureau of Employment and WELFARE DISPENSARY will be moved to 1417 Locust Street, on November 1st.

Brotherhood Welfare Association People's Meetings Announcement.

and San Francisco. The organization published a monthly newspaper, *Hobo News*, whose title—sixty years before identity politics—owned rather than shied away from a conventionally pejorative label. Sold on the street for five cents and providing a voice for the homeless, the paper contained information about labor organizing and employment opportunities as well as poems, essays and articles about the lore of hobo life.[498]

In hopes of further enhancing the "relief, edification and politicization of itinerant workers and homeless indigents," How founded a series of "Hobo Colleges," intended expressly for those on the down and out. Their unorthodox faculties consisted of certified professors but also "labor and leftist political leaders, doctors, and lawyers"; the "wide-ranging curriculum included courses in vagrancy laws, public speaking, and job-searching along with philosophy, literature, and religion."[499] The college's Los Angeles branch featured a room with pictures of Marx, Lenin, Jack London and J. Eads How.[500]

As with many utopian projects, including Harry Hay's and Ricardo Flores Magón's, the Hobo Colleges met with mixed results. On the hopeful side, a team of How's Chicago college students debated a contingent from the University of Chicago and reportedly "tore 'em to pieces." *Hobo News* failed to make it, however, and How's grandiose plan of organizing two million migrant workers into "one big brotherhood" fell far short of its goal.[501]

Silver Lake, and matrimony, entered the picture in tandem in 1924. At age fifty, Eads tied the knot with his secretary, twenty-nine-year-old Ingeborg Sorenson, and engaged none other than R.M. Schindler to design his young bride a house at at 2422 Silver Ridge Avenue. The house was one of Schindler's early successes, and through him, two other interconnections can be added to our book's long list. Access to the architect was likely gleaned through How's friendship with Aline Barnsdall. His kinship to James Leo Herlihy derives from their mutual compassion for the homeless. Herlihy

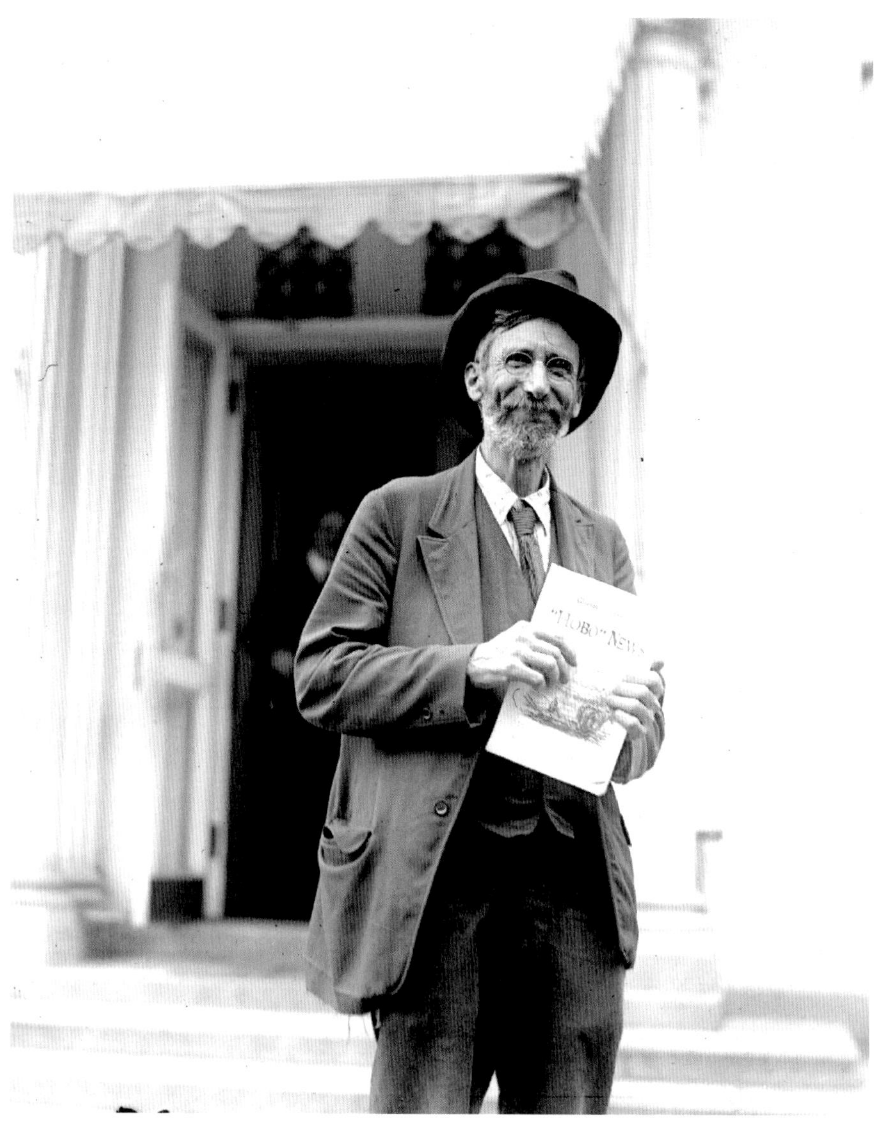

James Eads How holding a copy of the *Hobo News*.

allowed homeless people entry to his house and protected them from the police. How instructed Schindler to build his house within "sight and walking distance of the railyards where hobos would disembark, and that part of the basement bedroom floor be left unlocked and available" to those seeking shelter for the night.[502]

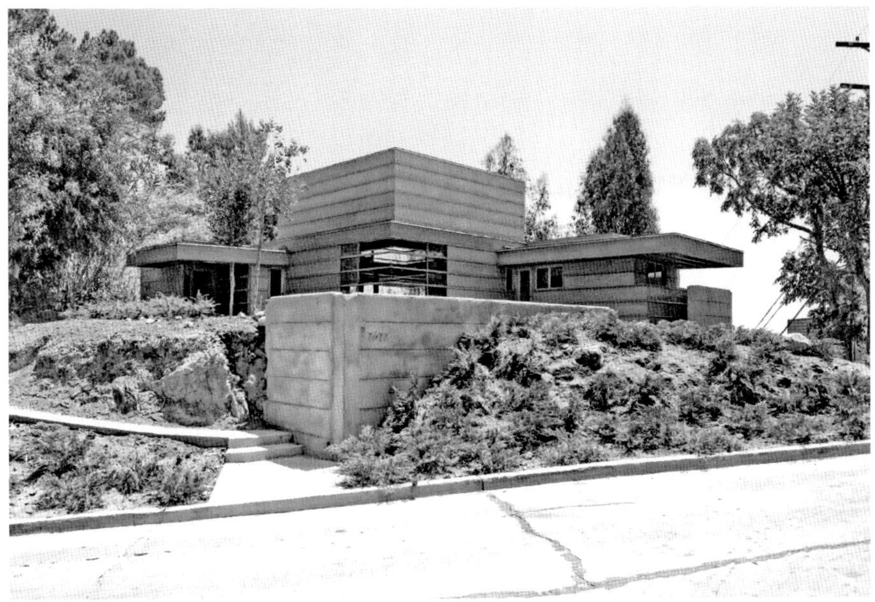

James Eads How House, 2422 Silver Ridge Avenue, R.M. Schindler, 1925.

Though he otherwise gave Schindler free rein in the Silver Ridge house's design, How apparently played fast and loose with payment, prompting Schindler to admonish the Hobo Millionaire in a letter: "It is astonishing how one who seems to feel keenly the brutality of the capitalist system can be entirely careless in his own dealings with his fellow man."[503]

The admonishment apparently applied to "his fellow woman" as well. In 1928, Ingeborg filed for divorce, claiming How had deserted her, "preferring to spend most of his time with his beloved hobos, to the point of staying with them in their seedy hotels."[504] The divorce was finalized two years later, four days before How's death. His eulogy in the August 4, 1930 edition of *Time* magazine read in part: "His death made much newspaper copy. Reporters interviewed hobos passing through their communities. Hobo 'kings' bragged that they would carry on his work, that hobos were hopping on freight trains for his funeral in Washington, D.C., that he was a 'good stiff.'"[505]

Washington police prepared for a "bum's rush" at the funeral held at All Souls Unitarian Church (where former president William Howard Taft was buried). Only one tramp, however, came to pay his respects—Harry W. Johannes Jr. of Baltimore, representing the International Brotherhood Association. Truer to How's spirit than those attending the service, Johannes

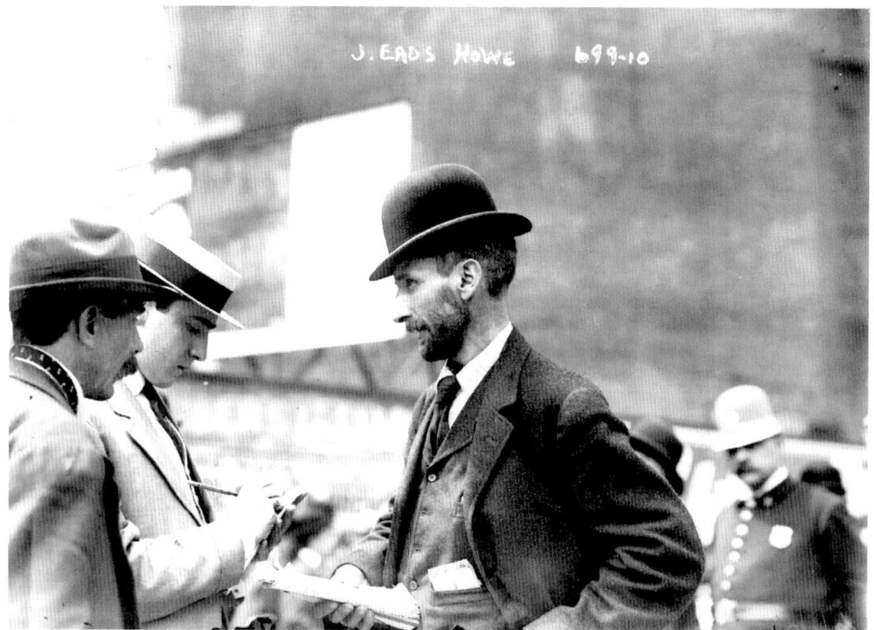

James Eads How, the Hobo Millionaire.

remained outside distributing copies of *Hobo News*. The only eulogy was a phrase from Matthew—"I was an hungred and ye gave me meat; I was thirsty and ye gave me drink"—spoken by the All Souls minister, Dr. Robert B. Day, one of How's classmates at Meadville Theological School. After the funeral, the body was cremated and sent to the family home in St. Louis.[506]

At the time of his death, How's remaining assets consisted of $4,000 in cash, the home in Silver Lake valued at $18,000 and a $600 interest in two empty factory buildings (not chump change in 1930, but a pittance compared to his former wealth).[507] His divorced wife's claim on a portion of the estate for her son, whom she alleged How had adopted, added posthumous insult to injury. But all that was granted to the thirteen-year-old boy, from the erstwhile riches of the Hobo Millionaire, was the sum of $5.[508]

Likely swayed more by his colorful life and selfless altruism than his acrimonious divorce or (comparatively) penurious end, the Los Angeles Cultural-Heritage Commission declared James Eads How's Silver Ridge Avenue house a Los Angeles Historic-Cultural Monument (No. 895) in 2007.

18

FROM HARLEM TO SILVER LAKE

Effa Manley

She was called the "Most Famous Woman in Baseball," was the first woman elected to the National Baseball Hall of Fame and played a significant role in the civil rights movement. Yet her contribution to Silver Lake Bohemia might have gone unrecognized save for a yellowed newspaper clipping found at the bottom of a cardboard box left behind by local historical archivist Ada Brownell.

Brownell planned to write a history of Silver Lake and had collected articles for that purpose when she passed away several years ago. The clipping on Effa Manley was written by Jim Murray, Pulitzer Prize–winning sportswriter for the *Los Angeles Times* from 1961 until his death in 1998. Murray had visited Manley in 1975, when baseball's free agency system just started to take effect. Before free agency, players, unless traded to another team, were contractually bound indefinitely to one team. The system began to fall apart in 1969, when St. Louis Cardinals outfielder Curt Flood appealed his trade to the Philadelphia Phillies all the way to the U.S. Supreme Court. Although the court, in *Flood v. Kuhn,* rejected the appeal, the incident led to the establishment of the current arbitration system in the mid-1970s, granting free agency to players after their contractual period had elapsed. Well aware of Effa's earlier struggle for equity in professional baseball, Murray went to her Silver Lake home to get her opinion of this sea change in the sport's business model.

"A delightful lady of seventy-seven going on thirty-nine" at the time of the Murray interview, Effa, and her since deceased husband, Abe Manley, had owned one of the first Negro League teams in the 1930s.[509] Despite the indignity of a segregated baseball system, black communities gained a measure of pride from their local teams and enjoyment from the high quality of play. Effa and Abe, along with the fans, were understandably ambivalent when Brooklyn Dodgers owner Branch Rickey, the man lauded for integrating baseball, raided the Negro Leagues in the late 1940s—leagues that, according to Murray, "put more great players in the majors than Charlie Finley, Connie Mack, the International League, American Association, Pony League and American Legion put together. Before them, black baseball was a kind of hit-or-miss proposition, a barnstorm through the barnyards; a very short money proposition, half carnival, half sport. The Manleys put the game on a solid business foundation and opened pipelines to keep good players from being sucked into the cotton mills, steel mills and coal mines."[510]

In the long run, of course, integrating baseball, and a few years later society as a whole, would benefit all Americans. And with the advent of free agency, Effa could see progressive change similar to that which she and her husband had fought for all their lives.

"Integrated" Birth

Effa Manley's entrance into the world in March 1897 came as a shock to polite Philadelphia society and to her mother's African American husband, Benjamin Brooks. Effa's birth to James M. Bishop, a wealthy Caucasian stockbroker, and Bertha Brooks, an African American seamstress in Bishop's employ, led Benjamin to divorce Bertha and successfully sue Bishop to the tune of $10,000.[511] Bertha subsequently married Benjamin A. Cole, and the family grew to include seven children, three via Cole. The odd girl out in the family due to her mixed-race background, Effa recalls being looked upon as "this little blond, hazel-eyed white girl, always with Negro children."[512] Her mother didn't reveal her true parentage until a white man's romantic interest in Effa moved her to do so.[513] Thereafter, although always claiming Bishop as her father and never denying her black heritage, Effa chose to straddle a fuzzy racial line. Defined by some as black, by others as white, she "used her ambiguous status to her advantage."[514]

Upon graduation from Penn Central High School in 1916, Effa moved to Harlem and began exploiting her racial duality. Landing a job in a millinery shop in Manhattan, from which she would have been turned away had the employer known she was part black, she found a second career as a fashion model, appearing in shows at Harlem's six-thousand-seat Manhattan Casino. She also married an African American, Charles Bush, though the marriage lasted only a few months.[515]

Effa had better luck with her second husband, Abe Manley, also an African American. A mutual love of baseball brought and held the couple together, though for Effa, at least at first, the love was less for the game itself than for Yankees superstar Babe Ruth. "I was crazy about Babe Ruth. I lived in Harlem, which was close enough to Yankee Stadium for me to walk. So I used to go see all the Yankee games just to see Babe Ruth come up to bat and hope that he'd hit the ball out of the park."[516] Abe's keen interest in the game had been demonstrated in 1929, three years before meeting Effa, when he purchased the all-black, if short-lived, Camden Leafs ball club.[517]

Not-So-Honest Abe?

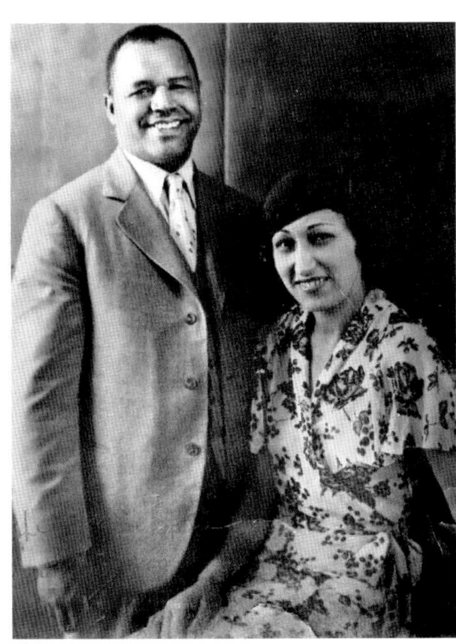

Abe and Effa Manley. *Courtesy of Negro Leagues Baseball Museum.*

Raised in a respectable North Carolina family, Abe had little taste for the stern Christian values imposed by his Quaker parents and left home at a young age. Moving to Norfolk, Virginia, he worked variously as a chauffeur, day laborer and barber, earning extra money running numbers and investing in real estate.[518] In 1925, he moved to Camden, New Jersey, and opened the Rest-A-While Club, a cover for a gambling operation whose clientele boasted politicians, doctors, lawyers and other members of Camden's African American elite.[519] The numbers racket could prove a lucrative but also a risky business, as Abe found out in 1932, when a bomb exploded in the club, blowing away the front of the building and driving Manley to take a friend's advice: "You'd better get out of town."[520]

Abe resettled in Harlem, where his wealth gave him entrée into the black district's upper-class society. Effa claimed she met Abe for the first time at a World Series game at Yankee Stadium in 1932. According to a newspaper report, the two were seen together in January that year at the Camden Charity Ball, where Effa stole the show from the other ladies, all dressed in white, with her "flowing black lace and pearls."[521]

Abe and Effa married in 1933 and settled in Harlem's Sugar Hill district, home to the area's upper crust, including black leaders W.E.B. Du Bois, Roy Wilkins, Walter White and young attorney Thurgood Marshall. Abe lavished Effa with mink coats, Lincoln Continentals and diamond rings, including a five-carat wedding ring purchased at Tiffany's. Effa got an extra kick out of the purchase when she overheard a salesgirl mutter that "this old Negro man had bought a ring for this pretty white woman."[522]

CIVIL RIGHTS AND ETHNIC PRIDE

Effa enjoyed the trappings of wealth, but noblesse oblige and her sense of social justice motivated her membership in several altruistic black organizations. She joined the NAACP's anti-lynching campaign and helped organize relief efforts for victims of the disastrous Ohio and Mississippi River floods of 1937.[523] She assumed leadership roles in the Edgecombe Sanitarium Renaissance Committee, working to save a private, black-run hospital from bankruptcy, and the Children's Camp Committee of New York, providing leisure activities for black youth. Her work with the Citizens' League for Fair Play, which organized boycotts of white-owned stores that denied employment to blacks, included involvement in its successful boycott of Blumstein's, Harlem's biggest department store, marking a critical moment in the early struggle for civil rights.[524]

Abe also sought to benefit blacks, and turn a profit, by purchasing a franchise in the nascent National Negro League (NNL) in 1934. His Brooklyn Eagles joined the New York Cubans as the city's second Negro League team. After an unsatisfactory start in Brooklyn, Abe moved the team to Newark, New Jersey, where it stayed for the next thirteen years. Effa was heavily involved in the club's day-to-day operations. According to Eagles pitcher Max Manning, "She ruled the roost." Besides administrative duties, she added a woman's touch: "She was interested in appearances—uniforms neat, shoes shined. She was particular about that."[525]

Under Effa's guidance, the Eagles became a source of pride for Newark's African American population and helped forge an important bond between baseball and the black community. The team's headquarters on Hamilton Avenue, the players' "home away from home" at the Grand Hotel and the team's ballpark, Ruppert Stadium, all became sacred places in the community's mythical folklore.[526] While Abe kept his eye on the bottom line, Effa never lost sight of civic obligations. She organized fundraisers at Eagles games on behalf of the community and even sponsored her own youth baseball team, the Cubs.[527] The peak of the Eagles' success came in 1946, when the team won the Negro League World Series.

After Jackie Robinson broke the color barrier in 1947 as a starter and eventual superstar with Branch Rickey's Dodgers, the Negro Leagues drifted into oblivion as its better players opted to join Robinson in the more prestigious, and lucrative, Major Leagues. Although it was certainly an honor to be inducted into the New Jersey Hall of Fame in November 1948 (along with Count Basie, Sara Vaughan and Paul Robeson), Abe and Effa disbanded the Newark Eagles with the words, "We're not quitters, it's just impossible to continue. Baseball has become a rich man's hobby and we're not rich."[528]

His health likely affected by the demise of the Negro Leagues he helped found, Abe Manley died in 1952.[529] Effa married again in 1953, to musician Henry Morton Clinton, former host at the Paradise Club in Atlantic City. But the marriage lasted less than a year and ended with Clinton making off with "a sizeable chunk of her money."[530]

Hoping to start things afresh, Effa moved to Los Angeles in 1958. With fourth husband Charles Wesley Alexander, an old boyfriend and a musician and singer, she settled down in a (still standing) bungalow at 4322 Kenwood Avenue in South Los Angeles. The marriage, sadly again, was short-lived, lasting about a year.

With the funds she had left, Effa, now in her sixties, purchased a four-unit bungalow court at 451 North Occidental Boulevard in Silver Lake. She hoped that some of her Philadelphia siblings (she had no children) might move in with her. Though none accepted the offer, the rent on the three other units covered the mortgage and other expenses, allowing Effa to live financially unencumbered in her Silver Lake sliver of paradise.[531]

Seemingly forgotten except by Jim Murray and other sports aficionados, Effa remained in Silver Lake for the next thirty-three years, ever a baseball

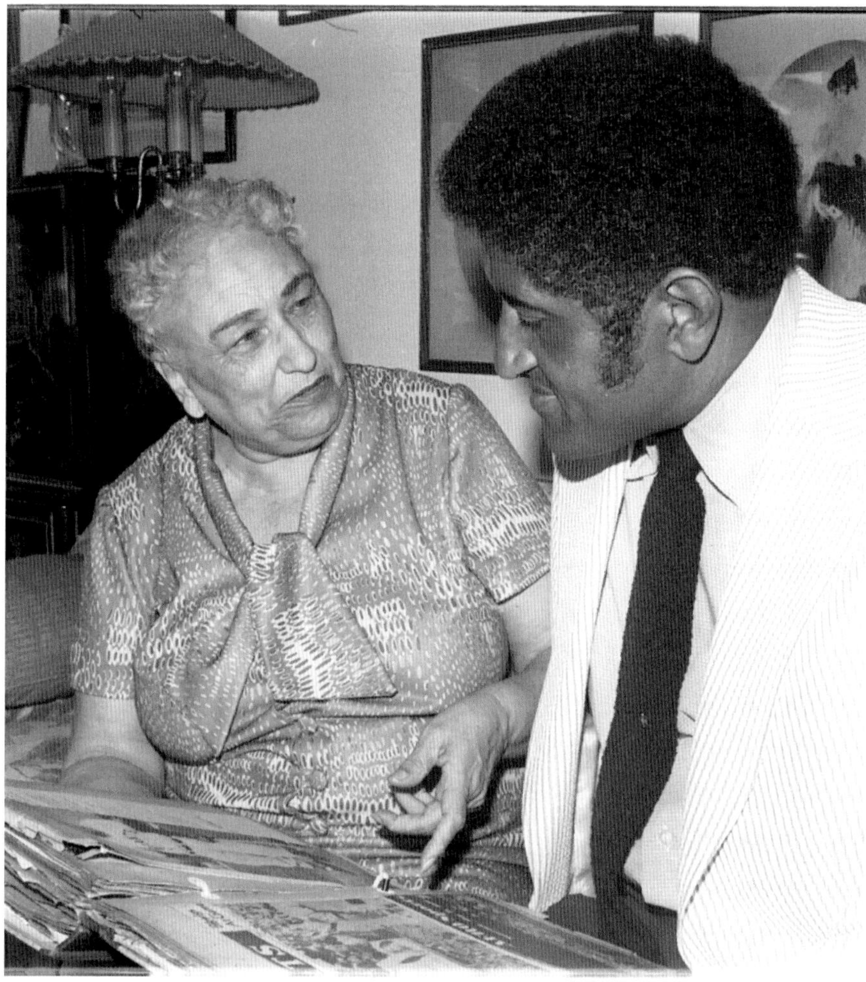

Effa Manley looks over a scrapbook with one of her former players, Don Newcombe, at her Silver Lake home, August 7, 1973. *AP Photo, courtesy of Negro Leagues Baseball Museum.*

fan and tireless worker for civil rights. She died on March 8, 1981, three weeks short of her eighty-first birthday, and was interred at Holy Cross Cemetery in Culver City. Effa Manley's induction into the National Baseball Hall of Fame, as the first woman to be so honored, took place posthumously in 2006.[532]

EPILOGUE

This book does not pretend to be an all-encompassing history of the cutting-edge cultural and political figures who helped turn Silver Lake into the bohemian epicenter of Los Angeles. Its aim is to highlight the most significant contributors to the area's avant-garde ethos, but several notable people and places surely slipped through the cracks.

Those we are aware of but were unable to fit into this volume include the following: noir novelist Raymond Chandler (1888–1959), who lived briefly in the Moreno Highlands section in the 1930s; Chicano educator/activist and Silver Lake resident Saul Castro (1933–2013), who organized the 1968 high school student walkouts to protest unequal conditions in East Los Angeles schools; psychologist Evelyn Hooker (1907–1996), whose research in Silver Lake in the late 1950s led to the American Psychiatric Association Manual's de-listing of homosexuality as a mental disorder in 1973; Monte Sano Hospital and Sanitarium, California's first osteopathic hospital, which served patients on Waverly Terrace from 1923 into the 1970s; explorer Antonia F. Futterer (1871–1951), likely inspiration for the Indian Jones character, who founded the still-active Holyland Bible Knowledge Society just down the street from Rose Scharlin School; architect James H. Garrott (1897–1991), cited but not extensively covered in the book, who designed Loren Miller's and his own Silver Lake home and shared an office with Gregory Ain; and artist Bernice Lee "Burr" Singer (1912–1992), prominent watercolorist and lithographer, whose Panorama Terrace home was designed by Garrott. In these and other worthy candidates lie the seeds of another book.

We also did not mean to suggest that Silver Lake is the only section in the city, or even in the immediate area, where a nexus of visionaries lived or plied their trade. Silver Lake is not a gated community. It is neither geographically nor demographically isolated. It shares a stretch of the Santa Monica Mountains, Sunset Boulevard and a vibrant character with several neighboring communities.

Had we expanded our parameters into Echo Park and Elysian Heights, premier printmaker Paul Landacre (1883–1963) and his artists circle, Communist leader Miriam Brooks Sherman (1910–1978) and her Red Hill brigade, *Nation* editor and historian Carey McWilliams (1905–1980) and the Semi-Tropic Spiritualists group (active in the early 1900s) would have come into play. Franklin Hills and Los Feliz would have offered a wealth of colorful movie people and additional modernist buildings.

And why stop with the immediate area? Los Angeles, for all the La-La Land epithets heaped upon it, has long been an incubator for radical ideas and practices. Charles Lummis's "Arroyo set" salons (which he called "noises") of the 1890s and early 1900s in Highland Park attracted a who's who of artists and intellectuals. Boyle Heights and other East Los Angeles communities, as the Gregory Ain chapter showed, were a hotbed of leftist activity from the 1920s to the '50s. Central Avenue in South Los Angeles, which Loren Miller frequented, became a hub of an African American musical and literary movement mirroring New York's Harlem Renaissance. Two bookstores, in particular, Larry Edmunds in Hollywood and Jake Zeitlin's downtown, held regular gatherings of major writers and other artists in the 1930s and beyond. Topping the list of gatherings in prestige and firepower were the Westside émigré salons attended by the cream of Europe's cultural elite, whose musical talent Peter Yates tapped for his Evenings on the Roof concerts.

Conceding other pockets of creativity and agitation does not detract from Silver Lake's status as L.A.'s historical Left Bank or Greenwich Village. No other community in the city boasted the range and concentration of this area's artists and activists. No other community matched their diversity of race, gender and sexual orientation. No other community—including those in Paris and New York—exhibited the unique interconnection of people and place, of individuals with one another but also with the built and natural environment.

Community and environment are key. Bohemianism, for all its emphasis on individuality and unconventionality, cannot thrive without common ground and a circle of like-minded souls. Silver Lake Bohemia, with a boost from the happenstance of history, managed to fuse these elements to an astonishing degree, producing a magic potion whose greatest impact may lie in the past but whose effects live on.

NOTES

Preface

1. For more on Silver Lake's more recent and ongoing bohemianism, see, from an architectural aspect, Bester, *Bohemian Modern*, and, more generally, the Silver Lake Neighborhood Council History Collective/Bob Herzog Memorial Archives, USC Libraries Special Collections, many of whose video interviews are available online at youtube.com.

Chapter 1

2. "Aline Barnsdall: The Ultimate Iconoclast."
3. On the house's naming for Aline's favorite flower, see Hoffmann, *Frank Lloyd Wright's Hollyhock House*, 1; on its naming for the flowers on the hill, see Secrest, *Frank Lloyd Wright*, 268.
4. Vankin, "L.A.'s Hollyhock House."
5. Karasnick, *Oilman's Daughter*, 2, 5, 17.
6. Herr, *Aline Barnsdall's Olive Hill Project*, 7.
7. Karasnick, *Oilman's Daughter*, 94.
8. Ibid., 19, 32.
9. Ibid., 20.
10. Ibid., 25.
11. Ibid., 25–27, 30.
12. Ibid., 32.

13. Ibid; Watt, *American Drama.*
14. Karasnick, *Oilman's Daughter*, 49, 10. Other Hollywood notables attending the premiere included Harold Lloyd, Gloria Swanson, Theda Bara, Marie Dressler, Wallace Beery, Bebe Daniels, Erich von Stroheim, Thomas Ince, Samuel Goldwyn, Jesse Lasky and Carl Laemmle.
15. Ibid., 61, 63. George was rewarded with a mortgage-free ranch in Arizona.
16. Ibid., 59. The agency became the Federal Bureau of Investigation in 1935.
17. Ibid., 44, 65–66, 196, 219–21.
18. Ibid., 70, 73.
19. Secrest, *Frank Lloyd Wright*, 266–67.
20. Karasnick, *Oilman's Daughter*, 95.
21. Ibid., 38.
22. Ibid., 77–78, 92.
23. Secrest, *Frank Lloyd Wright*, 265, 268.
24. Karasnick, *Oilman's Daughter*, 79–80.
25. Ibid., 87.
26. Ibid., 100, 73, 79, 91.
27. Ibid., 89, 90, 98.
28. Ibid., 191–92.
29. Ibid., 196–200, 208.
30. Ibid., 211.
31. Ibid., 215–17. In Betty's defense, Aline herself, to help finance the theater project, had planned "tall commercial buildings along Vermont Avenue and three-story buildings along Sunset Boulevard" (Herr, *Aline Barnsdall's Olive Hill Project*, 9).
32. Karasnick, *Oilman's Daughter*, 217–19.
33. Ibid., 219–20. Vincent Brook's wife, Karen, recalls that when she was a docent at Hollyhock House in the 1980s, Hjelte's disinformation was not part of her instruction.
34. Kim, "Behind the Scenes."
35. Karasnick, *Oilman's Daughter*, 222.

Chapter 2

36. "Vienna Secession." The motto was inscribed above the entrance to the Secession building.
37. McCoy, *Five California Architects*, 151.

38. Sheine, *R.M. Schindler*, 11; Long, "Alternative Path to Modernism," 21.
39. Gebhard, *Schindler*, 13.
40. Ibid., 15.
41. Ibid., 25.
42. Ibid., 15; McCoy, *Five California Architects*, 153.
43. Sheine, *R.M. Schindler*, 9, 38, 41.
44. Noever, *Schindler by MAK*, 10.
45. Crosse, "Pauline Gibling Schindler"; see also Sweeny, "Life at Kings Road."
46. Noever, *Schindler by MAK*, 1.
47. Hines, *Architecture of the Sun*, 253.
48. McCoy, *Five California Architects*, 150.
49. "Rudolph Schindler."
50. Ibid.
51. Hines, *Architecture of the Sun*, 254.
52. Ibid.
53. McCoy, *Five California Architects*, 152.
54. Lamprecht, *Neutra: Complete Works*, 10.
55. Ibid., 14.
56. McCoy, *Five California Architects*, 152.
57. Neutra, "Neutra Genius."
58. Hines, *Architecture of the Sun*, 275.
59. Ibid., 279, 283.
60. Ibid., 286.
61. Ibid., 286, 287, 306.
62. Lamprecht, *Neutra*, 16.
63. Sheine, *R.M. Schindler*, 124; Hines, *Richard Neutra,* 96.
64. Lamprecht, *Neutra*, 30.
65. Neutra, *Neutras Then & Later.*
66. Ibid., 573.
67. On the Chavez Ravine saga, see Lassett, *Shameful Victory*.
68. Lamprecht, *Neutra*, 7, 11.
69. Keeps, "A Bit of Genius."
70. Lubell, *Architect's Newspaper.*
71. Hines, *Architecture of the Sun*, 362.
72. Ibid., 605.
73. Author interview with Sarah Lorenzen, July 13, 2013.

Chapter 3

74. The Mensheviks were a socialist faction in pre-Soviet Russia opposed to Vladimir Lenin's Bolsheviks.
75. Hines, *Architecture of the Sun*, 432.
76. Cohen, "Community of Minsk," 74.
77. McWilliams, *Southern California*, 322.
78. Davis, *City of Quartz*, 24.
79. Ibid., 24, 25.
80. Ibid., 26.
81. McCoy, *Second Generation*, 86.
82. Hines, *Architecture of the Sun*, 432.
83. McCoy, *Second Generation*, 86.
84. Ibid., 87.
85. Denzer, *Gregory Ain*, 30.
86. Ibid., 38.
87. Ibid., 35, 39.
88. Ibid., 35.
89. Ibid., 63.
90. "Gregory Ain's Hay House."
91. Denzer, *Gregory Ain*, 94.
92. Ibid., 66.
93. Hines, *Richard Neutra*, 183; Denzer, *Gregory Ain*, 65.
94. Author interview with Antony Unruh, March 24, 2016.
95. Denzer, *Gregory Ain*, 109, 130.
96. Ibid., 169; McCoy, *Second Generation*, 144.
97. Antony Unruh interview.
98. Author interview with Marvin Malecha and Richard Chylinski.
99. Hines, *Architecture of the Sun*, 485.
100. Ibid., 486.
101. Ibid., 490.
102. Ibid., 488, 497.
103. Germany, *Harwell Hamilton Harris*, 64.
104. "Designated Historic-Cultural Monuments."
105. Wagener, *Soriano*, 41.
106. Hines, *Architecture of the Sun*, 485.
107. Ibid., 455, 456.
108. Ibid., 457.
109. Ibid.

110. Author interview with Michael Lehrer, January 11, 2010. Michael's wife, Mia Lehrer, is herself a celebrated landscape architect. She helped design the Silver Lake Meadow directly across from the VDL House and is among those, including Frank Gehry, involved with the revolutionary revitalization of the L.A. River.

Chapter 4

111. Nin, *Diary of Anaïs Nin*: *Volume Seven* (1980), 316; e-mail to the author from Phyl van Ammers, January 21, 2015.
112. Author interview with Ruth Ross, January 23, 2015.
113. As was falsely claimed in her lifetime, Nin's father, Joaquin Nin, was unrelated to the Spanish revolutionary Andres Nin (Bair, *Anais Nin: A Biography*, 525).
114. Ibid., 28–49.
115. Her diary writing had begun as early as 1914, and the short stories in the posthumously published *Waste of Timelessness* also were written before 1932 (see Bair, *Anaïs Nin*).
116. Nin, *Diary*: *Volume Seven*, 198, 236.
117. Bair, *Anaïs Nin*, 204, 351, 406, 483.
118. Ibid., 360, 590.
119. Ibid., 326, 437.
120. Fitch, *Erotic Life of Anaïs Nin*, 288, 351.
121. Bair, *Anaïs Nin*, 393.
122. Nin, *Diary: Volume Six*, 64.
123. Ibid., 337, 332. LSD guru Richard Alpert told Nin that he only gained true understanding of her work after dropping acid (Nin, *Diary: Volume Six*, 331).
124. Nin, *Diary: Volume Seven*, 4.
125. Ruth Ross interview; Bair, *Anaïs Nin*, 394; Fitch, *Erotic Life*, 330.
126. Bair, *Anaïs Nin*, 443, 499; Nin, *Diary: Volume Seven*, 53.
127. Nin, *Diary: Volume Seven*, 192, 153; "Eric Lloyd Wright" video interview.
128. Ruth Ross interview.
129. Kraft, *Anaïs Nin: The Last Days*, 6.
130. Ibid., 7.
131. Bair, *Anaïs Nin*, 516.
132. Ibid., 481.
133. Fitch, *Erotic Life*, 314, 383; Bair, *Anaïs Nin*, 514; Ross interview. We defer to Ross, who actually witnessed the event, in her assertion that the waters

near Catalina Island, not Santa Monica Bay (as Bair claims), are where Nin's ashes were scattered.
134. Bair, *Anaïs Nin*, 514, 520.
135. Ward, *Understanding James Leo Herlihy*, 3.
136. Bair, *Anaïs Nin*, 478.
137. E-mail to the author from Katya Meyer, March 6, 2015.
138. Kraft, *Anaïs Nin*, 4.
139. Author interview with Miriam Meyer, January 21, 2015; e-mail to the author from Miriam Meyer, March 6, 2015.
140. Nin, *Diary: Volume Seven*, 341.

CHAPTER 5

141. Nin, *Diary of Anaïs Nin: Volume Five*, 98.
142. Herlihy was also partly raised in Chillicothe, Ohio (Snyder, "James Leo Herlihy").
143. Ward, *Understanding James Leo Herlihy*, 8.
144. Ibid., 7. The plays were variously performed off-Broadway between 1965 and 1973.
145. Bonge, "Obituary of James Leo Herlihy," 16.
146. Ward, *Understanding*, 6.
147. Ibid., 3.
148. The first play, *Telephone Portrait of Scotty and His Three Women*, was unperformed and unpublished.
149. Nin, *Diary: Volume Five*, 5, 118.
150. Ward, *Understanding*, 21, 30.
151. Ibid., 4, 9.
152. Ibid., 11; Thoreau, *Walden*; Lowell, "Memories of West Street," 90.
153. Nin, *Diary: Volume Five*, 5, 53; Ward, *Understanding*, 38.
154. Ward, *Understanding*, 58, 54, 55; Herlihy, *Midnight Cowboy*, 41.
155. Ward, *Understanding*, 65.
156. Ibid., 8.
157. Ibid. 6, 7.
158. Ibid., 7.
159. Herlihy, *Season of the Witch*, 218.
160. Ward, *Understanding*, 8.
161. Bair, *Anaïs Nin*, 511.
162. Bonge, "Obituary"; Snyder, "James Leo Herlihy." Herlihy also appeared in the film *French Style* (1963).

Chapter 6

163. Viertel, *Kindness of Strangers*; Bilski, *Jewish Women.*
164. Yates, "Evenings on the Roof."
165. Crawford, *Evenings On and Off the Roof*, 36. For the first four years the regular admission charge was $0.50, $0.25 for subscribers; in 1944, it jumped to $1.10 regular, $0.45 for subscribers (36, 63).
166. Bilski, *Jewish Women*, 3; Brook, *Driven to Darkness*, 80.
167. Reinhardt, *Genius*, 284.
168. Frances's mother, Grace Mullen, founded the Redlands Bowl in 1924 (Crawford, *Evenings*, 14).
169. Ibid., 12.
170. Yates, "Column and a Roof," 11.
171. Crawford, *Evenings*, 18.
172. Ibid., 2.
173. Ibid., 2, 8.
174. Ibid., 24.
175. Ibid., 9.
176. Ibid., 20.
177. Ibid.
178. Ibid., 21. Yates eventually met Krishnamurti in the 1930s "and continued to be inspired by him in the 1940s and 1950s" (298, n42).
179. Ibid., 21.
180. Swan, *Music in the Southwest*, 284; Crawford, *Evenings*, 21.
181. Yates, "Evenings"; e-mail to the author from Peter "Bart" Yates, May 4, 2015.
182. Crawford, *Evenings*, 22, 23. Buhlig was also the young John Cage's piano teacher (Timmons, *Trouble with Harry Hay*, 75).
183. Crawford, *Evenings*, 34, 26.
184. Ibid., 4–5.
185. Ibid., 4; see also Smith, *Mary Carr Moore*, 175–85.
186. Crawford, *Evenings*, 17.
187. Yates, "Evenings."
188. Crawford, *Evenings*, 32.
189. Ibid., 1, 13, 8.
190. Crawford, *Windfall of Musicians*, 34, 53.
191. Crawford, *Evenings*, 9.
192. Morton, "A Remembrance of Peter Yates." From 1910 to 1961, the Los Angeles County Museum of Art was part of the Los Angeles County

Museum of History, Science and Art in Exposition Park. In 1961, it became a separate museum, and in 1965, it moved to its current location at 5905 Wilshire Boulevard.

193. Swed, "Weirdness," E6.
194. Yates, "Evenings," 31.
195. Crawford, *Evenings*, 44.
196. Founded in 1919, the Assistance League is dedicated "to improving the quality of the lives of at-risk children and families and providing vital social services in the Los Angeles community" ("Assistance League").
197. Crawford, *Evenings*, 81, 86, 96.
198. Ibid., 53–54.
199. Ibid., 71.
200. Ibid., 80, 146.
201. E-mail to the author from Phyl van Ammers, January 21, 2015.
202. Sontag, "Pilgrimage."
203. Van Ammers e-mail, January 21, 2015.
204. Author phone interview with Baylis Glascock, April 13, 2015; Crawford, *Evenings*.
205. E-mails to the author from Phyl van Ammers, March 30, 2015, and January 21, 2015.
206. Glascock interview; van Ammers e-mail, March 30, 2015. Peter "Bart" Yates, in a phone interview, April 7, 2015, reinforced Glascock's and van Ammers's statements about Yates's (and Mullen's) generosity.
207. The once-harmonious relationship between Yates and Morton soured once Morton took over the concert series, causing a feud that ensnared adherents on both sides (Crawford, *Evenings*, 287).
208. Yates, "Evenings."
209. "Peter Yates Papers." Yates had earlier published his poetry in *A Smaller Poem Book* (1946).
210. Swed, "All the Arts."
211. Percussionist Jonathan Helper took over as artistic director in 2015 (Swed, "Weirdness").
212. "Monday Evening Concerts."

Chapter 7

213. West Hollywood became a separate municipality within Los Angeles County in 1984.

214. Timmons, *Trouble with Harry Hay*, 3.
215. Ibid., 4–6.
216. Ibid., 18.
217. Ibid., 20.
218. His father's physical abuse caused Harry permanent hearing damage in one ear (Timmons, *Trouble with Harry Hay*).
219. Ibid., 21, 28.
220. Ibid., 27; White, *Pre-Gay LA*, 11; Hurewitz, *Bohemian Los Angeles*, 238.
221. Timmons, *Trouble with Harry Hay*, 32–33.
222. Ibid., 34.
223. Ibid., 36.
224. Ibid., 38, 40.
225. Ibid., 41–43; Faderman and Timmons, *Gay L.A.*, 109–10. The Berlin group was called the Scientific-Humanitarian Committee.
226. Timmons, *Trouble with Harry Hay*, 49, 53.
227. Ibid., 54.
228. Ibid., 57–59.
229. Ibid., 63–64, 78; Hurewitz, *Bohemian*, 153–54.
230. Timmons, *Trouble with Harry Hay*, 96.
231. Ibid., 80–81, 86–87; Roscoe, *Radically Gay*, 356.
232. Timmons, *Trouble with Harry Hay*, 100.
233. Ibid.
234. Ibid., 100, 102, 104, 106–12.
235. Ibid., 115–19.
236. Ibid., 116.
237. Ibid., 116, 123.
238. Ibid., 124–28.
239. Ibid., 116.
240. Hurewitz, *Bohemian*, 128, 140–41; Brook, *Land of Smoke and Mirrors*, 220.
241. White, *Pre-Gay LA*, 1–2.
242. Roscoe, *Radically Gay*, 60.
243. Hurewitz, *Bohemian*, 247.
244. Timmons, *Trouble with Harry Hay*, 136, 139.
245. Ibid., 129–30, 144; White, *Pre-Gay LA*, 16–18; Faderman and Timmons, *Gay L.A*, 106–8. Mattachine Society would not become the official name until April 1951, when it replaced the interim "Society of Fools." The French *mattachine* comes from the Italian *mattachino*, the name of a court jester character in *commedia dell-arte*; *mattachino* stems from the Arab *mutawajjihin*, meaning "mask wearer" (Johansson, *Outing*, 92).

246. Timmons, *Trouble with Harry Hay*, 130.
247. White, *Pre-Gay LA*, 15, 17.
248. Timmons, *Trouble*, 154.
249. Ibid., 147.
250. White, *Pre-Gay LA*, 14–15; Kepner, *Rough News*, 1; Myerhoff, *Number Our Days*, 32; Faderman and Timmons, *Gay L.A.*, 9–14.
251. Timmons, *Trouble with Harry Hay*, 104; Frieberg, "Harry Hay; "Gregory Ain's Hay House."
252. Timmons, *Trouble with Harry Hay*, 158, 160, 170–71, 174–76.
253. Ibid., 180, 183.
254. Ibid., 209, 214, 227, 230.
255. Ibid., 246.
256. Ibid., 249.
257. Ibid., 249, 282–84.
258. Ibid., 296.
259. Ibid., 287.
260. Joe, "Black Cat Bar," 4. The Los Angeles–centered gay organization ONE, Inc., and the magazine *ONE*, cofounded by Dale Jennings in 1952 and 1953, survive and themselves spawned the Homosexual Information Center (HIC), the Institute for the Study of Human Resources (ISHR) and the ONE National Gay & Lesbian Archives at USC Libraries.

Chapter 8

261. Boyd, *Take Off the Masks*, 14.
262. Ibid., 11.
263. Ibid., 21.
264. Boyd, *As I Live*, 8.
265. Ibid., 10. Malcolm was also part Jewish (Boyd, "My Jewish Grandfather").
266. Boyd, *As I Live*, 8, 9.
267. Thompson, *Advocate Days*, 12; author in-person interview with Mark Thompson, May 18, 2015.
268. Boyd, *As I Live*, 13–15, 19.
269. Ibid., 23, 34–35.
270. Ibid., 34; Boyd, *Take Off the Masks*, 50, 54.
271. Boyd, *Take Off the Masks*, 57; Boyd, *As I Live*, 3–5, 28.
272. Boyd, *As I Live*, 44–45; Boyd, *Take Off the Masks*, 72.

273. Boyd, *As I Live*, 61–63; Boyd, *Take Off the Masks*, 59, 61.
274. Boyd, *As I Live*, 70, 78.
275. Ibid., 114.
276. Ibid., 125.
277. Rourke, "Frank Priest."
278. Boyd, *Take Off the Masks*, 99.
279. Ibid.
280. Boyd, *As I Live*, 189, 190.
281. Ibid., 230–36; Rourke, "Frank Priest."
282. Boyd, *As I Live*, 268.
283. Ibid., 242, 250.
284. Integrity USA, founded in 1974, is a nonprofit organization of lesbian, gay, bisexual and transgender Episcopalians and their straight friends ("Integrity").
285. Boyd, *Take Off the Masks*, 123–24.
286. Rourke, "Frank Priest."
287. Thomas, *Disturber of the Peace* (documentary film).
288. Thompson, *Advocate Days*, 20–23; Thompson in-person interview.
289. Thompson, *Advocate Days*, 66.
290. Ibid., 101.
291. Thompson in-person interview.
292. Ibid.
293. Ibid; see also "Malcolm Boyd and Mark Thompson" video interview.
294. Thompson in-person interview.
295. Rourke, "Frank Priest."
296. Boyd, "We Are a Gentle, Loving People."
297. Thompson in-person interview. Thompson calls Kepner "one of the unsung heroes" of the LGBTQ movement (author phone interview, June 20, 2015).
298. Thompson in-person interview. The Episcopal Diocese of Los Angeles serves seventy thousand church members and 147 neighborhood congregations in six Southern California counties ("Episcopal Diocese of Los Angeles").
299. Thompson in-person interview.

Chapter 9

300. Jim Kepner and Stuart Timmons belong on the list as well, among many others.

301. Joe, "Black Cat Bar," 1. Several other gay protests, of various kinds and sizes, had taken place in the United States from at least as early as 1959 (see "List of LGBT actions").
302. Descriptions of the New Year's raid at The Black Cat and New Faces differ. The one here is a synthesis of those in Faderman and Timmons, *Gay L.A.*, 156; Burroway, "Temerity of a Kiss"; "Alexei Romanoff" video interview; "Alexei Romanoff and the LGBT Civil Rights Legacy."
303. Romanoff video interview.
304. Burroway, "Temerity." Hollywood dropped its content-policing Production Code in 1966, replacing it in 1968 with the current ratings system.
305. Romanoff video interview; "Alexei Romanoff and the LGBT," 5. Romanoff started New Faces (formerly Patty's Pub, another gay bar) with Lee Roy in 1962 but eventually sold his share.
306. Romanoff video interview.
307. Ibid. The Canyon Club is now a bucolic retreat called the Mountain Mermaid.
308. Faderman and Timmons, *Gay L.A.*, 155. Other gay groups involved in the protest and/or helping pay The Black Cat defendants' legal fees were the Southern California Council on Religion and Homophiles and the Tavern Guild of Southern California ("Alexei Romanoff and the LGBT," 8).
309. Faderman and Timmons, *Gay L.A.*, 155.
310. "Malcolm Boyd and Mark Thompson" video interview.
311. Faderman and Timmons, *Gay L.A.*, 157; Romanoff video interview; "Alexei Romanoff and the LGBT," 4; Wes Joe e-mail to the author, July 9, 2015.
312. Burroway, "Temerity."
313. Romanoff video interview; "Alexei Romanoff and the LGBT," 8.
314. The signs appear in photos of the protest hanging on the walls of the reopened Black Cat (courtesy of the ONE National Gay & Lesbian Archives at USC Libraries).
315. Faderman and Timmons, *Gay L.A.*, 157.
316. Ibid. Another important offshoot of The Black Cat raid (plus another raid at The Patch bar in August 1967) was the founding of the gay-oriented Metropolitan Community Church on Melrose, led by pastor Troy Perry (163).
317. "Alexei Romanoff and the LBGT," 6. Reagan was elected in November 1966 but took office in January 1967. According to David Fahar, Romanov's husband, there was actually a bit of a lull in gay bar harassment in the two years prior to Reagan's election.

318. Ibid., 3, 7–8.
319. Author interview with Charlie Conrad, Lindsay Kennedy and Dean Malouf, June 30, 2015.
320. Ibid.
321. Ibid.
322. Joe, "Black Cat Bar," 4, 5.
323. "Black Cat: Site of Black Cat Protest."
324. "Alexei Romanoff and the LGBT," 10, 12.
325. Bradley, "Lesbian Writers Series," 24.
326. Rabbi Ruth Podolsky e-mail to Wes Joe, July 2, 2015.
327. Ibid.
328. Whiting, "Different Light."
329. Boyd and Thompson video interview.
330. Whiting, "Different Light"; Podolsky, "Remembering."
331. Boyd and Thompson video interview.
332. Podolsky e-mail.
333. Bradley, "Lesbian," 27.
334. Whiting, "Different Light"; Faderman and Timmons, *Gay L.A.*, 172.
335. Whiting, "Different Light"; the notion of "creative destruction" is from Schumpeter, *Capitalism*.
336. "Silver Lake gay landmark"; Raymond, "Permit Existed"; "Silver Lake's A Different Light Bookstore."
337. Raymond, "Permit Existed."
338. Boyd and Thompson video interview.

Chapter 10

339. Romo, *East Los Angeles*, 3; Sanchez, "What's Good for Boyle Heights," 635; Estrada, *Los Angeles Plaza*, 209.
340. Bufe and Verter, *Dreams of Freedom*, 43.
341. Ibid., 30–31; Day, *Prison Notebooks*, 36–38. Day's book is a historical novel based on Ricardo's letters. Scholars disagree about Teodoro's Indian ancestry.
342. Bufe and Verter, *Dreams of Freedom*, 31.
343. Ibid.; Day, *Prison Notebooks*, 48.
344. Bufe and Verter, *Dreams of Freedom*, 32–33; Day, *Prison Notebooks*, 52. Scholars are divided on when precisely Ricardo embraced full-fledged anarchist ideals.

345. Bufe and Verter, *Dreams of Freedom*, 35; Day, *Prison Notebooks*, 103. Jesús had swung to the moderate left by this time and later sided with Madero in opposition to Ricardo.
346. Day, *Prison Notebooks*; Bufe, *Dreams of Freedom.* Ricardo stayed briefly in San Francisco and Sacramento before returning to and settling in L.A.
347. Bufe and Verter, *Dreams of Freedom*, 50, 57, 64.
348. Ibid., 70.
349. The Labor Temple, built in 1907, spurred "a briefly lively and vibrant scene of proletarian culture and politics" (Greenstein, *Bread and Hyacinths*, 44).
350. Day, *Prison Notebooks*, 220; Bufe and Verter, *Dreams of Freedom, 73.*
351. Day, *Prison Notebooks*, 154, 127, 76, 6.
352. Bufe and Verter, *Dreams of Freedom*, 74. Ricardo "never used the word 'anarchism' in any published document until after his release from prison in 1914" (ibid., 38).
353. Ibid., 74. The Narodniks were Russian agrarian populists of the 1860s and 1870s who influenced later revolutionary movements.
354. Estrada, *Los Angeles Plaza*, 250–51. Otis and Chandler owned 850,000 acres in Mexico, and Doheny owned the Mexican Petroleum Company. Hearst's *Los Angeles Examiner* initially courted labor but by 1907 had fallen out of favor with them (Greenstein, *Bread and Hyacinths*, 43–44).
355. Bufe and Verter, *Dreams of Freedom*, 69.
356. Greenstein, *Bread and Hyacinths*, 43–44.
357. Bufe and Verter, *Dreams of Freedom*, 84.
358. Day, *Prison Notebooks*, 230–31.
359. Ibid., 231–32.
360. Bufe and Verter, *Dreams of Freedom*, 85.
361. Ibid., 88.
362. Ibid., 89; Estrada, *Los Angeles Plaza*, 154–55; Monroy, *Rebirth*, 128–29.
363. Estrada, *Los Angeles Plaza*, 155.
364. Ibid.
365. Ibid., 157.
366. Ibid.
367. Ibid. Carranza became Mexico's third post-Diaz president in 1915, replacing Victoriano Huerta, who had overthrown and murdered Madero in 1913. Carranza himself would be sacked by Alvaro Obregon in 1920, marking the end of the revolution's most violent phase.
368. Ibid., 157–58.
369. Ibid.,158; Bufe and Verter, *Dreams of Freedom*, 99.

370. Estrada, *Los Angeles Plaza*, 159; Bufe and Verter, *Dreams of Freedom*, 100.

371. Bufe and Verter, *Dreams of Freedom*, 100. Following Ricardo's arrest in 1917, Enrique resigned from the PLM. After Ricardo's death, he returned to Mexico, where he helped found the progressive Confederación Campesina Mexicana (Confederation of Mexican Farmworkers). He died in Mexico City in 1954 (ibid., 96).

372. Ibid., 101. The names of the Oaxacan organizations are: Consejo Indigena Popular de Oaxaca—Ricardo Flores Magón, Coordinación Oaxaca Magonista Popular Antineoliberal, and Alianza Magonista Zapatista.

Chapter 11

373. Miller, *Petitioners*, dedication.

374. Hassan, *Loren Miller*, 14.

375. E-mail to the author from Robin Miller Sloan, August 11, 2015.

376. Author in-person interview with Robin Miller Sloan, December 5, 2015.

377. Miller, *Petitioners*, 422.

378. Hassan, *Loren Miller*, 37.

379. Ibid., 43–44; Sides, *L.A. City Limits*, 30; "Miller, Loren."

380. Miller, "Failure of the Fiesta," 8.

381. Hassan, *Loren Miller*, 48–76.

382. Ibid., 103–23.

383. Miller Sloan in-person interview.

384. Miller, "Failure of the Fiesta."

385. Sides, *L.A. City Limits*, 99.

386. Du Bois, "Colored California," 192–94.

387. Miller Sloan in-person interview; Miller Sloan phone interview with the author, August 11, 2015.

388. Bunch, "Past Not Necessarily," 119.

389. "Miller, Loren."

390. Miller, "Right Secured," 600.

391. "Victory on Sugar Hill"; Watts, *Hattie McDaniel*, 328.

392. Miller, "Right Secured," 600.

393. Miller, *Petitioners*.

394. Ibid.

395. *Shelley v. Kraemer*.

396. Robinson, "Race, Space, and the Evolution," 42.
397. Hassan, *Loren Miller*, 186.
398. "Miller, Loren."
399. O'Connor, "Negro," 139.
400. Bunch, "Past Not Necessarily," 119.
401. Dominic, *To Protect and to Serve*, 176.
402. Sides, *L.A. City Limits*, 4.
403. Miller, *Petitioners*, back matter.
404. "Passings."
405. Miller Sloan in-person interview.
406. Ibid.
407. "Loren Miller Legal Services Award."

Chapter 12

408. "Rose Scharlin"; Hewes, in *It's the Cameraderie,* lists Normandie Nursery School and its offshoot, Parents Cooperative Nursery School, founded in 1926 and 1931, respectively, as the first such schools in Los Angeles (104).
409. Author interview with Gilbert Brebes, October 2, 2015; Hurewitz, *Bohemian Los Angeles*, 171.
410. "Rose Scharlin."
411. Hurewitz, *Bohemian Los Angeles*, 171.
412. Robinson, "My Chain of Thoughts."
413. Timmons, *Trouble with Harry Hay*, 18.
414. Hurewitz, *Bohemian Los Angeles*, 171.
415. "Rose Scharlin Census Records."
416. Russian pogroms were the rule more than the exception, with another recent series of attacks occurring in 1881 after Czar Alexander II's assassination, for which, as usual, "the Jews" were blamed.
417. "Scharlin Census Records."
418. See, most recently, Mendes, *Jews and the Left.*
419. "Scharlin Census Records." The records spell Abraham's last name "Sharlin."
420. Brebes interview.
421. Hewes, *Cameraderie,* 3, 6, 7.
422. Ibid., 8, 10.
423. Ibid., 14.
424. Ibid., 15.

425. Ibid., 16, 18.
426. Ibid., 101–2.
427. Neighborhood Nursery School's first location was at the south end of Silver Lake Reservoir. It moved closer to Ivanhoe Reservoir in 1976. Two other local cooperatives are PLAY Silver Lake Preschool at Hyperion and Lyric and Camelot Kids Child Development Center on Rowena.
428. "Rose Scharlin."

Chapter 13

429. Hess, *Architecture of John Lautner*, 43.
430. Hines, *Architecture of the Sun*, 610.
431. Olsberg, *Between Earth and Heaven*, 38.
432. Ibid., 39.
433. Ibid., 40, 43.
434. Hines, *Architecture of the Sun*, 610.
435. Olsberg, *Between Earth and Heaven*, 45.
436. Ibid., 53.
437. Ibid. This included six small houses in Los Angeles.
438. Ibid.
439. Ibid.
440. Hess, *Googie REDUX*, 71.
441. Hines, *Architecture of the Sun*, 610.
442. Ibid., 619.
443. Ibid.
444. Hess, *Architecture of John Lautner*, 103.
445. Ibid., 105.
446. Hines, *Architecture of the Sun*, 641.
447. Beale, "John Lautner's Silvertop."
448. Olsberg, *Between Heaven and Earth*, 122.

Chapter 14

449. The bulk of this chapter is compiled from interviews with David Hyun and the handwritten notes he gave the author in September 2003.
450. Hyun, *Man Sei!*
451. Yi, "David Hyun."

452. Hyun interview.
453. Ibid.
454. Yi, "David Hyun."
455. Hyun interview.
456. Ibid.; Timmons, *Trouble with Harry Hay*, 184.
457. Cheung, *Breaking Ground*, 18.
458. Ibid.
459. Author interview with Kent Wong, April 16, 2016.

Chapter 15

460. Author interview with Momo Yashima and Ralph Brannen, April 12, 2016.
461. Ibid.
462. Yashima-Brannen and Kent Wong interviews. Beulah Quo, besides her prolific movie and television acting career, was an ardent activist on behalf of Asian Americans, of which her work with EWP was a part. She also passed on her progressivism to her children, most notably attorney and educator Stewart Kwoh, founding president and executive director of Asian Americans Advancing Justice, Los Angeles, and named among the one hundred most influential people in the city (Jun, "Service for a Cause").
463. Yashima-Brannen interview.
464. Ibid.
465. He published a sequel, *Horizon Is Calling*, in 1947.
466. Yashima-Brannen interview.
467. Pulvers, "Taro Yashima."
468. The country's anti-Asian immigration policies, beginning with the Chinese Exclusion Act of 1881 that barred both naturalization and further immigration, eventually also affected Japanese and Koreans and were codified in the Immigration Act of 1924.
469. Vincent Brook's wife, Karen, a longtime elementary school teacher, can vouch for the books' ongoing popularity.
470. Stewart, "Mako," 72.
471. Yashima-Brannen interview.
472. Ibid.
473. Ibid.
474. Ibid.

475. Ibid.
476. Ibid.
477. Taro and Mitsu Yashima died in 1994 and 1998, respectively.

Chapter 16

478. Farr, *History of Imperial County*, 369.
479. Pascal, *Kesling's Modern Structures*, 15.
480. Farr, *History*, 369.
481. Pascal, *Kesling's*, 17. No records support Kesling's claim.
482. "Modern San Diego."
483. Pascal, *Kesling's*, 12, 9.
484. Ibid., 13.
485. Ibid., 22.
486. Ibid., 27.
487. Ibid., 28.
488. Ibid., 28–29.
489. Ibid.
490. Ibid., 31.

Chapter 17

491. How, *James B. Eads*.
492. Anderson, *On Hobos*, 90.
493. Ibid., 91.
494. "End of an Idealist," 28.
495. Ibid.
496. Ibid.
497. Anderson, *On Hobos*, 91.
498. *Howley, Community Media*, 62.
499. Kusmer, *Down & Out*, 162.
500. Hines, *Architecture of the Sun*, 253.
501. Anderson, *On Hobos*, 92, 90.
502. Hines, *Architecture*, 254.
503. Ibid.
504. Wooldridge, "Mrs. How Wearies."
505. "End of an Idealist."

506. Ibid.
507. "James Eads How Died in Poverty."
508. "Former Wife Files Action in Behalf of Son."

Chapter 18

509. Murray, "Really Free Agents."
510. Ibid.
511. Luke, *Most Famous Woman*, 1.
512. Overmeyer, *Queen of Negro Leagues,* 6.
513. Ibid.
514. "Manley, Effa (1900–1981)."
515. Rogosin, *Invisible Men*, 108.
516. Richardson, *Retrospective*, 158.
517. Luke, *Most Famous Woman*, 5.
518. Ibid., 4.
519. Ibid.
520. Holt, "Women with a Mission."
521. "They Danced for Charity."
522. Holt, "Women."
523. "NAACP's Anti-Lynching Campaigns."
524. Overmeyer, *Queen*, 16; Luke, *Most Famous Woman*, 27.
525. Luke, *Most Famous Woman*, x.
526. Ibid.
527. Overmeyer, *Queen,* 61.
528. "Manleys Disbanding Club."
529. Luke, *Most Famous Woman*, 153.
530. Ibid., 154.
531. Ibid., 156.
532. Ibid.

BIBLIOGRAPHY

Albro, Ward S. *Always a Rebel: Ricardo Flores Magón and the Mexican Revolution.* Austin: Texas University Press, 1992.

Anderson, Nels. *On Hobos and Homelessness.* Chicago and London: University of Chicago Press, 1998.

Architectuul. "Richard Neutra." http://architectuul.com/architect/richard-neutra.

Art and Popular Culture Encyclopedia. "Vienna Secession." http://artandpopularculture.com/Vienna_Secession.

Assistance League, Los Angeles. http://assistanceleaugela.org.

Bair, Deirdre. *Anaïs Nin: A Biography*. New York: G.P. Putnam's Sons, 1995.

Beale, Lauren. "John Lautner's Silvertop Sells for Over Asking Price." *Los Angeles Times*, October 25, 2014.

Bestor, Barbara. *Bohemian Modern: Living in Silver Lake.* New York: Harper Design, 2006.

Bilski, Emily D., and Emily Braun. *Jewish Women and Their Salons: The Power of Conversation.* New Haven, CT: Yale University Press, 2005.

Black Past. "Manley, Effa (1900–1981)." www.blackpast.org/aah/manley-effa-1900-1981.

———. "Miller, Loren (1903–1967)." www.blackpast.org/aaw/miller-loren-1903-1967.

Bonge, Lyle. "Obituary of James Leo Herlihy." *Independent Observer*, October 29, 1993.

Boyd, Malcolm. *Are You Running with Me, Jesus?* Cambridge, MA: Cowley, 2006.

———. *As I Live and Breathe: Stages of an Autobiography*. New York: Random House, 1965, 1969.

———. "My Jewish Grandfather." April 28, 2012. www.huffingtonpost.com/rev-malcolm-boyd/my-jewish-grandfather-b_1291866.html.

———. *Take Off the Masks*. Philadelphia: New Society, 1984.

———. "We Are a Gentle, Loving People Singing for Our Lives." November 14, 2015. www.huffingtonpost.com/we-are-a-gentle-people-singing-for-our-lives.

Bradley, Ann. "Lesbian Writers Series." *UCLA Center for the Study of Women* (Fall 2014): 22–29.

Brook, Vincent. *Driven to Darkness: Jewish Émigré Directors and the Rise of Film Noir*. New Brunswick, NJ: Rutgers University Press, 2009.

———. *Land of Smoke and Mirrors: A Cultural History of Los Angeles*. New Brunswick, NJ: Rutgers University Press, 2013.

Bufe, Chaz, and Mitchell Cowen Verter, eds. *Dreams of Freedom: A Ricardo Flores Magón Reader.* Oakland, CA: AK Press, 2005.

Bunch, Lonnie. "A Past Not Necessarily a Prologue." In *Twentieth-Century Los Angeles: Power, Promotion, and Social Conflict*. Edited by Norman Klein and Martin J. Schiesl. Claremont, CA: Regina Books, 2000.

Burroway, Jim. "The Temerity of a Kiss." http://www.boxturtlebulletin.com/2006/12/27/171.

Carpenter, Edward. *The Intermediate Sex: A Study of Some Transitional Types of Men and Women*. Middlesex, GB: Echo Library, 2007.

Cheung, Floridia, Truong Long and Steven Y. Wong. *Breaking Ground: Chinese American Architects in Los Angeles (1945–1980)*. Exhibition catalogue at the Chinese American Museum, January 19–June 3, 2012.

Cohen, David. "The Community of Minsk from the End of the 19th Century until the Revolution of 1917." www.jewishgen.org/Yizkor/minsk/min1_074.html 74.

Crawford, Dorothy Lamb. *Evenings On and Off the Roof: Pioneering Concerts in Los Angeles, 1939–1971*. Berkeley: University of California Press, 1995.

———. *A Windfall of Musicians: Hitler's Émigrés and Exiles in Southern California*. New Haven, CT: Yale University Press, 2009.

Crosse, John. "Pauline Gibling Schindler: Vagabond Agent for Modernism, 1927–1936." http://socalarchhistory.blogspot.com/2010/07/pauline-gibling-schindler-vagabond.html.

Curbed Los Angeles. "Gregory Ain's Hay House in the Hollywood Hills." http://la.curbed.com/archives/2010/10/gregory_ains_hay_house_in_the_hollywood_hills.php.

Davis, Mike. *City of Quartz; Excavating the Future in Los Angeles*. London: Verso, 1990.

Day, Douglas. *The Prison Notebooks of Ricardo Flores Magón*. New York: Harcourt Brace Jovanovich, 1991.

D'Emilio, John. *Sexual Politics, Sexual Communities*. Chicago: University of Chicago Press, 1983, 1998.

Denzer, Anthony. *Gregory Ain: The Modern Home as Social Commentary*. New York: Rizzoli, 2008.

Discover Hollywood. "Aline Barnsdall: The Ultimate Iconoclast" (Winter 2005–6). www.discoverhollywood.com/Publications/Discover-Hollywood/2005/Issue-Winter-2005-2006/Aline-Barnsdall-The-Ultimate-Iconoclast.asp.

Dominic, Joe. *To Protect and to Serve: The LAPD's Century of War in the City of Dreams*. New York: Pocket Books, 1994.

Du Bois, W.E.B. "Colored California." *The Crisis*, August 1913.

Eastsider. "Silver Lake Gay Landmark Gets Bulldozed." September 25, 2011. www.theeastsiderla.com/2011/09/25/silver-lake-gay-landmark-gets-bulldozed.

Edsitement. "NAACP's Anti-Lynching Campaigns: The Quest for Social Justice in the Interwar Years." http://edsitement.neh.gov/curriculum-unit/naacps-anti-lynching-campaigns-quest-social-justice-interwar-years.

Episcopal Diocese of Los Angeles. http://www.ladiocese.org.

Estrada, William David. *The Los Angeles Plaza: Sacred and Contested Space*. Austin: University of Texas Press, 2008.

"Evenings on the Roof, 1939–1954." Interview of Peter Yates by Adelaide G. Tusler. Oral History Program of the University of California, Los Angeles, Department of Special Collections, University of California, Los Angeles, 1967.

Faderman, Lillian, and Stuart Timmons. *Gay L.A.: A History of Sexual Outlaws, Power Politics, and Lipstick Lesbians*. New York: Basic Books, 2006.

Farr, Finis C. *The History of Imperial County*. Berkeley, CA: Elms and Frank, 1918.

Fitch, Noël Riley. *The Erotic Life of Anaïs Nin*. New York: Little, Brown, 1993.

Frieberg, Leslie. "Harry Hay: Painful Partings." *Workers World*, June 28, 2005.

Gebhard, David. *Schindler.* San Francisco: William Stout, 1997.

Gebhard, David, and Robert Winter. *An Architectural Guide to Los Angeles*. Layton, UT: Gibbs Smith, 2003.

Germany, Lisa. *Harwell Hamilton Harris*. Berkeley: University of California Press, 2000.

Greenstein, Paul, Nigel Lennon and Lionel Rolphe. *Bread and Hyacinths: The Rise and Fall of Utopian Los Angeles*. Los Angeles: Classic Books, 1992.

Hassan, Amina. *Loren Miller: Civil Rights Attorney and Journalist*. Norman:

Oklahoma University Press, 2015.
Herlihy, James Leo. *All Fall Down*. New York: Dutton, 1960.
———. "The Art of Being a Person." In *Anaïs Nin: An International Journal I*, July 1983.
———. *Blue Denim*. New York: Random House, 1958.
———. "Letter to M.C. Richards, June 19, 1970." James Leo Herlihy Collection, Howard Gottlieb Archival Research Center, Boston University.
———. *Midnight Cowboy*. New York: Simon & Schuster, 1965.
———. *The Season of the Witch*. London: W.H. Allen, 1971.
———. *Sleep of Baby Filbertson, and Other Stories*. New York: Dutton, 1959.
———. *Stop, You're Killing Me*. New York: Dramatists Play Service, 1969.
Herr, Jeffrey. *Aline Barnsdall's Olive Hill Project*. Santa Monica, CA: Angel City Press, 2005.
Hess, Alan. *The Architecture of John Lautner.* New York: Rizzoli, 1999.
———. *Googie REDUX*. San Francisco: Chronicle Books, 2004.
Hewes, Dorothy W. *"It's the Camaradarie": A History of Parent Cooperative Schools*. Davis: Center for Cooperatives, University of California, Davis, 1998.
Heyworth, Peter. "Klemperer and the L.A. Philharmonic." In *Festival of Music Made in Los Angeles.* Edited by Orrin Howard. Los Angeles: Los Angeles Philharmonic Association, 1981.
Hines, Thomas P. *Architecture of the Sun: Los Angeles Modernism 1900–1970.* New York: Rizzoli, 2010.
———. *Richard Neutra and the Search for Modern Architecture*. New York: Rizzoli, 2005.
Historian4Hire. "The Black Cat: Site of the Black Cat Protest." http://historian4hire.com/black_cat.html.
Hoffmann, Donald. *Frank Lloyd Wright's Hollyhock House*. New York: Dover, 1992.
Holt, Henry. "Women with a Mission." *New York Post*, September 15, 1975.
Howley, Kevin. *Community Media: People, Places, and Communication Technologies.* Cambridge: Cambridge University Press, 2005.
How, Louis. *James B. Eads.* Boston: Houghton Mifflin, 1900.
Hurewitz, Daniel. *Bohemian Los Angeles and the Making of Modern Politics*. Los Angeles: University of California Press, 2008.
Hyun, Peter. *Man Sei!: The Making of a Korean American*. Honolulu: University of Hawaii Press, 1986.
Integrity USA. www.integrityusa.org.
Joe, Wes. "The Black Cat Bar." Unpublished manuscript, 2008.
Johansson, Warren, and William A. Percy. *Outing: Shattering the Conspiracy of*

Silence. New York: Hayworth Press, 1994.

Karasnick, Norman M., and Dorothy K. Karasnick. *Oilman's Daughter: A Biography of Aline Barnsdall*. Encino, CA: Carlston, 1993.

Keeps, David A. "Bit of Genius." *Los Angeles Times*, August 22, 2009.

Kepner, Jim. *Rough News, Daring Views: 1950's Pioneer Press Journalism*. New York: Harrington Park Press, 1998.

Kim, Nic Cha. "Behind the Scenes of the Hollyhock House Renovation." www.kcet.org/arts/artbound/counties/los-angeles/hollyhock-house-renovations-los-angeles.html.

Kraft, Barbara. *Anaïs Nin: The Last Days—A Memoir*. San Jose, CA: Pegasus Books, 2013.

Kusmer, Kenneth L. *Down & Out, on the Road: The Homeless in American History*. New York: Oxford University Press, 2001.

Lamprecht, Barbara. *Neutra: Complete Works*. Cologne, Germany: Taschen, 2000.

Lassett, John H.M. *Shameful Victory: The Los Angeles Dodgers, the Red Scare, and the Hidden History of Chavez Ravine*. Tucson: University of Arizona Press, 2015.

Lieberman, E. James. *Acts of Will: The Life and Work of Otto Rank*. New York: Free Press, 1985.

Locke, Michael, with Vincent Brook. *Silver Lake Chronicles: Exploring an Urban Oasis in Los Angeles*. Charleston, SC: The History Press, 2014.

Long, Christopher. "An Alternative Path to Modernism: Carl König and Architectural Education at the Vienna Technische Hochschule, 1890–1913." *Journal of Architectural Education* 55, no. 1 (2001).

Los Angeles Times. "Passings: Loren Miller Jr., Boris Chertok." http://articles.latimes.com/2011/dec/15/local/la-me-passings-20111215.

Lowell, Robert. "Memories of West Street and Leple." In Lowell, *Life Studies* (1959). Reprint, New York: Farrar, Strauss & Giroux, 2007.

Luke, Bob. *The Most Famous Woman in Baseball: Effa Manley and the Negro Leagues*. Dulles, VA: Potomac Books, 2011.

McCoy, Esther. *Five California Architects*. Santa Monica, CA: Hennessey + Ingalls, 1960.

———. *The Second Generation*. Salt Lake City, UT: Peregrine Smith, 1984.

McWilliams, Carey. *Southern California, an Island on the Land*. Layton, UT: Gibbs Smith, 1946, 1973.

Mendes, Philip. *Jews and the Left: The Rise and Fall of a Political Alliance*. New York: Palgrave Macmillan, 2014.

Miller, Loren. "The Failure of the Fiesta." *California Eagle*, September 4, 1931.

———. *The Petitioners: The Story of the Supreme Court of the United States and the Negro*. New York: Pantheon, 1966.

———. "A Right Secured." *The Nation*, May 29, 1948.

Modern San Diego. "William Kesling." www.modernsandiego.com/WilliamKesling.html.

Monroy, Douglas. *Rebirth: Mexican Los Angeles from the Great Migration to the Great Depression*. Berkeley: University of California Press, 1999.

Morton, Lawrence. "A Remembrance of Peter Yates." Monday Evening Concert Program Note, April 4, 1977. Morton collection in the Arnold Schoenberg Institute, University of Southern California.

Murray, Jim. "The Really Free Agents." *Los Angeles Times*, December 5, 1975.

Myerhoff, Barbara G. *Number Our Days*. New York: E.P. Dutton, 1979.

Neutra, Dion. "The Neutra Genius: Innovations & Vision." www.neutra.org.

———. *The Neutras Then & Later*. Barcelona: Triton, 2012.

Nin, Anaïs. *D.H. Lawrence: An Unprofessional Study*. Athens, OH: Swallow Press, 1964.

———. *The Diary of Anaïs Nin: Volume Five, 1947–1955*. New York: Harcourt Brace Jovanovich, 1974.

———. *The Diary of Anaïs Nin: Volume Seven, 1966–1974*. New York: Harcourt Brace Jovanovich, 1980.

———. *The Diary of Anaïs Nin: Volume Six, 1955–1966*. New York: Harcourt Brace Jovanovich, 1966, 1976.

———. *House of Incest*. Athens: Ohio University Press, 1994.

———. *Waste of Timelessness: And Other Early Stories*. Riverside, CT: Magic Circle Press, 1977.

Noever, Peter. *Schindler by MAK*. Munich, Germany: Prestel, 2005.

O'Connor, George. "The Negro and the Police in Los Angeles." Master's thesis, University of Southern California, 1955.

Office of Historic Resources. "Designated Historic-Cultural Monuments." http://presevtatio.lacity.org/commission/designated-historic-cultural-monuments.

Olsberg, Nicholas. *Between Earth and Heaven: The Architecture of John Lautner*. New York: Rizzoli, 2008.

Overmeyer, James. *Queen of the Negro Leagues, Effa Manley and the Newark Eagles*. London: Scarecrow Press, 1998.

Pascal, Patrick. *Kesling's Modern Structures*. Los Angeles: Balcony Press, 2002.

"Peter Yates Papers, 1927–1976, MSS 14." Special Collections, University of California, Santa Barbara. http://libraries.ucsd.edu/speccoll/findingaids/msss0014.html.

Philadelphia Tribune. "They Danced for Charity." February 4, 1932.

Pulvers, Roger. "Taro Yashima: An Unsung Beacon for All Against 'Evil on

This Earth.'" *Japan Times*, September 11, 2011. www.japantimes.co.jp/opinion/2011/09/11/commentary/taro-yashima-an-unsung-beacon-for-all-against-evil-on-this-earth/#.Vx6f-I-cFjp.

Queerty. "Silver Lake's A Different Light Bookstore Bites the Dust—Literally." October 10, 2011. www.queerty.com/silver-lakes-a different-light-bookstore-bites-the-dust%E2%80%94literally-20111003.

Raymond, Anthea. "Permit Existed to Demolish Site of Historic Gay Bookstore." September 27, 2011. http://patch.com/california/echopark/permit-existed-to-demolish-site-of-historic-gay-bookstore.

Reinhardt, Gottfried. *Genius: A Memoir of Max Reinhardt, by His Son Gottfried Reinhardt*. New York: Knopf, 1979.

Richardson, Allen. "A Retrospective Look at the Negro Leagues and Professional Negro Baseball Players." Master's thesis, San Jose State University, May 1980.

Robinson, Florence J. "My Chain of Thoughts." Unidentified press clipping, June 30, 1941. Rose Scharlin Cooperative School collection.

Robinson, Paul. "Race, Space, and the Evolution of Black Los Angeles." In *Black Los Angeles: American Dream and Racial Realities*. Edited by Darnell Hunt and Ana-Christina Ramon. New York: New York University Press, 2010.

Rogosin, Donn. *Invisible Men: Life in Baseball's Negro Leagues*. New York: Athenaeum, 1987.

Romo, Ricardo. *East Los Angeles: History of a Barrio*. Austin: University of Texas Press, 1983.

Roscoe, Will, ed. *Radically Gay: Gay Liberation in the Words of Its Founder*. Boston: Beacon Press, 1996.

Rose Scharlin Census Records. www.Rose%Sharlin%20Census%Records.docx2oref=e&n=195072119.

Rose Scharlin: LA's Oldest Cooperative Nursery School. http://rosescharlin.com.

Rourke, Mary. "Frank Priest Took to the Streets." *Los Angeles Times* obituary, February 28, 2015.

"Rudolph Schindler." www.ncmodernist.org/schindler.htm.

Salt Lake Tribune. "James Eads How Died in Poverty; Fortune Left Him." August 21, 1930.

Sanchez, George. "'What's Good for Boyle Heights Is Good for the Jews': Creating Multiculturalism on the Eastside During the 1950s." *American Quarterly* 56, no. 3 (September 2004).

Schumpeter, Joseph A. *Capitalism, Socialism and Democracy*. New York: Routledge, 2006.

Secrest, Meryle. *Frank Lloyd Wright: A Biography*. Chicago: University of Chicago Press, 1998.

Sheine, Judith. *R.M. Schindler*. London: Phaidon, 2001.

Sides, Josh. *L.A. City Limits: African American Los Angeles from the Great Depression to the Present*. Berkeley: University of California Press, 2003.

Silver Lake History Collective. "Alexei Romanoff" video interview. April 28, 2009. https://www.youtube.com/results?search_query=alexei+remanov+interview+silver+lake+history+collective.

———. "Eric Lloyd Wright" video interview. November 20, 2010. www.youtube.com/watch?v=itJWqKULxFc.

———. "Malcolm Boyd and Mark Thompson" video interview. July 7, 2013. www.youtube.com/watch?v=0r8zWzJ-518.

Smith, Catherine Parsons, and Cynthia S. Richardson. *Mary Carr Moore, American Composer*. Ann Arbor: University of Michigan Press, 1987.

Snyder, Michael. "James Leo Herlihy: The *Midnight Cowboy* in Key West." www.kwls.org/littoral/james_leo_herlihythe_midnight.

Sontag, Susan. "Pilgrimage." *The New Yorker*, December 21, 1987.

Sporting News. "Manleys Disbanding Club in Negro National Leagues." November 17, 1948.

State Bar of California. "Loren Miller Legal Services Award." www.calbar.ca.gov/AboutUs/Awards/LorenMillerLegalServices.aspx.

Stewart, Jocelyn. "Mako, 72: Actor Opened Door for Asian Americans." *Los Angeles Times*, July 26, 2006. http://articles.latimes.com/2006/jul/23/local/me-mako23.

St. Louis Post-Dispatch. "Former Wife Files Action in Behalf of Son—Personal Estate Involved." September 24, 1931.

Swan, Howard. *Music in the Southwest*. San Marino, CA: Huntington Library, 1952.

Swed, Mark. "All the Arts, All the Time." April 13, 2009. http://latimesblogs.latimes.com/culturemonster/2009/08/a-lesson-for-lacmas-film-program-from-the-monday-evening-concerts.html.

———. "Weirdness Makes for Amazing Show." *Los Angeles Times*, December 9, 2015.

Sweeny, Robert. "Life at Kings Road: How It Was, 1920–1946." In *The Architecture of R.M. Schindler*, 2001 MOCA exhibition catalogue.

Thirsty in LA. "Alexei Romanoff and the LGBT Civil Rights Legacy of The Black Cat." June 12, 2015. www.thirstyinla.com/2015/06/12/alexei-romanoff-lgbt-black-cat.

Thomas, Andrew, director. *Disturber of the Peace: The Life and Times of Malcolm Boyd*. Documentary film, 2016.

Thompson, Mark. *Advocate Days & Other Stories*. Hull's Cove, ME: Rebel Satori Press, 2009.

———. *Gay Body: A Journey through Shadow to Self*. New York: St. Martins, 1997.

———. *Gay Soul: The Heart of Gay Spirit and Nature*. New York: HarperCollins, 1994.

———. *Leatherfolk: Radical Sex, People, Politics, and Practice*. New York: Daedalus, 2004.

Thompson, Mark, ed. *Gay Spirit: Myth and Meaning*. New York: St. Martins, 1987.

Thoreau, Henry David. *Walden*. Reprint, New York: Oxford University Press, 1997.

Time. "End of an Idealist" (August 3, 1930).

———. "Victory on Sugar Hill" (December 17, 1945).

Timmons, Stuart. *The Trouble with Harry: Founder of the Modern Gay Movement*. Boston: Alysin, 1990.

Vankin, Deborah. "L.A.'s Hollyhock House Among Wright's Buildings Up for World Heritage List." *Los Angeles Times*, January 30, 2015. www.latimes.com/entertainment/arts/culture/la-et-cm-frank-lloyd-wright-world-heritage-list-20150130-story.html.

Viertel, Salka. *The Kindness of Strangers*. New York: Holt, Reinhardt & Winston, 1969.

Wagener, Wolfgang. *Soriano*. London: Phaidon, 2002.

Wang, Jun. "Service for a Cause." *China Daily*, January 4, 2013. http://usa.chinadaily.com.cn/epaper/2013-01/04/content_16081184.htm.

Ward, Robert. *Understanding James Leo Herlihy*. Columbia: University of South Carolina Press, 2012.

Watts, Jill. *Hattie McDaniel: Black American, White Hollywood*. New York: HarperCollins, 2005.

Watt, Stephen, and Gary Richardson, eds. *American Drama: Colonial to Contemporary*. Cambridge, MA: Heinle & Heinle, 1994.

White, C. Todd. *Pre-Gay LA: A Social History of the Movement for Homosexual Rights*. Chicago: University of Illinois Press, 2009.

Whiting, Sam. "A Different Light Gay Bookstore in Castro Closing." April 22, 2011. www.sfgate.com/news/article/A-Different-Light-gay-bookstore-in-Castro-closing-2374151.php.

Wikipedia. "List of LGBT Actions in the United States Prior to the Stonewall Riots." www.en.wikipedia.org/wiki/List_of_LBT_actions_in_the_United_States_prior_to_the_Stonewall_riots.

Wooldridge, A.L. "Mrs. How Wearies of Her Tramp DeLuxe." *St. Louis Post-Dispatch*, July 22, 1928.

Yashima, Taro. *Crow Boy*. New York: Puffin, 1974.

———. *Horizon Calling*. New York: H. Holt, 1947.

———. *The New Sun.* Reprint, Honolulu: University of Hawaii Press, 2008.

Yates, Peter. *An Amateur at the Keyboard*. New York: Pantheon, 1964.

———. "A Column and a Roof." *Arts and Architecture*, December 1952.

———. *A Smaller Poem Book*. Los Angeles: Roof Publications, 1946.

———. *Twentieth Century Music*. New York: Pantheon, 1967.

Yi, Eugene. "David Hyun: The Larger-than-Life Personality Saw Much of Korean History with His Own Eyes." June 2012. http://iamkoream.com/june-issue-david-hyun-first-korean-american.

INDEX

ABOUT THE AUTHORS

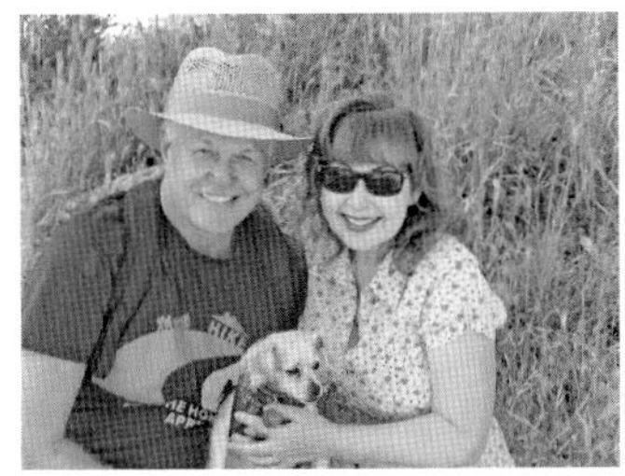

Michael and Donna Locke with Maggie, their pet Chihuahua mix. *Photo by Monique Frese.*

Michael Locke is a longtime resident of Southern California. He is a partner in the residential brokerage firm Deasy Penner & Partners. He served on the first Silver Lake Neighborhood Council as Region One representative and vice-chair. He is a regular contributing writer and photography chief for the *Los Feliz Observer* and an occasional writer and photographer for the *Los Feliz Ledger* and the *Los Angeles City Historical Society Newsletter.* He lives in the Durex Model Home (Los Angeles Historic-Cultural Monument No. 1025) with his wife, Donna Jean. Previously, he collaborated with Vincent Brook on the book *Silver Lake Chronicles: Exploring an Urban Oasis in Los Angeles*, also published by The History Press.

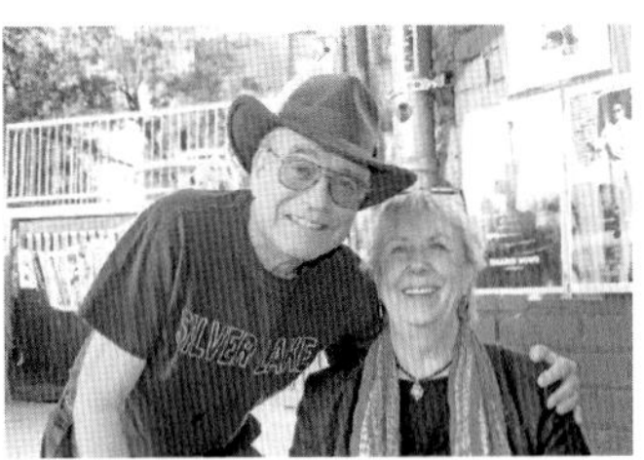

Vincent and Karen Brook portrait.

Vincent Brook has lived in Silver Lake since 1978 with his wife, Karen. A longtime community activist and university professor (UCLA, USC, Cal-State LA and Loyola Marymount University), he has written or edited eight books, most recently, besides *Silver Lake Chronicles* (2014, cowritten with Michael Locke), *Woody on Rye: Jewishness in the Films and Plays of Woody Allen* (2014, coedited with Marat Grinberg) and *From Shtetl to Stardom: Jews and Hollywood* (2017, coedited with Michael Renov).

Visit us at
www.historypress.net

This title is also available as an e-book